BUDDHIST TALES OF INDIA, CHINA, AND JAPAN

Indian Section

BUDDHIST TALES
OF INDIA, CHINA, AND JAPAN

A Complete Translation of the *Konjaku Monogatarishū*

Indian Section

Translated by

Yoshiko Dykstra

Kanji Press

HONOLULU

This publication is printed on acid-free paper and
meets the guidelines for permanence and durability
of the Council of Library Resources.

Print-ready copy prepared by Kanji Press.

DISTRIBUTED BY

UNIVERSITY OF HAWAI'I PRESS

2840 Kolowalu Street

Honolulu, Hawai'i 96822

www.uhpress.hawaii.edu

for
Professor Emeritus Enshō Ashikaga and
Provost Emeritus Andrew Dykstra

CONTENTS

INTRODUCTION TO THE INDIAN SECTION

This volume contains translations of 257 stories of the Indian section of the *Konjaku monogatarishū*. The works and variants related to the tales in the Indian section are in the appendix.

Since my major objective is to provide a readable translation of the complete work for general readers, I have minimized annotations and have taken certain liberties in rendering some awkward and repetitious expressions in the text into more natural English. The whole effect of the *Konjaku* style has been said to reside in its brevity and strength. I hope my English translation has retained somewhat these major traits of the originals.

Since many stories in the Indian section deal with the historical Buddha, the founder of Buddhism, a survey of his life will be useful for general readers. Śākyamuni identifies the *muni*, a holy man or sage, of the Śākya or the Sakka clan. He is popularly called Shaka, Gautama Buddha, or sometimes Prince Gautame Siddhārtha, and he is also referred to as Butsu (Buddha) or Nyorai (Tathāgata) in honorific Japanese terms. Hereafter in the translation, for the sake of convenience, Shaka will be used to refer to the historical Śākyamuni Buddha in particular.

The date of Shaka's birth is not definitely known, but April 8, 565 (or 563) B.C., is conventionally accepted. His father, Śuddhodana, king of the Śākya clan and the lord of Kapila Castle in the city of Kapilavastu, located near present-day Trionakoto in Tarai of Nepal, was a member of the Kṣatriya warrior cast.

There are two theories about the lineage of Shaka's mother. One is that his mother, Mahāmāyā or Lady Maya, was a sister of King Suprabuddha of Devadaha. She had a daughter called Yaśodharā (Gopika), who later married a first cousin. The other is that Shaka's mother was a daughter of King Suprabuddha or of King Anjara, who was also from Devadaha.

According to a well-known legend, on her way to her father's palace, the pregnant Lady Maya paused to rest at Lumbini Park, where she gave birth to Shaka. The tradition says that at his birth, Shaka took seven steps in each of four directions, saying each time, "I alone am honored in heaven and on earth. I will be the savior from these Triple Worlds of suffering." Lady Maya died seven days later.

During his youth, Shaka was given the conventional rearing of a crown prince and was trained in the ways of the court, in letters, and in the military arts. As the young prince grew, he tended to fall into deep meditation. His concerned father finally arranged his marriage at the age of nineteen to Yasodhara.

After the marriage, Shaka's meditations were deeper as he became preoccupied greatly with the transiency of life, and finally he decided to enter the priesthood.

Shaka pursued his enlightenment by visiting several famous masters, such as Bhārgava. However, he found their teachings unsatisfactory. Subsequently, he engaged in harsh ascetic practices for six years. Barely surviving his ascetic experiences, he went to the Nairañjanā River, cleansed his body, and gradually regained his strength.

Shaka proceeded to the north and meditated under a *pippala* tree, later known as the Bodhi Tree, near the village of Buddha-gaya. After overcoming many delusions and temptations, Shaka finally attained the enlightenment of the Middle Way at the age of thirty-five. He then crossed India until he reached Deer Park near Benares, present-day Sarnath. There he preached his first sermon, which expounded the doctrine of the Middle Way, the Four Noble Truths, and the Eightfold Path to five companions sent by his father, all of whom immediately were converted to Buddhism.

Shaka's career of teaching the Law is said to have lasted forty-five years. In his last journey, an offering from a smith named Cunda gave him a fatal case of food poisoning. As he realized his last moments were approaching, he preached his final sermon, the *Nirvana Sermon*, to his disciples and then passed away while lying on his right side with his head pointing north and his face looking west. Shaka is commonly said to have been eighty years old. His teachings have been transmitted by two routes, to the south via the Pali scriptures and to the north via the Chinese translations.

In this translation, since the term "heaven" appears quite frequently, a brief account of the Buddhist cosmology should be help-
ful for general readers. In early Buddhism, nirvana was important for
the clergy, while rebirth in the *devaloka*, heaven, was emphasized for
the laity. As the oldest sutra, the *Sutta-rupata*, mentions, anyone who
makes appropriate offerings according to one's ability and leads a mor-
ally good life is reborn in heaven.

The idea of heaven was not exclusively Buddhist, but it had
been popularly known to the Indian people, who believed that an ideal world, a Changri-la-like place, would exist after death. Buddhists
adopted this general view of heaven into their teachings, interpreted
it as the absolute state of mind, and developed it into something more
complex. Consequently, the *devaloka* was divided into three major
worlds or *trayo dhatavah*, the Three Worlds or Triple World, for un-
enlightened sentient beings: the World of Desire, whose inhabitants
have appetites and sexual desire; the World of Forms, whose inhabitants have neither appetites nor sexual desire; and the World of the
Formless, whose inhabitants have no physical form.

Each of the Three Worlds contains its own heavens: six heavens
for the World of Desire, four for the World of Forms, and eighteen for
the World of the Formless, thus totaling twenty-eight heavens. The
second of the six heavens in the World of Desire is the well-known
Trayasrimsa (the Thirty-three Heavens, or Tōriten in Japanese), located on the summit of Mount Sumeru, the highest mountain in the
ancient Indian cosmology. The summit of Mount Sumeru has four
peaks designating the four directions, each of which has eight heavens.
Thus the summit has a total of thirty-three heavens, including the
central one where Śakro-devānam-indraḥ (Taishauten or Tentaishaku
in Japanese) lives.

Another important heaven called Tuṣita Heaven (Tosotsuten in
Japanese) is the fourth of the six heavens of the World of Desire, and
various bodhisattvas who attain Buddhahood in the future reside in its
Inner Palace. Shaka also practiced there once, and at present Bodhisattva Maitreya (Miroku in Japanese) lives there. The life span of the
celestial beings in Tuṣita Heaven is four thousand years, since one of
their days is comparable to four hundred years for human beings.

Various Indian gods have been assimilated into Buddhism since
its early stage of development. The mentioned Taishakuten, as well as
Bonten or Brahmadeva, have been adopted into the Buddhist cosmol-

ogy as the two tutelary deities of the Law. Taishakuten, who resides in the Palace of the Correct View on the summit of Mount Sumeru, hears about the moral conditions of the people of the world from the Four Deva Kings (Shitennō in Japanese), the guardian deities of the four directions, north, east, south, and west, who inspect the world on the fourteenth, fifteenth and eighteenth days of each month. Taishakuten even tested Shaka several times by transforming himself into a demon.

In the translation, I have generally used Japanese readings for personal and place names, and have footnoted significant Sanskrit equivalents, which are often long and cumbersome, to maintain the brevity, flow, and flavor of the original.

The translation, transcriptions of personal and place names, and suggestions to fill the various textual lacunae are based upon the version in the *Nihon Koten Bungaku Taikei*, vols. 22–26 (Iwanami Shoten, Tokyo), edited by Yoshio Yamada et al. The reference materials for the notes include Nagazumi Yasuaki and Ikegami Junichi, *Konjaku monogatarishū*, vols. 9–10 (Heibonsha, Tokyo); and Kunisaki Fumimaro, *Konjaku monogatarishū*, vols. 6–7 (Kodansha, Tokyo).

This book is heartily dedicated to my late husband, Dr. Andrew H. Dykstra, emeritus provost and professor of the Kansaigaidai Hawaii College, who had read the entire manuscript several times. Without his efforts and cooperation, this book would not have been realized.

Likewise, the book is respectfully dedicated to Professor Enshō Ashikaga, emeritus professor of the University of California, Los Angeles, who introduced me to the most fascinating world of *sestuwa* narrative literature.

ABBREVIATIONS

BD	*Bukkyō daijiten*	仏教大辞典
BJ	*Bukkyōgaku Jiten*	仏教学辞典
DBZ	*Dainihon bukkyō zensho*	大日本仏教全書
Hokkegenki	*Dainihonkoku hokekyōkenki*	大日本国法華経験記
Konjaku	*Konjaku monogatarishū*	今昔物語集
KT	*Shintei zōho kokushi taikei*	新訂増補国史大系
NKBT	*Nihon koten bungaku taikei*	日本古典文学大系
NKZ	*Nihon koten zensho*	日本古典全書
Ryōiki	*Nihon ryōiki*	日本霊異記
Sanbō-e	*Sanbō ekotoba*	三宝絵詞
Taishō	*Taishō shinshū daizōkyō*	大正新修大蔵経

CHAPTERS OF THE INDIAN SECTION
OF THE *KONJAKU MONOGATARISHŪ*

CHAPTER 1

CHAPTER 3

CHAPTER 4

CHAPTER 5

ANNOTATED TRANSLATION
OF THE INDIAN SECTION
*OF THE **KONJAKU MONOGATARISHŪ***

CHAPTER 1

1:1   HOW SHAKA WAS CONCEIVED IN THE HUMAN WORLD

Long ago, before Shaka Nyorai[1] became the Buddha, he was called Bodhisattva.[2] Shaka and lived in the Inner Palace of the Tosotsu Heaven. He considered appearing in Enbudai.[3] At this time, he revealed the Five Deteriortions: First, he blinked although celestial beings do not blink. Second, the flowers of his necklace became wilted although those of celestial beings do not wilt. Third, his clothes were soiled with dirt and dust although those of celestial beings are not soiled. Fourth, he perspired under his arms although celestial beings do not perspire. Fifth, he appeared in various places and did not seek his original seat although celestial beings do not change their seats.

....

1. 如来. *Nyorai* or *tathāgata* is an epithet of the Buddha defined as "he who comes as do all other Buddhas," or "he who has followed the path and attained the perfect wisdom."

2. Bodhisattva or *bosatsu* identifies a being destined for enlightenment, a future Buddha who seeks enlightenment not only for himself but for others.

3. 須弥山. Mount Sumeru, the highest mountain in the ancient Indian cosmology, has three layers: the earth ring (or gold ring), the water ring, and the wind ring, in that order from the base of the mountain. The mountain is forested with scented trees, and the sun and the moon circle the middle part of the mountain. The nine mountains intermingled with the eight oceans extend from its outskirts. The furthest ocean contains continents in the four directions, north, east, south, and west. The human world is included in the south continent, Jambu-dvipa, or Enbudai (閻浮提) in Japanese, which includes sixteen great, five hundred middle-sized, and a hundred thousand small countries symbolizing India. The Enbudai inhabitants in the south continent have less pleasure than those in the east and the north continents, but Buddhas and bodhisattvas appear only in Enbudai to preach the joys of the Law.

Seeing these manifestations, the celestial beings felt strange and addressed Shaka, "We are deeply disturbed over your present condition. Would you please explain the cause?" Shaka replied to the celestial beings, including the deva kings, "One should know that no action is permanent. I shall leave this place and be reborn in Enbudai." Hearing this, the celestial beings lamented bitterly over him.

Shaka considered who the father and mother should be for his rebirth, and decided on King Jōbon[4] of the country of Kabirae as his father and Lady Maya as his mother. Shaka was conceived by Lady Maya on the eighth day of the seventh month of the Year of the Ox.[5]

That night, Lady Maya dreamed that a bodhisattva rode from the sky on a white elephant with six tusks and entered her body through her right side as if going into a translucent vase of lapis lazuli. The startled lady awakened and hurried to King Jōbon to tell him her dream. Hearing her story, the king said, "I just had a similar dream. We cannot interpret our dream by ourselves." He immediately called for a Brahman of the highest rank who was skilled in divination. The king offered the Brahman fragrant flowers and various delicacies and asked him about their dreams.

The Brahman answered the king, "There are various auspicious signs related to the conception by Lady Maya. I give a general explanation for the king's sake. The prince dwelling in Lady Maya will be a member of the illuminating Shaka clan. When he is born, he will release a great radiance, and all the deva kings in heaven, including Bonten and Taishakuten, will respect him. His auspicious signs guarantee that he will become the Buddha. If he does not enter the priesthood, he shall fill the world under the Four Heavens as the Holy King of the Turning Wheel and shall have thousands of children."

Hearing this, the overjoyed king and lady offered the Brahman various treasures, including silver and gold and carriages with horses and elephants.

It is said that the Brahman left the palace with all these treasures. Thus it was told and handed down.

....

4. 浄飯王. King Śuddhodana, a king of Kapilavastu in Central Asia, the crown prince of Simhahanu, and the father of Śākyamuni.

5. The Year of the Ox. The second of the twelve Chinese zodiac years starting from the Year of the Mouse.

1:2   HOW SHAKA WAS BORN INTO THE HUMAN WORLD

Long ago, in the early spring, on the eighth day of the second month, Lady Maya visited the Ranbini flower garden with her wealthy father, who belonged to the Zengaku, a collateral clan of the Shaka.

When the lady arrived at the garden, she alighted from her carriage, adorned herself with precious jewels, and went under a muuju tree.[6] She was attended by forty thousand ladies in ten thousand carriages and followed by nobles, ministers, and other officials.

The muuju tree had a thick stem and weeping branches with pliant leaves. The shining blue and green leaves reflected the light like the neck of a peacock. Just as the lady stood before the tree with her right arm uplifted and tried to break off a branch, the radiant prince was born from the right side of her body. Various celestial beings, including devas and evil kings,[7] priests and Brahmans, were all gathered under the tree.

After the prince was born, he took seven steps in each of the four directions with the help of the celestial beings. As the prince walked, lotus blossoms appeared and received his feet. The prince took seven steps toward the south to indicate that he would bless all sentient beings. He took seven steps toward the west to indicate that after his life was expended, he would become a bodhisattva transcending death and time. He took seven steps toward the north to indicate that he had passed through several births and deaths. He took seven steps toward the east to indicate that he would become the leader of sentient beings. He took these seven steps to the four corners to indicate that he would become the Buddha and be separated from many delusions. He took seven upward steps to indicate that he would not be defiled by the defiled beings. He took seven downward steps to indicate that he would give comfort to sentient beings by extinguishing the fires of hell with the rain of the Law. After having taken this series of seven steps, the prince composed an explanatory poem:

Having repeated numberless lives,

....

6. 無憂樹. The muuju tree or *aśoka* tree with red blossoms frequently appears in Indian literature, especially in connection with the legendary tale of Lady Maya delivering Śākyamuni under the tree.

7. They refer to the *maō* who live in the highest of the Six Heavens in the World of Desire, or *yokkai,* and often interfere with people's attainment of the Way.

> This is my terminal existence;
> Transcending all imperfection,
> I shall save all sentient beings.

The seven steps taken by the prince represented the seven kinds of enlightenment.[8] The lotus blossoms appearing from the ground were the incarnations of the terrestrial deities.

At that time, the four deva kings wrapped the prince with a fine silk cloth and placed him on a jeweled table.

Holding a jeweled canopy, Taishaku sat at the prince's left; holding a jeweled fan, Bonten sat at his right. The two dragon kings[9] Nanda and Batsunanda spouted purified water through the air and bathed the prince once in warm and again in cool water. A golden glow illuminated the prince, who possessed the thirty-two physical features of a Buddha.[10] The great radiance of the prince shone over all the world. The Eight Dragon Deities, the guardians of the Law, produced celestial music in the air. Celestial robes and jeweled necklaces fell from heaven like rain.

At that time, the great minister Makanama[11] reported the birth of the prince and the unusual accompanying phenomena to the king. The amazed king hurried to the garden. A woman there carried the prince before him and said, "The prince pays his respects to his father, the great king." "After paying respects to my Brahman teacher, come to see me," said the king. The woman took the prince to the Brahman, who said to the king, "This prince will surely become the Holy King of the Turning Wheel." The king took the prince to the Kapirae Palace.

Near the palace was the shrine of the celestial deity Zochō.[12]

....

8. 七覚支. The seven qualities of wisdom for attaining perfect wisdom include mindfulness, investigation of the Law, energy, rapture, repose, concentration, and equanimity.

9. The eight great dragon kings identified in the *Lotus Sutra* as the protectors of the Law include Nanda. They are Nanda, Upananda, Sagara, Vāsuki, Takṣaka, Anavatapta, Manas, and Utpala.

10. The thirty-two distinguishing marks on the body of a Buddha include slender fingers, slender limbs, round heels, and long legs.

11. 摩訶那摩. A disciple of the Buddha who is said to be a prince of the Koliya clan.

12. 増長天. Virūdhaka, one of the four deva kings, the guardian of the south. The other three deva kings include Dhṛtarāṣtra or Jikokuten, Virūpākṣa or Kōmokuten,

The Shaka clan members frequently visited there to pray for favors. "Now I am going to take the prince to pay homage at the shrine," the king said to his ministers. As a wet nurse carried the prince before the shrine, the goddess Mui, appearing from the hall of the shrine, came down to welcome the prince and said to the wet nurse, "The prince is superior to others. Don't ever make light of his life and make him worship me. Instead, I will pay homage to him," and the goddess paid her respects, throwing herself at the prince's feet. Afterward, the king, the prince, and his mother returned to the palace.

Seven days after the birth of the prince, his mother died and the king and the people of the country grieved and lamented greatly, wondering who would care for the small prince. The father of the deceased lady had eight daughters. Makahaja,[13] his eighth daughter and an aunt to the prince, looked after him like a true mother. Later the prince was named Shidda.

It is said that after her death the Lady Maya was reborn in the Tōri Heaven. Thus it was told and handed down.

1:3   HOW PRINCE SHIDDA WAS OFFERED PLEASURE IN THE PALACE

Long ago, when Prince Shidda,[14] a child of the Great King Jōbon, became seventeen years old, the king gathered many ministers and consulted with them, asking, "Is there anyone suitable for our prince, who is grown and should take a wife?" The ministers replied, "Makanama, a Shaka Brahman, has a daughter called Yashudara[15] who is said to be superior mentally and physically. She might be a suitable wife for the prince."

Hearing this, the pleased king sent a messenger to the Brahman father of Yashudara, saying, "Our prince is looking for a wife and we have decided on your daughter." The father respectfully received the message and consented.

The king chose a day of good omen after consulting the ministers

----

and Vaiśravaṇa or Tamonten or Bishamonten who respectively protect the east, west, and north.

13. 摩訶波闍. Mahāprajāpati, the stepmother of Śākyamuni.

14. Siddhārtha, the name of the Shaka Buddha before he entered Buddhahood.

15. Yaśodharā.

and sent numerous carriages to receive Yashudara. After Yashudara came to the palace, the prince and Yashudara were married like an ordinary man and wife. Numerous good-looking women were selected to serve and entertain the newlyweds during the days and nights. However, the prince never became intimate with the princess. At night, the prince was calm and composed. He had concentrated only on the Way of the ascetic since the time when he was unfamiliar with his new wife.

Each day, the king asked the attending ladies if the prince had become intimate with the princess. The attendants replied, "We have never seen the prince intimate with the princess." The concerned king added more good-looking women to entertain the prince with dancing and singing. But the prince never became intimate with the princess. The worries of the king increased.

Meanwhile, the prince heard about the blooming flowers and the clear fresh water of the spring in the garden. He sent a lady attendant to the king with the message, "I have seen in the palace for a long time and now I would like to go out to enjoy myself." Receiving the message, the pleased king ordered his ministers and hundreds of officials to construct and sanctify roads. Before leaving the palace, the prince went to the king to pay his respects. The king had an old but wise and learned minister accompany the prince. With numerous attendants and followers, the prince left the palace through the east gate, where the crowd of people, high and low, and of both sexes, gathered like clouds to pay their respects to the prince.

Just at that time, the deity Jōgoten[16] transformed himself into an old man with white hair and a crooked back. He staggered, relying on a stick. Seeing this old man, the prince asked one of his attendants, "What kind of person is he?" The attendant answered, "He is an old man." "What do you call being old?" asked the prince again. "Long ago, this man was young and strong. Now that he is aged, he appears to be weakening. This is what we call being old," replied the attendant. The prince asked him again, "Will only this person become old or will everyone become like this?" The attendant replied, "Everyone will become like this." The prince turned his carriage back and returned to the palace.

---

16. 浄居天. Jōgoten, the Fourth Heaven in the World of Form, where the one who reaches the third stage of enlightenment is reborn.

After a while, the prince again asked the king if he could go out to enjoy himself. Hearing this, the king worried and did not allow him to do so, thinking, "Last time, when the prince went out, he did not enjoy himself but returned lamenting after seeing an old man. Why should he go out again?"

However, the king gathered many ministers, discussed the matter, and finally allowed the prince to go out again, saying, "On the last occasion, the prince left the palace through the east gate, saw an old man, and did not enjoy himself. Now he wishes to go out again. This time, clear the way and don't let anyone like the old man be on his way."

So the prince, as on the previous occasion, left the palace. He passed through the south gate followed by hundreds of officials.

This time, Jōgoten transformed himself into a sick person with a swollen stomach, exhausted, panting, and gasping for breath. Seeing this, the prince asked one of his attendants, "What kind of person is he?" "He is a sick person," answered the attendant. "What do you call being sick?" asked the prince. The attendant answered again, "Though one eats, one will never be cured. Due to the disharmonies of the Four Elements of earth, water, fire, and wind, hundreds of his joints suffer pain. Though exhausted, he cannot sleep well. Though he has hands and feet, he cannot support himself but must rely on others when up or resting. This is what we call a sick person." Feeling pity, the prince lamented over the sick person and asked again, "Will only he become sick or will everyone become sick?" The attendant replied, "Everyone, regardless of class, will become sick." The prince turned his carriage toward the palace, deplored this more, and never enjoyed himself.

The king asked the attendant if the prince had enjoyed his last trip. The attendant answered that the prince became more unhappy after he left the palace through the south gate and saw the sick person on the road. Hearing this, the concerned king became more anxious about the prince leaving the palace and made more efforts to entertain the prince.

At that time, there was a wise and intelligent Brahman named Udai. The king called Udai[17] to the palace and said, "Our prince does not enjoy the Five Desires of color, sound, fragrance, taste, and touch

----

17. 憂陀夷. Udāyin, the son of the teacher of the king of Kapilavastu who later became an eloquent disciple of the Shaka Buddha.

in this world. I am afraid that he may leave the palace to follow the ascetic way of a holy man. From now on, you become his friend and teach him to enjoy the pleasures of this world. Try to stop him from going into the priesthood."

Receiving the king's order, Udai never left the side of the prince but always entertained him with singing and dancing. After a while, the prince wished to go out again. Thinking, "Since Udai is accompanying him, the prince may discard his ideas of detesting this world and entering the priesthood," the king allowed the prince to go out again.

The prince left the palace through the west gate, accompanied by Udai and hundreds of officials, who burned incense, scattered flowers, and entertained him with music and dancing.

Now Jōgoten thought, "Formerly, when I showed the prince the two things, old age and sickness, other people saw them and reported what they saw to the king. The king was angry since the prince did not enjoy himself. This time, I am going to show him death. If this is reported to the king, he may be so furious that he will punish these people. Today, I will show death only to the prince and Udai and not to the others." Jōgoten transformed himself into a dead person who was placed in a carriage with scattered flowers and incense and was escorted by the mourners. Only the prince and Udai saw this.

"What kind of person is he?" the prince asked Udai. Concerned over the king's words, Udai remained silent. The prince asked him three times, yet Udai gave no answer. Now Jōgoten, with his mysterious power, made Udai unconscious and had him answer, "This is a dead person." "What sort of person is a dead person?" asked the prince. Udai answered, "Death will dissolve the form with a wind as sharp as the point of a sword, separate one from consciousness and remove the source of the various senses and the soul. When this person was alive, he was attached to the Five Desires, loved treasure without realizing the transiency of all phenomena, finally departed from it, and now is dead. Those who were related to this person, including his parents, and relatives, will not follow him after his life is ended. The person will be like a plant. A deceased one like this is really pitiful."

Hearing this, the prince was greatly frightened and asked Udai again, "Will only this person die or will everyone die?" Udai replied, "Everybody will become like this." The prince turned his carriage toward the palace.

When the king asked Udai if the prince enjoyed himself, Udai said, "Shortly after we left the palace, there was a corpse on our way. We did not know from where he came and only the prince and I saw him." Hearing this, the king thought, "Only the prince and Udai saw the deceased. The others did not. Surely this must have been a heavenly revelation just as the Brahman interpreted the dream before the birth of the prince. It is not the fault of the ministers and the other people." The worried king sent a messenger to the prince day after day and comforted the prince saying, "This is your country. Why are you always so sad and never enjoying yourself?"

One day, the king told his various ministers, "Our prince has left the palace through the east, south, and west gates, but not through the north gate. When he wishes to take another outing, he will definitely leave by the north gate. Decorate the route and don't permit anyone such as those on his previous trips to appear." The king silently prayed, "Gods in heaven, when the prince leaves the palace next time, please don't annoy him with unfortunate displays."

The prince again told the king that he would like to go out. The king had Usai and hundreds of officials accompany the prince, who left the palace through the north gate. The prince came to a garden, dismounted, and went to a tree, leaving his attendants at a distance. The prince remained alone under the tree and meditated on the facts of old age, sickness, and death.

This time Jōgoten transformed himself into a priest. Dressed in a priest's robe with a stick and bowl for begging alms, he appeared before the prince. Seeing the priest, the prince asked, "Who are you?" The priest answered, "I am a priest." "What sort of person is a priest?" asked the prince. "A priest is one who has abandoned various delusions and will not receive another life. All in this world is transient. What I am learning is the right way of detaching myself from delusion. After being separated from secular life for a long period of time, being undazzled by color, unstartled by sound, unstimulated by scent, unaffected by taste, free of the senses, unconfused by laws, I have reached the shore of true enlightenment," said the priest and vanished into the air. After seeing this, the prince rode back to the palace.

Again the king asked Udai if the prince had enjoyed his trip. Udai replied, "This time, the prince saw no unfortunate signs on his way. When he arrived at the garden, he went to a tree. While he was sitting alone under the tree, a man with a shaven head, dressed in a dyed robe, appeared before the prince, and talked with him. After a while, this person disappeared in the sky. No one knew what this person said to the prince, but the prince appeared very happy while talking with this person. But after returning to the palace, the prince looked unhappy again."

When the king heard this, he did not recognize it as a good sign, and his grief over the situation increased. He reflected,"Our prince may leave the palace to learn the Way of a holy man." Thus it was told and handed down.

1:4   HOW PRINCE SHIDDA LEFT THE PALACE AND WENT TO THE MOUNTAINS

Long ago, the nineteen-year-old Shidda, son of King Jōbon, fervently wished to enter the priesthood. The prince went to have an audience with his father in a proper manner that displayed respect for Taisha-kuten and Bonten. A minister reported the prince's arrival to the king. The king, who had been sad during those days, was very pleased to see the prince. The prince bowed and paid his respects to the king, who seated the prince properly. Sitting down, the prince said to the king, "Separation is inevitable in love and affection. Please allow me to leave this secular life and enter the priesthood to follow the Way. I wish to deliver all sentient beings from their sufferings and from their attachment to love and this life."

Hearing this, the king grieved as though his heart were shattered by the crashing force of a iron mountain, and he had difficulty in sitting calmly. Clasping the prince's hands, the king wept silently with bitter tears. Seeing the king shedding bitter tears, the awestruck prince feared his desire would never be granted and left silently.

However, the prince, thinking only of the priesthood, never had any intention of enjoying himself afterward. Realizing the prince's strong determination, the king ordered his ministers to close all four gates of the palace so that the noise of the opening and closing would be heard for a distance of forty ri[18] from the palace.

One night, Yashudara had three strange dreams. The moon fell to the ground in her first dream, her teeth fell out in her second dream, and she lost her arm in her third dream. Yashudara woke up frightened

....

18. A Japanese league, approximately 2.44 miles.

and told her dreams to the prince, asking, "What do these dreams mean?" "The moon is still in the sky and you still have your teeth and arm. These dreams were nothing but dreams and not real. So don't be afraid," said the prince.

The prince had three wives, Kui,[19] Yashudara, and Rokuya.[20] Each was attended by twenty thousand ladies in a palace of her own. At that time, a heavenly deity who respected the Law descended to the king's palace. By his mysterious power, he controlled the mind, body, and dress of these attendants and made them act as he wished.

When the prince came by, some of these ladies had thrown off their dresses and were sleeping open-eyed as if dead. Others were asleep on their backs with their hands and legs spread and their mouths wide open. Others wore no decorations and ornaments and had urinated and defected while asleep.

Holding a light in his hand, the astounded prince saw this sight and thought, "The true appearance of women is impure and unsightly. They do not deserve to have one offer himself to them."

After midnight, Jōgoten and other deva kings filled the air with their voices and told the prince, "All the people inside and outside the palace are asleep. Now you should enter the priesthood!" The prince hurried to his valet Shanoku[21] and ordered him to saddle the horse called Kenjoku.[22] Shanoku, the only soul left awake by the deva kings' mysterious power, was confused and frightened by the prince's words and remained silent. After a time, Shanoku spoke tearfully, "I don't wish to oppose your order, prince. But I am afraid of neglecting the king's command. This is neither the time to go out for pleasure, nor the time to fight to conquer enemies. Why do you wish to ride at this hour? Where do you plan to go?" "I would like to go and subjugate evils, illusion, and delusion for the benefit of all sentient beings. Don't oppose me," said the prince. Shanoku shed tears like rain and refused many times, but finally brought the horse.

....

19. 瞿夷. The first wife of Prince Siddhārtha. Kui is sometimes considered another name for Yashudara or Yaśodharā.
20. A daughter of a rich man of the Shaka Clan.
21. 車匿. Chandaka, the servant of Prince Siddhārtha, who later became a disciple of the Buddha.
22. 犍陟. Kaṇthaka, the white horse that Prince Siddhārtha rode on the night when he renounced the world.

The prince approached Shanoku and the horse and said to them, "In this world, one must some day be separated from what one loves and from that to which one is attached. One should know and fear the transiency of this life. The priesthood is not easy to attain." To these words, Shanoku replied nothing and the horse did not neigh. At that moment, a radiance released by the prince shone in a hundred thousand directions. He declared, "Now I am going to enter the priesthood as did the Buddhas of the past."

The deva kings made the horse's legs move and made the stableman obey the prince. Taishaku held a silken canopy and the other deva kings followed the prince. The north gate of the palace opened silently by itself. When the prince departed through the gate, the deva kings admired the prince endlessly. The prince vowed, "Unless I terminate suffering in birth, old age, sickness, and death, I shall not return to the palace. Unless I shall achieve enlightenment and spread the teachings of the Law like a widely turning wheel, I will not return to see my father, the king. Unless I extirpate attachment and affection from my mind, I will not return to see Makahaja and Yashudara!"

Near dawn, after the prince had traveled about fifty *ri*, the various deva kings following him suddenly disappeared. The horse traveled as fast as Konjichō.[23] Shanoku also went the entire distance. The prince dismounted at a grove where Baka[24] was practicing the Way. He dismounted, patted the horse, and said, "I am pleased that you have brought me here." Turning to Shanoku, the prince said, "Some have a good mind but an unsatisfactory appearance; others present a good appearance but have an unsatisfactory mind. Your mind and appearance are harmonious. After leaving my country, I have come the entire distance to this mountain, and you are the only person who has accompanied me. I am very grateful. Now that I have reached this place of holy men, you take this horse and immediately return to the palace."

Hearing this, Shanoku threw himself on the ground. He grieved

....

23. 金翅鳥. Suparṇa, the Golden Winged Bird, the protector of the Law, is identified with Jarunda in the Indian myth. It feeds on dragons and its wings span 3,360,000 *ri*. The bird is said to be the incarnation of Mañjuśrī or Brahmadeva to save sentient beings.

24. 跋伽仙. Bhārgava, the first Brahman ascetic with whom the Shaka Buddha engaged in ascetic practices.

and wept with bitter tears. The horse, also, on being ordered, "Go back!" knelt on the ground and shed tears like rain. Shanoku said to the prince, "I disobeyed the king, took the horse, and came with you, prince. Grief and regret will greatly disturb the king. The confusion in the palace will be extraordinary. How can I leave you here like this and return to the palace?" The prince replied, "The Law of this world is: One dies and another is reborn. Is there anyone who remains forever?"

The prince continued, "I will discard my hair ornaments and tonsure my head to attain enlightenment like the Buddhas of the past." Speaking thus, he took a pearl from the jeweled crown ornamenting his coiled queue, handed it to Shanoku, and said, "Give this pearl from my jeweled crown to the king." Removing his ornaments, including his necklaces, the prince said, "Give my necklaces to Makahaja and my other ornaments to Yashudara. Don't regret my absence, but take the horse and quickly return to the palace!" However, Shanoku would not leave the prince; he lingered and wept.

At that moment, the prince cut his hair with his sword and tonsured his head. Taishaku came down and took his hair. All of the other celestial deva kings burned incense, scattered flowers, and praised the prince, saying, "It's wonderful! It's wonderful!"

Afterward, Jōgoten transformed himself into a hunter, wore a priestly robe, and appeared before the prince. The pleased prince spoke to the hunter, "You are wearing the robe of calm and silence; you have detached yourself from delusion and suffering. That is the robe worn by the various Buddhas of the past. Why do you sin by taking life while wearing such a sacred robe?" The hunter answered, "I am wearing this robe to allure the deer. Many deer see my robe and approach me. Then I kill them." "So you wear the robe to kill deer and not to attain enlightenment. I will give you my robe decorated with seven jewels. I would like to wear your robe and save all sentient beings," said the prince. The hunter agreed and they exchanged clothes. Now the prince wore the priestly robe. At the same time, Jōgoten assumed his original form and flew into the sky, releasing a radiance.

Seeing this, Shanoku understood and thought, "Our prince will not return to the palace with us." Kneeling on the ground, he sobbed with increasing sorrow. The prince repeated to the valet, "Quickly return to the palace and report what you saw to the king." Finally Shanoku and the horse started home, tearfully crying aloud.

When Shanoku informed those in the palace, the confusion and grief of the king and others were indescribable. It is said that Kenjoku was the prince's personal horse and Shanoku was his valet. Thus it was told and handed down.

1:5   HOW SHAKA PRACTICED ASCETICISM IN THE MOUNTAINS

Long ago, Prince Shidda entered the priesthood in the grove of Hermit Baka. The prince visited the place where Baka and other ascetics were practicing the way. Baka respectfully received the prince. The prince saw some ascetics wearing grass for clothing and saw others doing penances as they sat by fire and by water. The prince asked Baka, "What do they seek?" "They hope for rebirth in heaven after practicing these arduous ascetic ways," answered Baka. Thinking, "Though they endure such hardship, they will not attain the way of Buddha. I should not stay here," the prince said to Baka, "I am leaving." Hearing this, many ascetics suggested, "If you leave here, you should go north to the great hermits, Arara and Karan."[25]

Meanwhile, Shanoku, leading the horse, visited other palaces and gave reports of the prince to Makahaja and Yashudara, both of whom received the news in tears. The king, too, was so upset that he lost consciousness for a moment. After a while, having recovered his senses, the king ordered a thousand carriages filled with food to be sent to search for the prince in every direction. The king said, "Take and offer this food to the prince so he will never want for food." Shanoku took the food to the prince and offered all the food to the prince, but the prince did not accept any of it. Shanoku sent back the thousand carriages to the king. He remained with the prince and never left him, whether it was morning or night.

The prince went to Arara. The various deva kings again told Arara, "After leaving his father and country, Prince Shidda has come here to learn the true Way and to save sentient beings." After hearing these words from heaven, Arara met the prince and found him extremely noble and stately.

....

25. In the *Konjaku* text, Arara and Karan are the names of two hermits, while in other Buddhist writings, such as the *Butsuhongyōshū-kyō*, they appear as the name of one person.

Arara received the prince respectfully, showed him a seat, and said, "Many kings of the past, when young, enjoyed the Five Desires of this world as much as they wished. They never left their countries and never renounced the world to seek the Way. Though still young, you have come here, leaving the Five Desires behind you. This is truly unusual." The prince said, "I am very pleased to hear this. Please instruct me so that I may end the cycle of birth, age, sickness, and death." Arara commenced, "All beings begin with an independent self, from which arises consciousness of the self, from which arises ignorance, from which arises desire. From desire arise the five delicate sensory elements of color, sound, fragrance, taste, and touch. From these arise the five great elements of earth, water, fire, wind, and space. From these arise various delusions such as greediness and anger. Thus one repeats the cycle of suffering of birth, age, sickness, and death. I have given you a general explanation, prince." The prince said, "I know the karma of life and death, which you just explained. But in what manner will you terminate it?" "If one wishes to terminate its causes, one should renounce the world, keep the precepts well, practice forebearance, and avoid evil desires by practicing meditation in a quiet place. This is what we call enlightenment," answered Arara. "When did you renounce the world and for how many years have you been practicing the Way?" the prince asked. Arara replied, "I entered the priesthood at the age of sixteen, and ever since then for one hundred and four years I have been practicing the Way." The prince thought, "One hundred and four years of practice have left this person in this condition. I shall seek a better way." The prince stood up, told Arara good-bye, and left. Two ascetics on that spot saw the prince leaving. They thought, "The prince's wisdom is so deep that no one can fathom it," and paid him respect by joining their palms.

The prince arrived at the place where the ascetic Karan and other five ascetics, including Kyōjinnyo,[26] were practicing the Way. After that, the prince came by the Nirenzenga River[27] and began his arduous and strict ascetic practices, which included meditation. One day the prince ate only one sesame seed, and on another day he ate only one grain of rice. Sometimes, the prince ate only a grain of rice for one to

....

26. 憍陳如. Kaundinya was one of the five monks who were the Shaka Buddha's first disciples after his enlightenment.

27. Nairañjanā River.

seven days. Other ascetics, including Kyōjinnyo, out of respect for the prince, joined him and practiced the Way.

Thus six years passed, and one day the prince thought, "Since I have started to practice the Way, six years have already elapsed, and I have not yet attained the Way. If I die from exhaustion before I attain the Way, all heretics would say that I had died of starvation. I will take food and seek the Way." The prince left his seat, walked to the river, and bathed. After bathing, the prince felt very exhausted and could not climb the riverbank. A celestial deity came down and assisted the prince with a tree branch. There was a large arina tree by the river. Another celestial deity, Kakuba, stretched out his jeweled arm to receive the prince. Relying on his arm, the prince could cross the river. After the prince finished his meal of rice mixed with sesame, he threw the golden bowl which he used for eating into the river and walked toward the bodhi tree.

In the forest was a woman, Nandahara, caring for a cow. Jōgoten came down to her and said, "The prince has arrived in the forest. Go and pay your respects." The woman rejoiced at this news. Then thousands of lotus blossoms unfolded in the pool, and the woman saw rice gruel with sesame seeds in milk on the blossoms. Thinking this remarkable, the woman took the gruel and respectfully offered it to the prince.

After eating the food, the prince regained his spirits and his body was radiant just as before. Seeing this, the other five ascetics who had followed the prince were amazed, thinking, "If we accept this woman's offering, our merit achieved after so many years of ascetic practice will be lost," and they returned to their original places of practice. So it is said that the prince went alone under the bodhi tree. Thus it was told and handed down.

1:6   HOW TENMA[28] TRIED TO DETER THE BODHISATTVA
        FROM ATTAINING THE WAY

Long ago, when Bodhisattva Shaka came under the bodhi tree, he thought, "How did the past Buddhas attain the most superi-

....

(28) 天魔. Tenma or *Mara* demons interfere and distract those who are trying to attain the Way.

or Way?" Shaka realized that he should sit on the grass. At that time, Taishakuten assumed human form and brought Shaka some soft grass. "Who are you?" asked Shaka, and the person answered, "I am Kichijō, the Good Sign."[29] Shaka was pleased to hear this and said, "So I have dispelled the omens of evil and brought auspicious signs. Could I have the grass that you brought?" Kichijō offered him the grass and asked, "Bodhisattva Shaka, when you attain the Way, will you help me first of all?" Accepting the grass, Shaka sat upon it with his legs crossed just as past Buddhas had done. He vowed, "I will not rise from this seat unless I attain the right Way." Hearing Shaka's firm resolve, all the celestial deva kings, including the Eight Guardians of the Law, the Dragon deities, were exalted and greatly praised him.

At that time, the palace of the demon king was shaken. The demon king thought, "The ascetic Kudon under the tree, leaving the Five Desires, meditating in a correct position, is trying to attain the right Way. If he attains the right Way and saves sentient beings, he will trespass on my territory and surpass me. Before he does this, I shall disturb him and interfere."

The demon king had a son called Satta,[30] who, seeing his father worried about Shaka, asked, "What worries you so much?" The demon king told Satta his intention. "Bosatsu[31] is pure and rectified. He is incomparable. With the support of all the Eight Guardians of the Law, Bosatsu's miraculous wisdom will never be obscured. Why are you trying to invite punishment by creating evil?" asked the son of the demon king, scolding him.

The demon king had three daughters, all more beautiful than other celestial women. They were called Zenyoku, or Indulging Desire; Nōetsuin, or Capable of Pleasing; and Kairaku, or Capable of Love. These three daughters went to Bosatsu and said, "Your virtue is so highly esteemed that all celestial beings admire you. We are young and the most attractive. Our father sends us to you as gifts. We would like to serve you by day and by night." Bosatsu replied, "You are tem-

....

29. 吉祥. It also refers to Śrīmahādevi, the wife of Vaiśravana, who brings happiness and virtue.

30. 薩埵. Satta or Sattva means sentient beings.

31. It refers to Bodhisattva Shaka.

porarily born as celestial beings as the result of some small merit accumulated in your former existences. Though your appearance is good, your minds fail to recognize the transiency of life, the right Way of Buddha. You will surely fall into the Three Evil Realms of hell, of the hungry ghosts, and of animals. I will not accept you." Thus Bosatsu refused them. At that moment, the three women suddenly aged. Their hair turned white, their faces became wrinkled, their teeth fell out, their mouths shriveled up, their hips became crooked, and their stomachs became swollen like hand drums. They became tired and could not walk, but staggered, clutching their canes.

Seeing this, the demon king thought of alluring Bosatsu with soft words. He said, "If you don't like the realm of human beings, ascend to our palace in heaven. I will renounce and offer you any position and means which will enable you to enjoy the Five Desires." "Due to some small merit in your former existence, you were born into the status of a deva king who is free to do anything. Yet after your fortunate moments are over, you will sink into the Three Evil Realms and will have no chance to escape. This is the cause of sin and I shall not accept your offer," said Bosatsu.

The demon king said, "You know the consequence of my acts. Who knows that of yours?" "The consequence of my acts is known by heaven and earth." As Bosatsu said this, the earth was shaken by six kinds of roaring sounds and a terrestrial deity filled seven jeweled vases with lotus blossoms. He placed them on the ground and told the demon king, "Bosatsu has given his mind, country, and family to others and has been single-mindedly pursuing the Way of enlightenment. For this reason, you should not interfere with him!" Hearing this, the demon king was so frightened that he felt all of his hair standing on end. The terrestrial deity offered the blossoms, paid his respects to Bosatsu, and disappeared.

Now the demon king thought, "I cannot distract Bosatsu. I will try another method. I will gather many armies and attack him with power!" Immediately, with his mysterious power, the demon king filled the air space around Bosatsu with monstrous warriors. They held spears, swords, and metal rods. Some carried huge trees on their heads for weapons. Others had the heads of wild boars and of dragons.

Two demon sisters, Mika and Kari, joined the warriors too. They appeared before Bosatsu holding human skulls and produced various ghastly creatures. Other demons also attempted to distract Bosatsu by exhibiting frightful forms and fearful figures. Yet Bosatsu was not disturbed; not a single hair became displaced. The demon king became more and more disturbed by his increasing frustration.

At that time, Inta,[32] a deity, making himself invisible in the air, spoke to the demon king, "I have been watching Bosatsu all this time. His mind is calm and peaceful without any evil thoughts. Don't conceive malicious ideas and force your evil intentions on him, you demons!"

The demon king, who heard these words in the air, became greatly ashamed and returned to his palace. It is said that the demon king was not arrogant or jealous for a long time. Thus it was told and handed down.

1:7   HOW THE BODHISATTVA ATTAINED ENLIGHTENMENT UNDER A TREE

Long ago, although the demon king employed various means to interfere with Bosatsu's attainment of the Way, the king could neither agitate nor alter Bosatsu's mind even by so little as the size of a poppy seed. By the power of mercy, Bosatsu overcame the demons and destroyed the influence of the annoying celestial women and avoided evil plots involving the use of swords.

Finally, on the night of the seventh day of the second month, after practicing meditation, Bosatsu succeeded in attaining the highest knowledge of the absolute truth. About midnight, Bosatsu acquired the Buddha Eye[33] with which he could perceive every phenomenon of the universe. On the third night, after overcoming ignorance and delusion, Bosatsu gained the perfect wisdom of Buddha. From this time on, Bosatsu was called Shaka, or the Buddha.

While Shaka sat meditating, the Great Brahma descended and said, "Teach the Law for the sake of all sentient beings!" With his Buddha Eye, which perceived every phenomenon of this world, for

....

32. 員多. It refers to a thunder god.

33. 天眼. It refers to *divyacakṣus*, the "penetrating eye" in the Buddhist tradition which distinguishes the Buddha and bodhisattva from ordinary men. With such an eye, one can perceive all the phenomena of this world, including those in the past, present, and future.

twenty-seven days the Buddha observed sentient beings of high, middle, and low status, and high, middle, and low bodhisattvas.

First the Buddha thought, "I shall help the ascetic Arara[34] to enter the gate of the wonderful law." Then he heard a Buddha's voice in the air saying, "Arara ended his life last night." "So Arara ended his life last night. Then I shall help another ascetic, Karan,[35] who is wise and intelligent by nature," thought the Buddha. He heard another voice in the air, saying, "Karan ended his life last night." So it is said that the Buddha told himself that Karan, too, had ended his life. Thus it was told and handed down.

1:8   HOW THE BUDDHA TAUGHT THE LAW TO THE FIVE PRIESTS

Long ago, the Buddha went to the country of Harana[36] to visit at the place where five priests, including Kyōjin-nyo[37], were living. These five priests, seeing the Buddha coming in the distance, said to each other, "He may be giving up his asceticism and coming here for food. We should not be disturbed, but should welcome him." When the Buddha arrived, these five priests stood up and paid their respects to the Buddha. The Buddha said, "With your limited wisdom and knowledge, don't regard my attainment of the Way lightly. If you wish to know the reason, I will tell you: If one engages in arduous asceticism, his mind will be disturbed by physical suffering. If one seeks pleasure, one's mind becomes attached to it. By abandoning these two ways of suffering and of pleasure, and by following the Middle way, the Right way, I have finally attained enlightenment." The Buddha expounded to the priests on the Four Truths; on the four sufferings of birth, age, sickness, and death; on ignorance, the cause of these sufferings; on enlightenment after leaving ignorance and suffering; and on the Way to attain enlightenment.

Having listened to the Buddha, these five priests finally ended their suffering and acquired the right view, which enabled them to see

....

34. See note 25.

35. See note 25.

36. 波羅奈国. Vārāṇasī was an ancient country in central India, west of Magadha and north of Kośala. The capital called Vārāṇasī is present-day Benares.

37. See note 26.

the absolute truth. These five priests were Kyōjinnyo, Makakashō,[38] Ahei,[39] Badai,[40] and Manankuri.[41]

In their previous existence, these five priests were five students among the nine at the time of Kashō Buddha. The other four students were intelligent by nature and had already attained the Way, while these five had not. Therefore it is said that these five students, wishing to meet the Buddha in the future, were reborn, became priests, and were helped by the Buddha after he had attained Buddhahood. Thus it was told and handed down.

1:9 HOW SHARIHOTSU[42] PITTED HIS SKILLS AGAINST THE HERETICS

42 number / diciple to Buddha

Long ago, Sharihotsu, a disciple of the Buddha, was the son of a heretic. While still in the womb, he was so smart and strong that he attempted to break out of his mother's stomach. So it was said that his mother had to wear an iron sash around her stomach. After he was born, he was named Sharihotsu and studied under Chōsōbonji, the Long-Nailed Ascetic.[43]

When Sharihotsu heard Priest Ahei preaching about the Four Truths, the four sufferings, ignorance, enlightenment, and the Way to attain enlightenment, he abandoned the heretical teachings, became the Buddha's disciple, and finally attained the right Way. Later, Sharihotsu came to the Buddha. Seven days later, he attained the stage of *arhat*,[44] the highest stage for Buddhist ascetics.

Hearing about Sharihotsu, all the heretics became immensely

....

38. 摩訶迦葉. Mahā-kāśyapa, a son of a Brahman, became one of the ten great disciples of the Buddha and presided over the first council after the demise of the Buddha.

39. 頞鞞. Aśvajit, or the Master of the Horse, was one of the five disciples of the Buddha.

40. 跋提. Bhadrika, a son of King Amrtodana.

41. 摩男拘利. He is sometimes referred to as Makanama. See note 11.

42. 舎利仏. Śāriputra.

43. 長爪梵志. An uncle of Śāriputra who vowed not to cut his nails until he attained scholarship comparable to that of Śāriputra.

44. 阿羅漢. It refers to the one who is free from all craving and rebirth and the one who attains the fourth and highest stage of enlightenment in Hīnayāna Buddhism. See notes 72 and 74.

jealous, and planned to pit their skills against Sharihotsu. They set the date and prepared for the contest.

The people of the sixteen countries of India all heard about the contest and gathered around like a crowd in a marketplace. When the day arrived, the competition began before King Victor.[45] Sharihotsu sat alone while the numberless heretic participants sat in a line facing Sharihotsu.

First, the heretics produced a huge tree on top of Sharihotsu's head and tried to crush it. Sharihotsu created a storm and blew the tree away. Next the heretics caused a flood, whose waters were immediately drunk and dried up by a giant elephant which Sharihotsu produced. Then the heretics produced a blue dragon, which was driven off from the side of Sharihotsu by the Golden Winged Bird. Next a huge ox was produced by the heretics, but a lion produced by Sharihotsu would not allow him to approach. Bishamonten,[46] the guardian deva of the Law, produced by Sharihotsu, instantly subjugated a great demon which had followed the ox.

Thus the heretics were completely defeated and the Buddha's honor maintained by Sharihotsu's victory. The power of the Law became renowned throughout the Five Parts of India, including the east, west, south, north, and central sectors. Ever since, many heretics are said to have followed and respected the Way of Buddha. Thus it was told and handed down.

bad guy Devadatta

1:10   HOW DAIBADATTA[47] FOUGHT AGAINST THE BUDDHA

Long ago, Prince Daibadatta was a cousin of Shaka and a son of King Kokubon.[48] At that time, Shaka was called Prince Shidda.

One day, Daibadatta shot an arrow, which pierced a goose. The goose flew erratically and fell into the garden of Prince Shidda. The merciful Prince Shidda felt great pity for the goose. He took it in his hand, extracted the arrow, and cared for it. Daibadatta came and asked for the goose. Prince Shidda refused to surrender it. Daibadatta became very angry, and the two princes were permanently estranged.

....

45. 勝軍王. King Prasenajit.

46. 毗沙門天. Vaiśravaṇa. See note 12.

47. 提婆達多. Devadatta.

48. 斛飯王. King Droṇodana, a prince of Magadha.

After Prince Shidda had attained Buddhahood, Daibadatta learned the heretical teachings. Daibadatta thought his learning was superior, and he felt increasingly competitive toward the Buddha.

When the Buddha was preaching on Mount Ryōjusen,[49] Daibadatta paid him a visit and proposed, "Since you have so many disciples, you should share them with me." The Buddha refused. Daibadatta spoke cunningly to the five hundred new disciples of the Buddha and secretly transferred them to his residence, Mount Elephant Head.[50] By interfering with the Buddha's preaching and causing disturbance and commotion in heaven and on earth, Daibadatta committed the first of the Five Sins, that of causing dissension within the priestly community.

Some time later, at Mount Elephant Head, Daibadatta preached on the Five Laws and the Eight Treatises of the heretical teachings. Sharihotsu, one of the Buddha's disciples, launched a surprise attack when Daibadatta was sound asleep in order to recover the five hundred disciples. Mokuren,[51] another disciple of the Buddha, used his mysterious powers to put the five hundred disciples in a bag, placed the bag in a pot, and flew back to the Buddha with it.

Seeing this, Kukari,[52] a disciple of Daibadatta, took his shoe and slapped the face of his master. Daibadatta finally woke up and was very disturbed to learn that his five hundred disciples had been taken.

Daibadatta went to the Buddha. He threw a boulder which was thirty pairs of outstretched arms in circumference. The intervention of a mountain deity caused the rock to miss the Buddha. Yet a broken piece of the shattered rock hit Buddha's foot, and his toe began to bleed. Of the Five Sins, this was the second committed by Daibadatta.

Next Daibadatta put poison on his fingertips. Pretending to pay

....

49. 霊鷲山. It refers to the Vulture Peak located on the southern side of Śailagiri, east of Rajigi. Since the appearance of the peak resembles a vulture, it has been popularly called Vulture Peak.

50. It refers to Mt. Gajaśīrṣa in Gaya, a city of Magadha.

51. 目連. Maudgalyāyana, a son of a Brahman, who closely associated with Śāriputra, finally became one of the ten great disciples of the Buddha. Mokuren especially excelled in his spontaneity and mysterious powers. A popular legend tells how he saved his mother, who had fallen in hell in connection with the origin of the *bon* festival.

52. 倶迦利. Kokālī, who fell into hell due to his interference with the Buddha's teaching.

his respects to the Buddha, he knelt at the Buddha's feet and rubbed the poison into the Buddha's wound. The poison was transformed into medicine, and the Buddha's wound was cured instantly.

Later, at the evil instigation of Daibadatta, King Ajase[53] had a gigantic elephant drink a great deal of liquor and drove it at the Buddha to harm him.

Seeing the drunken elephant charging, the five hundred *arhats* of the Buddha flew into the sky from fear. At the same moment, the Buddha produced five lion heads from his hands. The elephant turned and ran when it saw them.

Later, the Buddha went to the palace of King Ajase. Here, he preached and cultivated the king, who finally paid homage to the Buddha. Daibadatta, who was also in the palace, left with increasing frustration and jealousy. Later Daibadatta hit the head of the Nun Lotus, also called Flower Color, an arhat of the Buddha. Of the Five Sins, this was the third committed by Daibadatta. The arhat nun died.

Finally, the earth exploded and Daibadatta fell into hell. It is said that the hole through which he fell is still extant. Thus it was told and handed down.

1:11   HOW THE BUDDHA VISITED A BRAHMAN CITY TO BEG ALMS

Long ago, when Buddha went to a Brahman city to beg alms, the heretics of the city assembled and said to each other, "Priest Kudon[54] is visiting each house and begging alms. This is truly disgusting. They say that he was originally a son of King Jōbon and was supposed to inherit the crown, but an obsession caused him to go to the mountains and become a Buddha. Since he has allured many people and distracted their minds, we should pay no attention to him." These heretics had gone about the city telling the people, "If any of us breaks his promise and pays respect to Priest Kudon, he or she should be expelled from our city!"

So when the Buddha came to a house in the city, he could not

....

53. 阿闍世王. King Ajātaśatru, the son of King Bimbisāra, later supported the First Buddhist Council.

54. 瞿曇. Kudon is the Japanese appellation for Gautama, another name for Śākyamuni before he entered Buddhahood.

enter because the gate was closed. The Buddha stood at the entrance
to another place for a long tme since the family did not answer. Another family drove him away, saying that he had no reason to come to
them. The Buddha could collect no alms, even when the sun was high.
The exhausted Buddha started back, vainly holding his begging bowl
against his chest.

A woman came out of a certain house with a pail of water. She
was going to throw away a bucket of spoiled water which had been
used to wash rice some days before. Seeing the Buddha returning
without alms, this woman felt pity and thought, "What can I offer
him?" She was too poor to offer anything to the Buddha. "What shall
I do?" thought the woman and tears fell from her eyes. Seeing this, the
Buddha asked the woman, "Why are you crying?" "I saw you returning home with no alms at this time of the day. I would like to offer
you something, but I am so poor that I have nothing. This is why I
feel sad and miserable."

The Buddha asked, "What is in your pail?" "Spoiled water which
has been used to wash rice," replied the woman. "You can offer me the
water, which should taste good with the rice flavor," said the Buddha.
"It seems strange to give you this, but I will do whatever you say,"
and the woman poured the old water into the Buddha's begging bowl.
Receiving the water in his bowl, the Buddha offered a prayer, "This
has great merit. Because of this, you will become a deva king of the
Tosotsuten if you are reborn in the heaven, or the king of a country if
you are reborn in the human world."

A heretic on a building had been watching the Buddha. He saw
the Buddha visit each house to beg alms, being driven away, returning
exhausted without any alms, receiving the spoiled water, and offering
a prayer for the woman. The heretic came down to the Buddha and
said scornfully, "Why do you disturb people by saying nonsense like
'You will be reborn in heaven and become a king' after receiving the
spoiled water? These are all lies."

"Have you ever seen a seed of the pippala tree[55]?" asked the Buddha. "Yes, I have," replied the heretic. "How was it?" asked the Buddha. "Smaller than a poppy seed," answered the heretic. "How big
is the tree?" questioned the Buddha. The heretic answered, "It can

....

55. The *pippala* tree (*Ficus religiosa*) under which the Buddha is said to have attained
enlightenment.

shelter five hundred carriages under its branches and have more shade left." "Then this parable should help you understand. A tree growing from a seed smaller than a poppy seed shelters five hundred carriages and still has shade remaining. The merit accumulated by a small offering to a Buddha is invaluable. Things are all like this in the world. Needless to say, likewise are things in the world of future existence," the Buddha explained to the heretic.

Hearing this, the heretic was very impressed and thought it noble. When the heretic paid his respects to the Buddha, his hair fell out instantly as if he had shaven his head. He had attained the stage of *arhat*. After having heard the Buddha predict her future, the woman also paid her respects to the Buddha and departed. Thus it was told and handed down.

1:12   HOW THE BUDDHA VISITED SHŌMITSU, A HERETIC

Long ago, a heretic called Shōmitsu lived in India. After thinking over various schemes, he decided to invite the Buddha and harm him. He assured himself, "If the Buddha accepts my invitation, I will know he is only an ordinary person. If he refuses, he must be a wise man."

Shōmitsu sent a messenger to the Buddha, who immediately accepted the invitation. The pleased Shōmitsu waved his hands at his excited men saying, "Be quiet, be quiet." He had them dig a large trap inside the gate. They set fires and planted swords pointing upward. They scattered sand over thin boards hiding the sword points. Shōmitsu waited for his guest.

One of Shōmitsu's children saw this and said, "It is ridiculous for someone like you to do this, father! The Buddha will never be deceived by such simple scheme. Even one of the Buddha's disciples of the lowest rank will perceive such a trick. It is needless to say that the Buddha will detect it with his immeasurable wisdom. You should stop this nonsense immediately!" The father, Shōmitsu, said, "If the Buddha were wise, he would know of our trap and not come. Since he accepted our invitation so readily, he deserves our trap. So say nothing, but stay there!" The child remained silent after being soundly scolded.

All the preparations for injuring and killing the Buddha were completed. Shōmitsu and his people anxiously waited for the Buddha. The radiant Buddha walked quietly, followed by many disciples of higher and lower ranks. When they arrived before the gate, the Buddha said to his disciples, "You should never walk before me, but should always follow my steps. When eating, too, don't eat or use chopsticks before I do." After warning his disciples, the Buddha stepped through the gate. The heretic and his people all waited attentively by the gate, excitedly watching the Buddha as they thought, "Now he will fall into the hole, he will be burned and will be pierced by the sword blades!" Large lotus blossoms bloomed from the hole in the ground and received the Buddha's feet. The disciples, too, followed the Buddha, stepping on the lotus blossoms. The heretic and his people watched. They thought this extraordinary and regretted their actions.

When the Buddha was properly seated, he was offered various poisonous foods which had been prepared by the heretics. They had thought, "Certainly the Buddha cannot survive after eating the poison!" As Buddha ate the food, all the poison was changed into sweet liquor. The Buddha and his disciples finished all the food and nobody was poisoned.

Seeing this, the heretic felt sad and pitiful, and confessed his ridiculous plots in detail. The merciful Buddha cultivated the heretic and his people by teaching the Law. It is said that the heretic and his people all attained *arhat* status after listening to the Buddha preaching. Thus it was told and handed down.

1:13 HOW THE BUDDHA VISITED A WEALTHY MAN NAMED
      MANZAI

Long ago, a wealthy man in India named Manzai had a son. Another rich man called Shudatsu[56] had a daughter. When Manzai visited Shudatsu, he saw his radiant and good-looking daughter. Manzai asked Shudatsu, "I have an only son. Will you have him marry your daughter?" Shudatsu rejected the proposal. Manzai asked, "Why don't you want them to be married?" "Since I have given my daughter to the Buddha, she is no longer my concern. Besides, your son has accepted heretical beliefs. Wives usually follow their husbands, and my daughter, too, may become a heretic. This is why I don't wish her to marry your son," Shudatsu replied. Since Manzai insisted on the marriage, Shudatsu said he would see the Buddha.

....

56. 須達. Sudatta, a rich man or Śrāvastī, was devoted to Śākyamuni and later constructed Jetavanavihāra, where Śākyamuni stayed more than twenty years.

When Shudatsu explained the situation, the Buddha said, "It's all right. You may have them married immediately. I, too, will go to Manzai and cultivate him." Meanwhile, Manzai kept saying to Shudatsu, "If you can give your daughter to my son, we will receive and welcome her by decorating the route for a distance of sixteen *ri* with gold and seven different treasures." So, finally, Shudatsu had his daughter marry Manzai's son. The route was decorated by scattering gold and other treasures. It is needless to say that Manzai and his people did their best to receive and welcome the new bride.

At that time, the Buddha said to Anan (Ānanda), his cousin, "Go to Manzai and observe the situation and try to convert them to the right way. If you fail, they may beat you and drive you away. Then come back using your mysterious power." Anan received the Buddha's order and went to Manzai. The people were excited and confused to see Anan and said, "Here comes an evil man whom we have never seen before. Is he Priest Kudon?" and they tried to drive Anan away.

Manzai's daughter-in-law stopped them. Her husband asked her, "Is this your master?" "No, he is Anan, the Buddha's disciple," replied his wife. The husband said, "This priest must have come to court you. Send him away!" The wife defended him, "No, you are very wrong. This person left the sufferings of love and desires of this world a long time ago. Just watch when he leaves." Then Anan, by his mysterious power, flew into the sky and disappeared as he released a radiance.

A few days later when the husband saw Sharihotsu coming, he asked his wife, "Is this your teacher?" The wife replied, "No, this person is also a disciple of the Buddha." After a while, Sharihotsu, too, disappeared into the air, releasing a mysterious light. Later the Buddha sent more disciples, including Furuna,[57] Shubodai,[58] and Kashō,[59] who also manifested their miraculous powers by releasing radiance.

Manzai and his son became anxious to meet the Buddha, thinking, "All of the Buddha's disciples have marvelous powers which excel our heretical arts. How would it be with their master, the Buddha? We would like to see him!" At that time, the Buddha revealed mysterious signs. He allowed the radiance released from the white hair in

----

57. Pūrṇa, one of the ten great disciples of the Buddha, was noted for his eloquence.

58. 須菩提. Subhūti, one of the ten great disciples of the Buddha, explained the doctrine of the void.

59. Mahā-kāśyapa. See note 38.

the middle of his forehead to shine on Manzai's house. He shook the earth up and down and in all the Eight Directions, including the east, west, south, and north, with six kinds of roaring sounds. Four kinds of unusual flowers fell from heaven, and the world was filled with the fragrance of sweet daphne and sandalwood.

At that time, Sanmaya, another heretic, came to Manzai's place and said to Manzai, "An evil person came to your place. He is going to harm you and kill thousands of your people. Aren't you aware of it?" "No, I am not," replied Manzai. The heretic continued, "The earth was greatly shaken, and there is no safe place anywhere. Evil objects have fallen from the heaven and have manifested various ill omens. This is truly a strange thing unknown until this time." Manzai asked the heretic, "Why in the world does Priest Kudon wish to kill me?" The heretic answered, "Your daughter-in-law was originally given to Priest Kudon. Does anyone feel calm when his woman is taken away?" "What shall I do?" asked Manzai. "Chase your daughter-in-law out of your place immediately," answered the heretic.

So Manzai told his son, "Get her out of this family. If you live long, you may find a better wife than this woman." However, his son would not give up his wife. He insisted on keeping her, saying, "It is customary in this transient world for parents to depart before their children. My parents are already quite aged and they may die at any time. Yet I cannot spend even a moment without my loving wife. We will die together, hand in hand. I cannot possibly let her go."

The heretic warned Manzai, "The Buddha's men are coming. It will be of no use if you are caught and killed by them. You should end your life before they take you." Manzai agreed and said to one of his men, "I have five hundred swords. Bring the first one!" When the sword was brought before Manzai, he took it and said to his men, "I want to kill myself, but I am too timid. I have three hundred spears. Bring one and cut off my head with the sword and stab my stomach with the spear."

Some of his men brought a spear. When they took the sword and spear and were about to kill Manzai, suddenly lotus blossoms bloomed from the points of the sword and the spear. At that time, the Buddha came down from Mount Spirit Eagle. The Buddha appeared indescribably solemn and dignified with two flanking attendants. Fugen[60] rode

....

60. Samantabhadra, mounted on a white elephant, typifies the teaching, meditation, and practice of the Buddha.

a white elephant with six tusks on his left, and Monju[61] rode an awesome lion on his right.

The Buddha was preceded and followed by numberless bodhisattvas and priests and was also attended by Bonten, Taishaku, and the Four Deva Kings. Nobody knew how many more were included in the procession. When the Buddha visited Manzai in this grand manner, hundreds and thousands of Manzai's people were all said to have rejoiced and to have paid their respects to Buddha. Thus it was told and handed down.

1:14 HOW THE BUDDHA VISITED THE CITY OF THE BRAHMANS AND TAUGHT THE LAW

Long ago, the people of the city of the Brahmans were ignorant of the Law. All had learned and followed heretical teachings. The Buddha decided to visit and cultivate the people in the city.

Sanmaya, a heretic, was in the city and went about telling the people, "Priest Kudon, an evil person, is coming. He will cause a rich man to lose his possessions and become poor by telling him, 'This world is transient. Accumulate more merit.' He will make a married couple in love separate by telling them, 'Life is mutable. Practice the Way.' He will persuade a young and good-looking woman to shave her head by telling her, 'This life is futile. You should become a Buddhist nun.' He will teach the people and cause them to lose what they have; he will estrange the people, and cause their appearance to deteriorate."

"If he comes, what shall we do?" asked the people. The heretic answered, "Priest Kudon likes to stay by fresh flowing streams, by the pure water of pools, and under the serene shade of a fine tree. Pollute the rivers and pools with urine and excrement. Chop down all the trees in the city and close your doors. If he still approaches your places, shoot him with bows and arrows."

The people of the city defiled the water of the rivers and pools, felled their trees, and prepared their bows and arrows.

The Buddha arrived in the city with many disciples. The Buddha said to the people, "It is a pity that you don't believe my teachings

....

61. Mañjuśri often appears astride a lion, representing knowledge and wisdom. Fugen and Monju flank the Buddha and lead the group of *bodhisattvas*.

and will fall into the Three Bad Realms,[62] suffering incessantly for an immeasurable time."

As soon as the Buddha had spoken, the rivers and pools became pure and clear, shining like gold and silver. Lotus blossoms floated on the waters, and plants and trees grew profusely nearby.

The people's bows and arrows were transformed into lotus blossoms, which were eventually offered to the Buddha. The people of the city prostrated themselves and did penance with their foreheads touching the ground, saying, "We heartily pay homage to Shaka Buddha." It is said that the people of the city all attained enlightenment by these deeds. Thus it was told and handed down.

1:15 HOW A WEALTHY MAN NAMED DAIKA[63] RECEIVED PRINCE JINEN

Long ago in India a wealthy man named Daika and his wife had become aged, but had not been blessed with children. One day Daika said to his wife, "Parents are regarded as wealthy and fortunate in heaven and on earth. Unfortunately, we have no children. We should pray to the deity for a child," and they did so.

His wife became pregnant. Daika was immensely pleased. Sharihotsu was visiting Daika, who asked, "Do you know if our child will be a boy or a girl?" "It will be a boy," answered Sharihotsu. The delighted wealthy man immediately called for musicians and celebrated the occasion with great festivity.

One of the six influential heretics of India visited Daika and asked, "Why are you celebrating at this time of the year?" "Sharihotsu told us that our child will be a boy. We became so happy that we decided to celebrate," replied Daika. The heretic became jealous of Sharihotsu, and said to Daika, "The baby will be a girl," and left the place. Some time later when Sharihotsu returned, Daika told him the prediction of the heretic. Sharihotsu said, "The baby will be a boy." The heretic insisted, "The baby will be a girl."

Daika went to the Buddha and asked for his judgment. The Buddha said, "The baby will definitely be a boy who eventually will persuade his father to follow the Way of Buddha!" Hearing this, the

....

62. They refer to the Three Lower Realms of hell, animals, and hungry ghosts.

63. 樹提伽. Jyotiṣka, a wealthy man of Rājagṛha, gave all his goods to the poor.

heretic became more jealous and said to Daika, "This argument is like whipping a running horse without having a goal. We have known each other for a long time, you as my patron and I as your teacher. I will use my miraculous power to change your child from a girl to a boy!" Daika was extremely pleased.

The heretic returned to his people and consulted with them. He decided, "The baby will be a boy and the Buddha will win. This is not what we want. It is better to kill the infant than to have it born." The heretic made some fatal medicine in the form of pills. He sent them to Daika by a messenger, who said, "If your wife takes one of these pills each day, the girl in her body will change into a boy." The pills were red and as large as citrons. Daika's wife took the pills but she died without a word three days later. The wealthy man's grief was indescribable.

Daika and Sharihotsu went to see the Buddha and described the situation. The Buddha asked Daika, "Which do you wish, your wife or child?" Daika replied, "If only I can have a boy, I will not grieve any longer." "You have not lost your child," said the Buddha.

On the day of the funeral, the Buddha and the heretic were present. When the ceremony commenced, the mourners saw a noble and handsome boy, thirteen years of age, standing in the flames of the fire made for the occasion.

The boy was taken immediately by Bishamonten, one of the Four Deva Kings, and was carried to the lap of the Buddha. Since the boy had appeared in this world without his mother, he was named Jinen, Prince Nature. The Buddha gave this boy to Daika. The heretic had lost and returned to his place. The people of the city, including Daika, now regarded the Buddha's words highly. Daika's son eventually aided him in following the Way of the Buddha. Thus it was told and handed down.

Aŋgulimaya

1:16 HOW AUKUTSUMARA[64] HAD BUDDHA'S FINGER CUT OFF

Long ago in India, a man named Aukutsumara believed the heretic teachings which he had learned from his master, Shiman.[65] One day,

....

64. 鴦掘魔羅. Aṅgulimālya was a disciple of Manibhadra.

65. 指鬘. Manibhadra, a king of the Yakshas, is the tutelary deity of travelers and merchants.

Shiman told Aukutsumara, "You go out today and cut off the fingers of a thousand people, offer them to the celestial deities, obtain the throne, and govern the world!"

Hearing this, Aukutsumara rejoiced like a dragon returning into the water. Holding a sword in his right hand and a rope in his left, Aukutsumara ran on his way. By an interesting coincidence, Aukutsumara, planning to do evil, met the Buddha, the prince of King Jōbon, intending to practice the Way after leaving his father's palace.

Seeing Aukutsumara coming toward him, the Buddha began to retreat. Aukutsumara shouted and chased the prince. The prince ran so fast that Aukutsumara could not catch him. Finally exhausted, Aukutsumara shouted loudly, "Prince, I have heard of your vow to save all sentient beings and that you have renounced the throne to enter the priesthood. I want to obtain the throne by offering the celestial deities the severed fingers of a thousand people. Why do you wish to preserve only one of your fingers in opposition to your original desire to help others?"

The prince heard this and stopped running. He cut off his finger and gave it to Aukutsumara. Seeing this, Aukutsumara immediately felt pity, regretted his intention, and returned the way he had come. Thus it was told and handed down.

1:17   HOW THE BUDDHA HAD RAGORA ENTER BUDDHAHOOD

Long ago, the Buddha thought of having his son, Ragora, enter Buddhahood, and sent Mokuren as his messenger. Learning of the Buddha's intention, the mother of Ragora, Yashudara, climbed a high building and had the gatekeeper close the gates, saying, "Don't ever open the gates."

The Buddha gave a message to Mokuren, who was to bring Ragora to the Buddha, saying, "The mother loves the child out of her ignorance, but it will not last long. After death separates them, the mother and the child will suffer endless pain in hell without seeing each other. It will be too late to repent after having fallen in hell. If Ragora attains the Way; returns to his mother to deliver her in the Buddhist Way; cuts the cycle of birth, age, sickness, and death; and attains the arhatship, he will become like me. Now Ragora is already nine years old. I want him to enter Buddhahood and learn the Way." With this message Mokuren went to Yashudara's palace.

Meanwhile Yashudara was calmly sitting in the edifice with the gates closed. Mokuren jumped up in the air and descended to Yashudara as if flying down from the sky. After Yashudara heard the Buddha's message from Mokuren, she said in reply, "Although the Buddha married me when he was still a prince, I have served him as if a god. However he has left me even before three years have passed. Since then, he has neither returned to his country nor seen me. I have been left like a widow, and now does he wish to take my son away? You talk about becoming a Buddha to deliver sentient beings with mercy. Isn't it merciless to separate a mother from her child?" Saying this, Yashudara bitterly cried in tears.

Mokuren found no words to answer Yashudara, and he went to see King Jōbon and told him the situation. The great king called his wife, Hajahadai, and said, "My son, the Buddha, has sent Mokuren for Ragora to have him enter Buddhahood. However, out of her ignorant attachment to her child, the mother would not let the child go. You go and talk to her so that she will understand and regain her reason."

Hajahadai went to Yashudara and delivered the king's words. In reply, Yashudara again spoke in tears, "When I was in my native country, kings of eight countries asked for me, but my parents would not allow any of them to have me except Prince Shaka, who had excelled others in his talents. However, the prince, giving up secular life, has entered Buddhahood. We shall have our son, Ragora, reign over this country. If we have him also enter Buddhahood, what shall we do?" Hearing this, Hajahadai remained wordless.

At that time, the Buddha somehow understood Yashudara's grudge and again sent Mokuren to her. Mokuren came as if flying to Yashudara and delivered the Buddha's words. Yashudara said, "Ragora's entering Buddhahood will disrupt the succession to the throne of the country forever."

Mokuren replied, "The Buddha said, 'Long ago, at the time of Nentō Buddha,[66] I was practicing the way of boddhisattvas. I bought five stalks of lotus flowers with five hundred pieces of gold and offered them to the Buddha. At that time, you, too, offered two lotus flowers

---

66. 燃燈仏. Dīpaṃkara-buddha, the twenty-fourth predecessor of Śākyamuni, appeared in the past and testified that Śākyamuni would attain Buddhahood in the future.

to the Buddha. We vowed to each other that we would be married to each other for one generation after another. Due to that vow, we have become husband and wife in the present life. So now you should not hold a grudge over giving up Ragora out of your ignorance, but have him enter Buddhahood and learn the way of the holy man.'"

Hearing this, Yashudara felt as if she remembered what had happened in her past existence as if it were yesterday or today, and handed Ragora to Mokuren without a word. When Mokuren was about to take Ragora out of the palace, Yashudara, taking Ragora's hands, shed tears like rain. Ragora spoke to his mother, "Do not lament, since I will see the Buddha in the morning and evening. I will soon return to the palace to see you."

In order to console the grieving Yashudara, King Jōbon gathered all the heads of the important clans in the country and said to them, "My grandson, Ragora, is going to join the Buddha, enter Buddhahood, and learn the Way of the holy man." Then the king had each family of the town offer a son to accompany Ragora and to enter Buddhahood with him.

Anan as a messenger shaved the heads of the fifty boys, including Ragora. Sharihotsu and Mokuren, as the priests in charge, granted the precepts to each of the fifty boys. Now the Buddha explained the relationship between the sendara[67] class and retribution in this life. Hearing the Buddha, all the young priests became greatly distressed and lamented, saying to the Buddha, "Venerable Sharihotsu with his great wisdom and virtue has been successfully receiving veneration and offerings in the country. On the contrary, we, the ignorant and virtueless children, may have the same retribution as the sendara in the future as we take other's foods and drink. So we beg of you, Buddha, to forgive our sins in abandoning the Way and returning home!"

Hearing these young ones' anxieties, the Buddha again explained to them by narrating a parable. "Suppose two persons suddenly found food, of which they consumed more than they should. One of them, being intelligent, went to the doctor, took a medicine, got rid of the food and pain in his stomach, and prolonged his life. However, the other one, being ignorant, was unaware of his excessive eating, took no medicine, and, wishing to save his life, sacrificed lives to make

....

67. 旃陀羅. Caṇḍāla is the lowest Indian caste and includes fishermen, jailers, and butchers.

offerings to demons. The food in his stomach caused pains as sharp as the swords of wind. Finally, the person died and fell into hell. If you, young ones, wish to go home out of your fear of sin, you will become like the ignorant one in the parable. But now that you have met me thanks to your good karmic relation, you will be like the intelligent one in the parable who met the doctor, got rid of the pain, and maintained his life." Hearing this, Ragora finally opened his mind to acquire enlightenment.

Thus it was told and handed down.

1:18   HOW THE BUDDHA CULTIVATED NANDA TO HAVE HIM ENTER BUDDHAHOOD

Long ago when the Buddha's younger brother, Nanda, was a layman, he was deeply attached to his wife, whose beauty surpassed anyone in all of India. Being infatuated with his love, he neither believed in the Law, nor listened to the Buddha's advice.

At the time when the Buddha was at Nikuruion,[68] he went to Nanda's place with Anan to cultivate Nanda. Nanda from a high place saw the Buddha in the distance begging alms by holding a bowl in his hands. Quickly descending, Nanda hurried to the Buddha and said, "You were born as a Wheel-Turning King. Why did you discard your sense of shame and pride, and go around begging for food with a bowl?" Nanda took the Buddha's bowl, went inside his house, filled the bowl with delicious food, and returned to the Buddha to offer it. However, the Buddha without accepting the bowl said to Nanda, "I will take your offering if you enter Buddhahood," and went back to Nikuruion.

Hearing the Buddha's words, Nanda thought of following the Buddha's advice. At that time, his wife came out of the house and said, "Quickly come home." However, Nanda, with the idea of entering Buddhahood, went to the Buddha and offered the bowl to him, saying, "Please accept this." The Buddha replied, "Now that you are here, shave your head, wear a priestly robe, and never think of returning to your home."

With his mysterious power, the Buddha pressed Nanda hard and

68. 尼拘類. *Nikurui* refers to the *pippala* or *bodhi* tree under which the Buddha attained enlightenment.

finally had Anan help Nanda enter Buddhahood. While Nanda was in a quiet room, the Buddha appeared and soothed him so well that finally Nanda became happy.

However, Nanda was soon caught with the desire to see his wife. When the Buddha was absent, Nanda tried to go out. But as he tried to leave, the doors to the exit closed instantly and the other doors opened. As soon as Nanda reached the opened doors, the doors immediately shut while others opened. Thus Nanda was unable to go out. Meanwhile, the Buddha had returned and Nanda could not leave the place.

"Next time, as soon as the Buddha goes out, I will go back to my wife," thought Nanda. Just before the Buddha went out, he gave Nanda a broom saying, "Sweep here." Trying to finish his sweeping job quickly, Nanda worked hard. But every time he swept, the wind blew and scattered the dust all around, and Nanda could not finish his job before the Buddha returned.

At another time when the Buddha was away, Nanda came out of the priests' quarters, thinking, "I am going to see my wife while the Buddha is out. The Buddha will surely return by the same route he has taken. So I will take the other route." As Nanda started to take the other route, somehow the Buddha became aware of Nanda's intent and began to take the same route Nanda was taking. When Nanda saw the Buddha coming toward him in the distance, he hid himself behind a large tree. But since the deity of the tree lifted the tree up in the air with his mysterious power, Nanda was fully exposed to the Buddha, who immediately took him back to their temple. So, this time too Nanda could not go to see his wife.

At one time, the Buddha advised Nanda, "You should study the Way. Ignoring one's future life is most foolish. I will take you and show you heaven." So the Buddha with Nanda ascended to the Tōri Heaven, where Nanda saw many palaces of various deities who were amusing themselves greatly with Heavenly Ladies. As Nanda saw a palace which was decorated with innumerable jewels and housed five hundred Heavenly Ladies but no master, he asked the Buddha, "Why does this palace have only Heavenly Ladies but not a Heavenly Man?" The Buddha asked the same question of one of the Heavenly Ladies in the palace, who replied, "In Enbudai, the Buddha's younger brother called Nanda has recently entered Buddhahood. Due to this merit, he will be reborn to this palace as his life span in Enbudai is ended. Since he will be the Heavenly Master of this palace, we have no master in this palace yet." Hearing this, Nanda thought, "It is me."

The Buddha asked Nanda, "How would you compare your wife's beauty with these Heavenly Ladies?" Nanda replied, "In comparison with these Heavenly Ladies, my wife looks like a monkey, and I must likewise look like one!" As soon as Nanda saw these Heavenly Ladies, he forgot about his wife, conceived a wish to be reborn in this heaven, and decided to become one who would maintain the precepts.

Next the Buddha took Nanda to hell. On their way, they passed through the Iron Mountain, and outside the mountain they encountered some women called the Monkey Women whose beauty was incomparable. When Nanda caught sight of one of the women, Sondari,[69] the Buddha asked Nanda, "How would you compare your wife with Sondari, the Monkey Woman?" "A hundred thousand times more beautiful and utterly incomparable." "How about comparing Sondari with these Heavenly Ladies?" asked the Buddha again. "A thousand million times more beautiful and absolutely incomparable!" replied Nanda.

Finally the Buddha led Nanda to hell and showed him various cauldrons in which the sinners were suffering in the boiling water. The sight frightened Nanda immensely. When he saw a cauldron with boiling water but not a person in it, he asked a demon attendant, "Why does this caldron have no one in it?" The demon answered, "In Enbudai, the Buddha's younger brother called Nanda will be reborn in the Tōri Heaven due to his merit in entering Buddhahood. As soon as his life span in the heaven ends, he will fall into this hell. So I am waiting for him by blowing on the fire for the cauldrons."

The terrified Nanda asked the Buddha, "Please quickly take me back to Enbudai and protect me." "You observe the precepts and practice good to enter heaven," said the Buddha. Nanda spoke again, "Right now, I do not think of the rebirth in heaven, but please do not let me fall into this hell!"

The Buddha took back Nanda to Enbudai, preached the Law for him during seventeen days, and finally had him attain arhatship.

Thus it was told and handed down.

....

69. Sondari later became Nanda's wife.

Mahaprajapati

1:19   HOW KYŌDONMI,[70] SISTER OF THE BUDDHA'S MOTHER, ENTERED BUDDHAHOOD

Long ago, Kyōdonmi was a younger sister of Shaka Buddha's mother, Lady Maya. When the Buddha was in the country of Kabirae,[71] Kyōdonmi said to him, "I hear that a woman who engages in ascetic practices will attain the Four Stages of Buddhahood.[72] I very much would like to hear your teachings and enter Buddhahood."

The Buddha said, "You should not wish to enter Buddhahood."

Kyōdonmi asked three times, but the Buddha did not give his permission. Lamenting, Kyōdonmi left.

Later, when the Buddha was again in the country of Kabirae, Kyōdonmi asked the Buddha to permit her to enter Buddhahood. This time, too, the Buddha did not allow her to enter Buddhahood. When the Buddha was leaving with his disciples after spending three months in that country, Kyōdonmi came again with many old women and followed the Buddha. Suddenly the Buddha stopped, and Kyōdonmi again asked permission to enter Buddhahood, the Buddha refused as before. Clad in dirty clothes, the old and tired Kyōdonmi went outside the city gates and sat there crying.

Seeing her, Anan[73] asked, "Why are you crying here like this?"

"I am sad and lamenting since I cannot enter Buddhahood because I am a woman," replied Kyōdonmi.

"Wait here for a while. I will tell this to the Buddha," said Anan. He asked the Buddha about her. "My lord, I have followed you, and have heard that a woman engaged in ascetic practices can attain the Four Stages of Buddhahood. Kyōdonmi wishes with atmost sincerity to receive and enter Buddhahood. Please grant your permission."

"No. She should not seek that. Women should not enter Buddhahood

---

70. 僑曇弥. Muhāprajāpatī.

71. Kapilavastu, the capital of the country of the same name. Kapilavastu, in central India, is present-day Tilonakot in Nepal. The Buddha was born at Lumbini on the outskirts of the city when his father, Suddhodana, was the king of the country.

72. 四果. The Four Stages of Buddhahood or enlightenment (*shudaonka* 須陀洹果, *shidagonka* 斯陀含果, *anagonka* 阿那含果, and *arakanka* 阿羅漢果) may be attained by a Hinayāna Buddhist. Refer to notes 44, 125, and 126.

73. 阿難. Ānanda, a cousin and one of the ten great disciples of the Buddha, accompanied the Buddha for more than twenty years. Due to his excellent memory, he recited the *Sutrapiṭaka* at the First Council.

through my teachings. If women remain pure and engage in ascetic practices, the Buddhist law will not survive in this world. Many sons ensure a family of prosperity. We should have these boys practice the Way and maintain the Law forever. If women are allowed to enter Buddhahood, they will not produce children and mankind will perish. I will not allow this," said the Buddha.

Yet Anan insisted, "Kyōdonmi has a good heart. When you, the Buddha, were born, she took care of you, and she looked after you until you were fully grown."

The Buddha was finally convinced. "Kyōdonmi is certainly full of goodness, and I am obligated to her. Now that I have become a Buddha, I feel more obligated to her. She has been relying solely on my virtue, believing in the Four Noble Truths[74] and maintaining the Five Precepts.[75] However, if a woman wishes to enter Buddhahood and become a nun, she should learn and practice the Eight Precepts. This is like constructing a strong dike to prevent leaks. Kyōdonmi should try hard if she wishes to enter Buddhahood."

Anan clearly understood the Buddha's words, paid his respects, went outside the gates, and told Kyōdonmi, "Stop lamenting. The Buddha has granted permission."

Hearing this, Kyōdonmi rejoiced immensely. She immediately entered Buddhahood, kept the precepts, and became a nun. After hearing the teachings, she attained arhatship.

This was the beginning of women's Buddhahood. Kyōdonmi was called Daiaidō, the Great Way of the Law, and also Hajahadai.

Thus it was told and handed down.

1:20   HOW THE BUDDHA MADE YASHUDARA ENTER
        BUDDHAHOOD [LACUNA]

....

74. 四諦. The Four Noble Truths, one of the first doctrines preached by the Buddha after his enlightenment, are that all existence is suffering, desire and illusion are the cause of suffering, *nirvāna* frees one from suffering, and *nirvāna* is attainable by practicing the Eightfold Noble Truths.

75. 五戒. The Five Precepts include not taking life, abstaining from intoxicants, accepting only what is given to one, not committing adultery, and not telling lies.

1:21   HOW ANARITSU[76] AND BADAI[77] ENTERED BUDDHAHOOD

Long ago, King Kokubon, a younger brother of King Jōbon, Shaka Buddha's father, had two sons. Makanan[78] was the elder son and Anaritsu was the younger. Their mother loved Anaritsu so much that she would not let him leave her sight. She constructed three palaces for him according to the three seasons, and entertained him with many court ladies.

One day, Makanan said to Anaritsu, "Many Shaka men have entered Buddhahood, yet none of our clan has become a priest. All have succeeded to their family occupations. You should enter Buddhahood. Otherwise, continue our family occupation and I shall go into Buddhahood."

Anaritsu replied, "Fine. I find it quite troublesome to engage in the family occupation. I think I will enter Buddhahood." He went to his mother and asked her permission. His mother did not grant it. Anaritsu asked three times. Yet, being so much attached to him, the lamenting mother would not permit him to enter Buddhahood but tried to stop him by various means.

At that time, King Kanrobon,[79] a younger brother of King Kokubon, had two sons. Baba was the elder and Badai was the younger. Their mother especially loved Badai and never would allow him to enter Buddhahood.

Anaritsu's mother said to him, "I will not permit you to enter Buddhahood unless Badai does." Anaritsu went to Badai and encouraged him to become a priest, saying, "My entry into Buddhahood depends on you."

Following Anaritsu's suggestion, Badai begged his mother for permission to become a priest. His mother did not allow it and said

---

76. 阿那律. Aniruddha, a cousin and one of the ten great disciples of the Buddha, lost his eyesight and acquired the Miraculous Eye, one of the Six Abhijñā, Mysterious Powers, by which he saw everything intuitively. He recited the *Abhidharmapiṭka* at the First Council.

77. See note 40.

78. Mahānāman, or Makanama. See note 11.

79. 甘露飯王. King Amṛta-rāja, an uncle of the Shaka Buddha, is sometimes identified with Amitābha-tathāgata or Amida Buddha.

to him as a condition, "If Anaritsu's mother gives him permission to enter Buddhahood, I will give you mine."

Thus the two mothers were reluctant, but finally both granted their sons permission to enter Buddhahood. Badai said to Anaritsu, "Although I have received permission, I will enter Buddhahood after seven years when I have enjoyed the Five Kinds of Desire."[80] "You speak nonsense. One's life is so uncertain. Why should one wait seven years? Allow yourself seven days," said Anaritsu.

Following Anaritsu's suggestion, Badai together with eight other Shaka men and a younger brother of Ubari[81] left seven days later to enter Buddhahood. They were of the same mind. They started off in fine clothes and were mounted on horses and elephants.

As they passed the boundary of the country of Kabirae, they took off their clothes and robes, which were decorated with jewels, and gave them with the elephants and horses to Ubari, saying, "You always have been with the nine of us. Since we are going to enter Buddhahood, we give you these robes, horses, and elephants, which will bring you a fortune."

Ubari parted from the nine others and headed toward his home with the robes, horses, and elephants. Suddenly, on his way, the idea struck Ubari that he, too, should enter Buddhahood with the nine others instead of returning home and engaging in his family occupation.

Ubari hung the robes on a branch and tied the horses and the elephants to the tree, thinking to give them away to anyone who passed by. However, since no one came along, Ubari just left the robes and the animals there and hurried to follow the nine others. As he caught up with them, he expressed his wish to enter Buddhahood with them.

When they all arrived at the Buddha's place, Anritsu and Badai spoke to the Buddha, "Since we have our parents' permission, we would like to enter Buddhahood." Hearing this, the Buddha thought of ordaining Ubari first in order to rid the nine men of their arrogance, and he did. Then the Buddha ordained Anaritsu, Badai, Nandai, Kon-

....

80. 五欲. Five Kinds of Desires include the desire for property, sexual love, food, fame, and sleep.

81. 優婆離. Upāli was one of the Buddha's ten great disciples. He was known for firmly upholding the precepts.

bira, Nanda, and the others in that order. Since the Buddha ordained Ubari first, he made Ubari an elder of his religious order.

Thus it was told and handed down.

1:22   HOW PRINCE HIRASENNA[82] ENTERED BUDDHAHOOD

Long ago, when the Buddha was begging alms with Anan in a city, Prince Hirasenna was enjoying himself with several court ladies on a tall building.

Hearing the amused voice of the prince, the Buddha said to Anan, "The prince will die in seven days. Unless he enteres Buddahood, he will fall into the hells and suffer."

Anan immediately went to the building, cultivated the prince, and encouraged him to enter Buddhahood. Accepting his advice, the prince enjoyed himself for six days and entered Buddhahood on the seventh day. He kept the precepts of purification for a day and a night and died.

The Buddha said, "Because of his merit in practicing the Way for one day, the prince will be reborn in the Four Deva Kings' Heaven, will become a child of Bishamon,[83] and will enjoy the pleasures of the Five Desires with various Heavenly Ladies. After his life of five hundred years in that heaven is ended, he will be reborn in the Tōri Heaven, will become a child of Taishaku, and will be blessed with a life span of one thousand years. After that, he will be reborn successively as a child of Yama[84] with a life span of two thousand years, as a child of the king of the Tosotsu Heaven with a life span of four thousand years, as a child of the King of the Keraku Heaven[85] with a life span of eight thousand years, and finally as a child of the king of the Takejizai[86] Heaven with a life span of sixteen thousand years. Thus the prince will

....

82. Unknown.

83. See note 12.

84. King Yama-rāja is the lord of the world of the dead.

85. 化楽天. Keraku Heaven or Nirmāṇarati is the fifth of the Six Heavens in the World of Desire (*yokkai*), which provides various pleasures.

86. 他化自在天. Takejizai Heaven, Paranirmita-vaśa-vartin, is the sixth and the highest heaven in the World of Desire, which has the palace of the great Māra King and provides pleasures and beneficial environments for its residents.

be reborn and will enjoy pleasures seven times in the Six Heavens, in each of which he will complete an entire life span.

The merit of one day's Buddhahood deserves rebirth in the heavens with happiness and pleasures and guarantees the avoidance of sufferings in the Three Lower Realms[87] for the period of twenty thousand *kalpa* years. Finally, the prince will be reborn in the human realm with abundant treasures, will abandon secular life in his old age, will enter Buddhahood, will practice the Way, and finally will become the Hyakushi Buddha[88] called Bitairi and will extensively benefit the sentient beings of the heavens and the human realms.

So the merit of entering Buddhahood is truly marvelous.

Thus it was told and handed down.

1:23 HOW KING SENDO[89] WENT TO THE BUDDHA AND ENTERED BUDDHAHOOD

Long ago in India, there were two capital cities which respectively became prosperous and declined. One was called Keshi and the other Shōon.

All the people of Shōon once enjoyed comfort and wealth. King Sendo governed the country, which bountifully produced the five cereals and rarely had sickness or disease. His queen was called Gakkō, Moonlight, and his prince Chōkei, Top Knot. The king had two ministers called Riyaku, Benefit, and Jogen, Troublefree.

The king of Ōsha[90] was called Yōshō, Shadow of Victory; the queen, Shōshin, Victory; the prince, Mishō,[91] Grudgeless; and the minister, Gyōu, Falling Rain.

King Sendō held a great Buddhist service, gathered many people, and asked, "Does the other country have comforts and pleasures such as ours?"

---

87. Three Lower Realms; see note 62.
88. 辟支仏. It refers to Pratyeka Buddha, a Buddha who has been emancipated without any teacher.
89. Unknown.
90. 王舎城. It refers to Rājagrha, the capital of Magadha, which is present Rajgir, Behar, India.
91. 未生怨. Mishō refers to King Ajase.

A merchant of the country of Makada[92] was at the service and replied, "The city of Ōsha to the east of here is like this." King Sendō asked him, "Is there anything that they lack?" "Treasures are scarce there," answered the merchant.

King Sendō filled a golden chest with precious treasures, and had a messenger take it with a letter to King Yōshō.

King Yōshō read the letter, opened the chest, was immensely pleased, and asked, "What does that other country lack?" Many people answered, "That country is very prosperous, but does not have woolen cloth."

Hearing this, King Yōshō immediately placed a large woolen cloth produced by his country in a box and had his messenger take it with a letter to King Sendō.

King Sendō was amazed at the size of the cloth and asked the messenger, "How does your king look?"

He replied, "Our king is as large as you. He is brave and talented in the ways of war."

King Sendō immediately had a suit of armor made. The armor had the five merits, including luster, coolness, and resistance to being cut by swords or pierced by arrows. The king had his messenger take the armor with a letter to King Yōshō.

King Yōshō read the letter, looked at the armor, and felt extraordinary. When the king had the armor appraised, he found that it was worth ten billion gold coins. The king became sad since he had nothing its equal to return to King Sendō.

Seeing the king lament, Minister Gyōu asked, "King, why are you so sad?"

The king described his problem. The minister said, "King Sendō sent you a valuable suit of armor. But, king, you have the Buddha in your country, who surpasses any treasure in the human realms and is matchless in all the worlds of the ten thousand directions."

"That is true. What should be done about it?" asked the king.

"You should have the Buddha's image painted on the wool cloth and send it by messenger," suggested the minister.

"In that case, I will tell this to the Buddha," said the king and did so.

....

92. 摩竭提 or Magadha.

The Buddha responded, "How wonderful to make a painting of the Buddha to send to that country. The painting should be
done according to the rules. The text on faith in the Three Treasures
should appear below the painting, followed by the text of the Twelve
Causations[93] of karmic cycles and *nirvana* with two verses which
should be written above the painted image:

> Seeking to leave the mundane world,
> One should endeavor by the Buddha's teachings
> To overcome the armies of life and death
> Just as an elephant tramples grass huts.
> The one practicing the Law
> Should never lose himself in idleness.
> He should successfully cross the seas of delusion
> And finally reach the end of suffering.

The king finished inscribing the verses on the painting as instructed by the Buddha and said to his messenger, "Take this painting
to a large and light place in that country for display under a decorated
canopy and banners. Burn incense and scatter flowers. If any one asks,
'What is this?' you will tell them, 'This is a painted image of the Buddha who gave up his throne and attained enlightenment.' You should
also explain the verses above and below the painted image." The king
put the painting in a box ornamented with gold and silver and for-
warded it with his letter to King Sendō.

The messenger took the painting to the other country. He first
delivered the letter to the king, who read it and somehow felt angry,
and said to his minister, "I still don't understand the conception of
good and evil held by the people of that country. Why has the king
sent me such a superior object?"

The minister replied, "Judging by what I have heard of the king,
I don't think he meant to insult you by sending this gift. So you
should do as described in the letter."

....

93. Twelve Causations refers to the twelve-linked chain of dependent origination:
(1) ignorance, the cause of illusions; (2) action produced by the preceding; (3)
consciousness; (4) mental functions and matter; (5) the five organs and the mind;
(6) contact; (7) perception; (8) desire; (9) attachment; (10) existence which causes
future reward; (11) birth; (12) old age and death. These twelve links are generally
thought to span the past, present, and future.

The messenger of King Yōshō set up and hung a canopy and banners on the street, decorated the place beautifully, burned incense, scattered flowers, and gathered many people.

Leading his army, King Sendō saw this fine display in an ornate place. He did not trust what he saw but felt insulted. He said to the minister, "Quickly gather soldiers. I am attacking the country of Makada." The minister warned the king, "You should consider this more carefully."

Taking the minister's advice and following the message in the letter from King Yōshō, King Sendō returned to his country and opened the painting of the Buddha's image. Merchants from the central part of India saw the painting and recited, "Faith in the Buddha!" in unison. Hearing this, King Sendō was so awestruck that he felt as if all his body hairs were standing on end.

The king asked the meaning of the phrase and the merchants explained it to him. Reciting the phrase, the king returned to his palace. As he had meditated greatly on the phrase, he attained the stage of *shudaonka*,[94] enlightenment, while sitting up until dawn.

Later, King Sendō sent King Yōshō a letter saying, "Thanks to you, I now can see the absolute truth. Next I would like to see a priest. Please send one."

King Yōshō read the letter, went to the Buddha, and suggested, "King Sendō has already attained the first stage of enlightenment. He also would like to see a priest. I think Priest Kataenna[95] has a connection with that country. He should be sent there immediately."

At the Buddha's instructions, Kataenna led five hundred priests to the city of Shōon and said to the king, "The Buddha has sent five hundred priests at your request, since you have already attained the first stage of enlightenment. Come out yourself and receive us. You also should construct a temple with five hundred rooms. The future benefits will be countless."

....

94. 須陀洹果. *Shudaonka* refers to the stage in which one has entered the stream of sanctification (*srotāpanna*), the first of the four stages of enlightenment pursued by a Hīnayāna disciple. This stage can be attained by entering the stream of sanctification (*nyūru*) or by going against the stream of birth and death (*gyakuru*), and the one who has attained this stage is free from all false views of the Three Lower Realms. Refer to notes 72, 125.

95. 迦多演那. It refers to Kātyāyana, who later became one of the ten great disciples of the Buddha.

Each of the five hundred priests preached the Law to the listeners as individuals. Some attained arhatship, and others were converted to the teachings of the Greater Vehicle.[96]

Some palace women invited Kataenna. He did not allow himself to preach the Law to the women. Yet he said, "If there are nuns, I will preach for them." King Sendō sent King Yōshō a letter on account of this. King Yōshō explained the situation to the Buddha and said, "We should send five hundred nuns, including Sera."[97] At the Buddha's instruction, the five hundred nuns, including Sera, went to the city of Shōon, and the Buddha preached for them.

Some time later, the queen, Lady Gekkō, suddenly passed away, was reborn in the heaven, descended, and reported her experiences to King Sendō. King Sendō wished to retire from secular life and thought, "I will give my throne to Prince Chōkei, and I will enter Buddhahood." He communicated his plans to his two ministers. The ministers grieved tearfully over the king's retirement from secular life and told the prince, who also mourned greatly. The king told his people, who likewise lamented greatly over his abdication, collected many treasures, and held a national grand service in honor of the king to repay his favors. The service was held with great offerings made to the general public of all ranks and both sexes.

After that, King Sendō, accompanied by a single attendant, walked to the city of Ōsha. Even though the distance was great and the trip on foot strenuous, the king would not change his mind because he strongly yearned for the Way. The king forced his escorts, including the prince, ministers, and hundreds of officials to cease following him. They bade him farewell and tearfully sent him off.

The king and his single attendant finally arrived in the city of Ōsha. This was reported to King Yōshō.

On hearing this news, King Yōshō immediately had the road prepared. At the head of his ministers, his hundred officials, and his soldiers, King Yōshō asked King Sendo why he came.

....

96. Great Vehicle refers to the Three Vehicles in Mahāyāna. They include *śrāvaka- yāna* in which one correctly understands the Four Noble Truths and becomes an *arhat* (*shōmon*); *pratyeka-buddha-yāna*, in which one correctly understands the Twelve Causations and becomes a *pratyeka-buddha* (*enkaku*); and *bodhisattva-yāna* in which one attains bodhisattvahood after innumerable years of religious practices.

97. Śaila.

King Sendō replied, "Thanks to your virtue, I am inclined toward the Way. I wish to visit the Buddha and enter Buddhahood. So I have come here after relinquishing my throne to the prince." Hearing this, King Yōshō was immensely affected and tearful. He accompanied King Sendō into the city.

The Buddha was in Chikurin Temple.[98] King Yōshō took King Sendō to the Buddha to explain his intention, and said to the Buddha, "He would like to enter Buddhahood." As soon as the Buddha said to King Sendō, "You are welcome," Sendō's hair fell out of its own accord and he looked like a one-hundred-year-old priest. He received the precepts and became a disciple of the Buddha. King Yōshō thought this most noble. He paid homage to the Buddha and left.

Thanks to the virtue of King Yōshō and of Minister Gyōu, King Sendō entered Buddhahood. Even though he had not known the Law, he was benefited because he saw the Buddha.

Thus it was told and handed down.

1:24   HOW YUGA, A WEALTHY MAN, VISITED THE BUDDHA
        AND ENTERED BUDDHAHOOD [LACUNA]

1:25   HOW WARATA[99] WENT TO THE BUDDHA AND BECAME
        THE BUDDHA'S DISCIPLE

Long ago, a man called Warata lived in India. His parents were very wealthy with abundant treasures. They had never been poor.

Being pious, Warata wished to enter Buddhahood and become the Buddha's disciple. Warata asked his parents for a leave of absence, but was refused. "Unless I am permitted to enter Buddhahood, I will die soon," said Warata. He lay down, and took no food for three days. He did not eat on the fifth nor on the seventh day, and said, "I am about to die."

Someone warned his parents, "Warata is going to die after starving for seven days. Allow him to enter Buddhahood rather than grieve over his death." Accepting this advice, the parents gave Warata their permission.

....

98. The temple refers to Veṇuvana, the Bamboo Grove Monastery built by King Bimbisāra.

99. A rich man of Śrāvastī.

Warata got up and took his meal as usual. When he was about to go to the Buddha, his parents said, "Even after you are the Buddha's disciple, be sure to come and see us three times a year to maintain our relationship as parents and child. Not to see you for a long time will be unbearable for us."

Warata went to the Buddha, entered Buddhahood, and became the Buddha's disciple. His parents waited for one year. Warata did not visit them. The parents waited in vain for a few more years. Twelve years had passed since Warata left them.

Finally Warata separated himself from the delusions of this world and received his arhatship. One day he said to the Buddha, "I am thinking of visiting my parents." "Go quickly," said the Buddha. Warata reached his home and begged for alms by the gateway.

Although he saw him, his father did not recognize him and chased him away, saying, "What priest has come here?"

Later Warata again stood by the gate. A female servant who was sweeping the yard watched him and asked, "Priest over there, aren't you our master Warata?" "Yes," Warata answered. The servant hurried to tell her master, "Don't you know that the priest standing by the gate is Warata?"

His parents tearfully received Warata, seated him properly, dressed him in good clothes, gave him delicious food, and said, "You have already attained your purpose. Now you should remain and succeed to our family occupation. We have accumulated countless treasures only for you," and the parents placed various treasures, including gold and silver, before Warata. They continued, "Your wife has been missing you all these years. She is gracefully coming from her room. You should look at her. All these thousands of treasures are in your hands. Use them as you wish."

"Are you really offering me these treasures? In that case, please load them in a carriage," said Warata. His father filled a carriage with the treasures and gave it to him.

Warata took the treasures to the River Gōga[100] and threw them into the water, saying, "Because of treasures, people never leave the Three Lower Realms!"[101] Afterward, Warata ascended into the air and revealed the Eighteen Mysterious Changes.

....

100. The Ganges River.
101. See note 62.

When Warata was sitting on the grass under a tree, a neighboring king came while hunting. One of the king's men said to the king, "My lord, isn't the priest under the tree your playmate Warata?"

The king came to Warata and asked, "Why have you become a priest?" "I have entered Buddhahood for three reasons," replied Warata. "What reasons?" inquired the king.

Warata asked the king, "First: Can you very well substitute for your parents when they are sick?" "No," replied the king. "Second: Can you substitute for a dying old man?" asked Warata. "No," the king answered. Warata continued, "Third: Can you substitute for suffering sentient beings in the hells?" "No, I cannot," said the king. "Having observed these three things, I have entered Buddhahood," said Warata.

The king suggested, "I remember that you are one of my old playmates. I will offer you the first of my twenty thousand queens and half of my country. So return to secular life."

"I want neither twenty thousand queens nor one thousand kingdoms. All I wish to is become a Buddha, to assume the sufferings of sentient beings such as you and to make them all Buddhas." Saying this, Warata ascended into the air and disappeared.

Thus it was told and handed down.

1:26   HOW A MAN FIRST ENTERED BUDDHAHOOD AT THE AGE OF ONE HUNDRED AND TWENTY

Long ago, an old man in India first developed a pious mind at the age of one hundred and twenty. He went to the Buddha, entered Buddhahood, and became his disciple.

Since he was a new disciple, the other five hundred disciples had him run their personal errands. Being old, the new disciple had difficulties in getting up and down and was slow in bringing the water for others to wash their hands.

The distressed old priest thought of throwing himself from a mountain. He climbed to a summit and jumped, saying, "I am not throwing myself down because I have broken the precepts, nor because I don't wish to serve the Buddha, but only because I am unable to get around due to my old age."

Seeing this, the merciful Buddha stretched out his hands adorned by one hundred blessings, received the old priest, and placed him with

Anan, saying, "The priest threw himself down because of his igno-rance. Quickly have him practice the Way and enlighten him." At the Buddha's order, Anan accompanied the old priest.

On the way, they saw a beautiful young woman lying dead on the roadside. Parts of her body had decomposed and large worms crawled in and out through her eyes, nose, and mouth. "What is this?" asked the old priest, but Anan continued on his way without replying.

After a while, they saw another woman walking ahead of them. She carried a huge cauldron from which fierce flames ten feet high ap-peared of their own accord. The woman entered the cauldron, cooked herself well, left the cauldron, ate part of her own flesh, and continued on her way, carrying the cauldron.

Seeing this, the old priest thought it most extraordinary, but he kept on his way with Anan. Soon they saw a ten-foot-high fire pole in the distance. As they came closer, they found that the pole had a human shape. Hundreds and thousands of worms had attached themselves to it and were sucking and biting with their iron jaws and teeth.

The old priest thought this strange but continued on his way. Finally they arrived at a great mountain. They climbed to its summit and sat on the grass seats for the leaders of the priests.

The old priest asked, "What were these strange sights we saw on our way?" Anan replied, "The first dead woman was a queen of this country, who fell into the sea and was washed ashore by the waves. Since she was egotistical about her appearance, she became worms af-ter her death and protected her appearance by crawling in and out of her corpse.

"The woman who carried the cauldron and ate her own flesh had served a master in her previous life. When her master sent her to a priest with an offering of food, the woman ate part of the food on her way.

"Noticing that part of the food was missing, the priest asked, 'I wonder if you have eaten some of the food?' 'No, if I did, I will eat my own flesh for generation after generation,' replied the woman. For her sin, she has been sentenced to eat her flesh for ninety-one years.

"The burning fire pole with a human shape resulted from the act of a person who committed thefts in the priests' community and who extinguished temple lights. He has burned like that for countless *kalpa*[102]. This high and great mountain is your accumulated bones and relics from the times when you were born in your former lives as dogs, foxes, hawks, crows, mosquitoes, and flies during one *kalpa* of years. You can imagine how great a pile of your bones remains from your suffering and pain after falling into the Four Realms of hell, hungry ghosts, animals, and *asura*[103] during countless years."

Hearing this, the old priest understood the transience of everything, immediately attained enlightenment, and became an arhat.

Thus it was told and handed down.

1:27   HOW AN OLD MAN WENT TO THE BUDDHA AND ENTERED BUDDHAHOOD

Long ago, a very poor old man who had not accumulated even a particle of dust during his life lived in India. Naturally his wife and children had abandoned him and he had no one to serve him. The sad old man thought in distress, "I have no savings and am too poor to carry on my family occupation. I have no recourse other than to become the Buddha's disciple."

The old man visited Gionshōja[104] and first saw Sharihotsu and said, "I would like to enter Buddhahood and receive the precepts."

"Wait for a while. I will first go into meditation and see whether you have a karmic cause to become a priest or not," said Sharihotsu and practiced meditation for three days. When Sharihotsu emerged from his meditation, he rejected the old man saying, "Examining your past during eighty thousand *kalpa* years, I have found no karmic causes for you to enter Buddhahood. You have never done a single good deed. On what basis can I allow you to enter Buddhahood?"

The old man went to Mokuren[105] and asked him. Mokuren also rejected him since he had no valid reason. The old man went to other

102. *Kalpa* refers to a long duration of time sometimes described as the period required for a celestial woman to exhaust a ten-cubic-mile stone as she touches it with her robe.
103. 阿修羅. *Asura* in Buddhism are regarded as demons who like fighting. Originally in Brahmanism and Hinduism, the *asura* fight with the gods headed by Śakra of India.
104. 祇園精舎. Gionshōja, Jetavana-vihāra, the first monastery of the Buddhist order, was built by a rich man, Sudatta.
105. See note 51.

disciples, such as Furuna[106] and Shubodai[107], but they all refused, saying, "How can we permit you to become a priest after all our superiors have rejected you?"

The five hundred disciples of the Buddha took sticks and stones. They rejected and chased the old man from the temple compound. The helpless old man was crying by the temple gate.

Seeing this, the Buddha came out from the gate and asked, "Why are you crying here? If you have any wish, I will try to grant it."

The old man replied, "I have neither savings nor clothes and food. My people, including my wife and children, have abandoned me. I thought of becoming your disciple, came here, and asked permission. All your five hundred disciples, including Sharihotsu and Mokuren, have rejected me. They have driven me out, saying that I have no valid reason to become a priest. So I am crying here like this."

The Buddha approached the old man, stroked his head with a golden-hued hand, and said, "I made a vow and became a Buddha just to benefit a sentient being like you. I will realize your wish." The Buddha took the old man inside the temple.

First, the Buddha called Sharihotsu and said, "Have this old man enter Buddhahood."

"I have examined his past during eighty thousand *kalpa* years" said Sharihotsu, "This old man has no valid karmic reason. On what basis, my lord Buddha, will you permit him to enter Buddhahood?"

"Just have him enter Buddhahood," insisted the Buddha.

Obeying the Buddha's order, Sharihotsu had the old man enter Buddhahood, granted him the precepts, and again inquired of the Buddha, "The good and evil that happens to people all results from causes in their previous lives. Why have you allowed this old man to enter Buddhahood?"

The Buddha explained, "You listen to me well. Many years ago, prior to the *kalpa* years, each of which can be estimated as equal to a dust particle which has appeared during the past eighty thousand years, this old man was born as a hunter. Once when he was stalking a deer, a tiger suddenly appeared and was about to devour him. To escape his predicament, the hunter uttered one phrase, "Faith in the Buddha!" That hunter is this present old man. Because his single good

106. See note 57.
107. See note 58.

deed in uttering the Buddha's name is still valid, I allowed him to enter Buddhahood. Failing to perceive this, you refused him entry into Buddhahood."

Hearing this, Sharihotsu had nothing to say. Thanks to his merit in entering Buddhahood, the old man immediately attained arhatship.

Thus it was told and handed down.

1:28   HOW A DRUNKEN BRAHMAN UNINTENTIONALLY ENTERED BUDDHAHOOD

Long ago in India, a drunken Brahman who had lost his senses while intoxicated went to Gionshōja and said to the Buddha, "I would like to enter Buddhahood." The Buddha had Anan bring the Brahman into Buddhahood. Afterward, the Brahman awoke and found himself in a priestly robe with his head shaved. Shocked and suspicious, the Brahman ran away.

"Why was the Brahman so surprised and why did he run away?" asked the Buddha's disciples. "That Brahman had no intention of becoming a priest during countless *kalpa* years. Yet when he lost his senses while drinking and intoxicated, he entered Buddhahood and wore the priestly robe. After he awoke, he was surprised and fled. However, thanks to his entry into Buddhahood, he will attain future enlightenment," replied the Buddha.

So, even though the Buddha usually prohibits drinking, the Buddha approved of this Brahman's drinking, which enabled him to enter Buddhahood.

Thus it was told and handed down.

1:29   HOW KING HASHINOKU[108] FOUGHT KING AJASE[109]

Long ago in India, King Hashinoku of the country of Shae and King Ajase of the country of Makada became unfriendly and began to fight. Each king enrolled thousands of troops, including riders on horses and elephants, and foot soldiers. Encouraging the morale of their numerous soldiers, the two kings developed their tactics.

....

108. 波斯匿王. Prasenajit, the king of Śrāvasti in Kośala, Central Asia, a devoted Buddhist, was deposed by his son Virūdhaka at the age of eighty and died of hunger.

109. See note 53.

On the battlefield, King Hashinoku's army was defeated and his camps were destroyed. The war continued, but Hashinoku's army lost three times. The distressed king returned to his palace and grieved immensely without eating during the day or sleeping at night.

Shudatsu,[110] a wealthy man of the country of Shae, heard of the king's grief. He came to the palace and suggested to the king, "I hear that even though its morale was high, your army lost every battle since it was inferior to the enemy. Here is my thought. I have many treasures in my storehouse. If I take out these treasures and offer them to the soldiers for fighting, naturally the enemy soldiers will hear of it and may even join your army. Even though the enemy army is strong, if your army is greater numerically, the enemy will be inferior."

Hearing this, the rejoicing king sent messengers to Shudatsu's place and had them bring many treasures, which he offered to his soldiers. The news reached his enemies in the country of Makada and brought King Hashinoku soldiers as numerous as the clouds.

When the battle commenced, King Ajase fought fiercely at the head of his soldiers. King Hashinoku placed his strong soldiers in the first camp and the rest in the second and third camps according to their ability. Both armies fought. Due to its inferior quality and size, the Makada army lost. Its camps were destroyed. King Ajase was caught by the Shae soldiers and was brought to King Hashinoku's camp.

The overjoyed King Hashinoku summoned King Ajase, put him on a flying carriage, accompanied him to the Buddha, and said, "Since King Ajase has been my foe, I should cut off his head. But since responding to enmity with favors is a superior policy, I will not kill him."

"How wonderful! How wonderful!" praised the Buddha and continued, "Great king, you have thought it out well. A grudge will end if one responds with favors and virtue. Even enmity continuing for three generations will disappear. It is very wise and merciful of the great king to comprehend such a good policy and to free his enemy, King Ajase!"

King Ajase, who was forgiven instead of losing his head, forgot his enmity against Hashinoku and behaved well toward him. The news reached neighboring countries, and no one thought lightly of King Hashinoku.

....

110. See note 54.

Now King Hashinoku invited Shudatsu and said, "Thanks to your suggestion, I won the battle. Quickly ask me for whatever you wish. I will grant it."

Clasping his hands together, the kneeling Shudatsu said to the king, "It is very gracious of you to say this. What I wish is to become king of this country for seven days. Please grant this."

The king issued an edict, "Shudatsu shall be king of the country of Shae seven days. All taxes shall be paid to Shudatsu. State affairs, whether significant or trivial, shall be decided by Shudatsu." Like bending plants in the wind, the people of the country all obeyed Shudatsu's orders.

At that time, Shudatsu had an order proclaimed to the accompaniment of beating drums and blowing trumpet shells, "All the people of the country, whether high or humble, shall venerate the Buddha and only obey his precepts." So the entire population of the country respected the Buddha and firmly upheld his precepts. On the seventh day, Shudatsu returned the throne to the king.

The Buddha explained, "Thanks to Shudatsu who encouraged the people to practice virtue while he was king for seven days, countless sentient beings will be delivered and attain Buddhahood in the future."

Thus it was told and handed down.

1:30   HOW TAISHAKU FOUGHT ASHURA

Long ago, Taishaku had a wife, Lady Shashi,[111] who was a daughter of Rago, King Ashura. King Ashura constantly fought Taishaku to regain his daughter.

Once King Ashura was pursuing the defeated and retreating Taishaku. Taishaku fled to the north of Mount Shumi.

On his way, Taishaku saw many ants crawling on the road ahead of him for a distance. He thought, "Even if I am caught and killed by Ashura, I should not violate the precepts. If I continue to run, I will kill many ants by stepping on them. Violating the precepts will never bring me rebirth in good places. Now can one expect to attain Buddhahood by violating the precepts?"

Taishaku reversed his course and approached King Ashura. See-

....

111. Śaśī.

ing Taihsaku returning, Ashura misunderstood and thought Taishaku was leading another army to attack him. Ashura immediately retreated and confined himself in a cell of lotuses.

Although Taishaku had been defeated, he won in the end since he did not kill the ants. The Buddha explained that obeying his precepts would prevent one from falling into the Three Lower Realms and aid one to escape sudden predicaments.

Thus it was told and handed down.

1:31 HOW THE WEALTHY SHUDATSU BUILT THE TEMPLE IN GIONSHŌJA

Long ago, Shudatsu, a wealthy man of the country of Shae in India, became poor seven times and became rich seven times during his life. His seventh impoverishment was worse than the others. Both he and his wife had no clothing, not even of rough hemp, and no food, not even seasoning. As Shudatsu and his wife grieved over their situation, the people, including their neighbors and relatives, become unfriendly and shunned them.

They starved for three days and were near death from hunger. They had no treasure in their empty storehouse. With a faint hope of finding something, they went to examine their storehouse. They found a chipped sandalwood measuring cup for rice.

Shudatsu took it to the market, sold it for five *shō*[112] of rice, and brought it home. He took one *shō* of the rice to the marketplace to sell so he could buy some greens. Meanwhile the wife cooked another *shō* of rice and waited for her husband.

One of the Buddha's disciples, Shubodai,[113] the expert on the concept of nothingness, came and begged alms. The wife offered him all the cooked rice in the bowl.

Later, Mokuren, who excelled others in his mysterious powers, came and begged alms as the wife was cooking another *shō* of rice. The wife offered him the rice as she had done for Shubodai.

The wife was cooking another *shō* of rice and was waiting for her husband. Anan, most knowledgeable disciple of the Buddha, came to beg alms and the wife made another offering of the cooked rice.

....

112. A *shō* equals 1.805 liters.
113. See note 58.

Afterward, the wife thought, "Only one *shō* remains. I can cook and enjoy the pure white rice with my husband. I will not make another offering, no matter which of the Buddha's disciples comes and begs alms."

Strongly determined to prolong their own lives, the wife cooked the last *shō* of the rice. Before her husband returned home, the greatest master, the Shaka Buddha, came and asked alms.

In spite of her determination, the wife was overwhelmed with joy and offered her last *shō* of rice with tearful respect. The Buddha left after reciting and explaining the verse:

It is difficult to make offerings when impoverished;
It is difficult to be patient when wealthy;
It is difficult to obey the precepts in adversity;
It is difficult to restrain desire in one's youth.

When Shudatsu returned home, his wife told him of the visits of the arhats and the Buddha. Hearing her story, Shudatsu was immensely pleased, saying "You will be my good leader and teacher for generation after generation!" At that time, Shudatsu's three hundred seventy storehouses all became filled as before with the seven kinds of jewels, and he and his wife again had unequaled wealth. For a long while, their wealth surpassed that of the previous six times. Shudatsu was famous in the world for his incomparable wealth.

Shudatsu thought sincerely, "I would like to acquire some beautiful land, build a temple for Shaka Buddha and his disciples, and make daily offerings for the rest of my life."

Prince Gida[114] owned some beautiful land with water, bamboo groves, and various trees and plants. Shudatsu asked the prince for the land, saying, "I would like to build a temple for the Buddha on this ideal land. Please let me have it."

"This land extends ten *ri*[115] from east to west and seven hundred paces from north to south. Even though influential and wealthy men of this and neighboring countries have asked, I haven't given it up. Yet since you say that you will build a temple for the Buddha, I have

....

114. 祇陁. Jeta, the son of King Prasenajit (Hashinoku) of Śrāvasti (Shae), together with Sudatta (Shudatsu), donated Jetavanānāthapiṇḍadārāma (Gidarin) to Śākyamuni.

115. See note 18.

no reservations about surrendering it to you. Spread gold pieces six inches high on the ground as my price for the land," agreed the prince.

The immensely pleased Shudatsu immediately had his men and horse carriages bring and spread the gold pieces as high as five inches on the ground and offered them to the prince. He finally obtained the land as he had wished.

Shudatsu built a temple with more than one hundred buildings in its compound. All were decorated and ornamented, stately and beautiful. He welcomed the Buddha in the central building and welcomed accomplished and learned bodhisattvas and five hundred arhats in the living quarters of the other buildings. These buildings became called the Gionshōja, the Temple of Gion. There Shudatsu served and venerated the Buddha, bodhisattvas, and other priests as he had wished with a hundred kinds of tasty dishes and rare treasures for twenty-five years.

Thanks to his good teacher, his wife, Shudatsu attained his final opulence, built temples, and venerated the Buddha as he had wished.

Thus it was told and handed down.

1:32   HOW SHŌGI[116] OF THE COUNTRY OF SHAE BECAME
       WEALTHY BY MAKING AN OFFERING

Long ago, Shōgi's was the poorest of nine hundred million families in the capital of Shae in India. He and his wife barely managed to live by begging alms as they visited each of the nine hundred million houses in the city.

To cultivate Shōgi, the Buddha sent Kashō[117], the best in ascetic practices among his disciples, to beg alms at his house.

Seeing Kashō, Shōgi said, "Though you are the Buddha's disciple, you are merciless. I am so poor that I have accumulated not even a dust particle. We barely prolong own lives by begging alms at the nine hundred million houses in the city. Why have you come here to beg alms? I have nothing at all to offer."

"Give me whatever you have," insisted Kashō. "I have absolutely nothing to offer," said Shōgi. "A particle of dust will be fine; let me have it," begged Kashō, but Shōgi refused.

....

116. Unknown.
117. See note 38.

Shōgi's wife appeared and scolded her husband, "Why don't you make an offering to this priest. We have kept a hemp robe between us. He is not asking for anything beautiful, but something as insignificant as a dust particle. Offer him the hemp robe!"

"How foolish you are. This is the only robe we have. When I go out, you remain naked and when you go out, I remain naked. Offering it will shorten our lives," disagreed Shōgi.

The wife insisted, "You are narrow-minded. Our life is transient and ends as we expire. No matter how much we care for ourselves, we eventually become dust and are reduced to nothing. Since we had no intention of making offerings in our former lives, we are now the poorest of the nine hundred million families in the city. Don't you see that this is all the karmic result of our previous lives? If we die as we are in this life, we will undergo unbearable hardships and sufferings by falling into the hells and become hungry ghosts. I am going to offer this hemp robe right now." Even though her husband was reluctant, the wife coaxed him, took off the robe, folded it, and said to Kashō, "Please close your eyes. I will be embarrassed when unclothed. Don't look at me."

As Kashō closed his eyes, the wife came closer and offered him the robe. Kashō chanted incantations as he accepted it.

Kashō returned and reported to the Buddha. "Shōgi's wife made this offering." The Buddha released a radiance and invited Buddhas from north, east, south, and west and praised Shōgi's wife, uttering incantations together with these Buddhas.

King Hashinoku, surprised by the radiance, visited the Buddha. The king first asked Mokuren about the auspicious radiance. Mokuren replied, "Shōgi and his wife were so poor that they barely managed to live by begging from the nine hundred million families in the city. When Kasho went to their place and begged alms, Shōgi refused to make an offering. But his wife freely offered Kashō their only clothing, a hemp robe. Seeing this, the Buddha praised her and released his radiance."

The king tearfully heard Mokuren's explanation. He removed his clothes and sent them to Shōgi. The king also ordered, "All public wealth shall be sent to Shōgi."

Shōgi immediately became wealthy with countless treasures. Without reluctance, one should offer treasures to priests and venerate the Buddha.

Thus it was told and handed down.

1:33   HOW A POOR WOMAN VENERATED THE BUDDHA BY OFFERING THREADS

Long ago, a poor woman lived in India. Her main activity was to run errands for many families. She left in the morning daily and returned in the evening.

The Buddha lived near her place. The woman venerated him by offering threads, which she hung on a tree branch every evening when he returned home.

The Buddha asked, "Why do you venerate me with these threads? If you wish something, tell me quickly."

The woman replied, "I wish that, by pulling these threads, I could bring together, read, and recite all the teachings and the Laws preached by the various Buddhas during three generations, and finally become a Buddha by that merit and benefit all sentient beings."

The impressed Buddha recorded her desire and exclaimed, "How wonderful! How wonderful!" The Buddha continued, "Thanks to your merit in venerating me by your fine idea, you will attain Buddhahood. Later you will be called the Future Buddha of Good and will benefit all sentient beings as you wish."

The woman immensely rejoiced over what the Buddha had recorded concerning her future attainment and returned home.

Thus it was told and handed down.

1:34   HOW A WEALTHY MAN'S COW MADE AN OFFERING TO THE BUDDHA

Long ago, a wealthy man lived in India. He was greedy, held incorrect views, and had no intention of making offerings. Being older than ninety, this wealthy man was near the end of his life.

To cultivate him, the merciful Buddha stood in the wealthy man's gateway. However, the evil wealthy man had his people chase away the Buddha by striking him with sticks and by throwing stones. Though chased away daily, the Buddha still stood in the gateway. The wealthy man became more angry and tried to drive him farther from the house. Yet the Buddha patiently stood by the gate for three years.

The wealthy man kept five hundred cows, which were driven in and out every morning and evening. One of the cows thought, "My evil and ignorant master does not venerate the Buddha. After I deliver my child, I will offer the Buddha my milk." Soon the cow delivered a calf. Later the cow wished to offer her milk to the Buddha, but she could not realize her wish since she was constantly driven away by the cowherds.

The cow thought, "When I return tonight, I will try to make my offering." As she returned and again stopped before the Buddha, she was driven on and could not offer her milk.

At the dawn of the third day, the cow resolutely decided, "Since I had had no intention to make offerings in my previous lives, I have fallen into the status of an animal and have been undergoing unbearable sufferings. This time, I will make my offering to the Buddha, withstand the pain of being struck by the sticks, and practice the way of the bodhisattvas."

In the morning, the cow, instead of accompanying the herd, stepped out and stood before the Buddha. She offered her milk and said, "I offer you all my milk except a little for my child." The Buddha received the cow's milk in his bowl. The calf came near her mother cow and said, "I will feed myself on grass. So quickly offer the Buddha the rest of the milk," and the calf disappeared into the bushes.

The Buddha said, "Thanks to her merit, this cow will be reborn in the heavens." After that, the people began to offer milk to the Buddha.

Thus it was told and handed down.

1:35   HOW THE PEOPLE OF SHAE VENERATED THE BUDDHA BY PLAYING MUSIC

Long ago, many people of the capital of Shae in India adorned and dressed themselves in a stately manner. They were leaving the capital to amuse themselves by singing and playing music.

Before they reached the city gates, they saw the Buddha entering the city. He begged alms as he led many of his disciples. The rejoicing people paid their respects as they left and venerated the Buddha and his disciples by singing and playing music.

The Buddha smiled at these people and said to Anan, "Thanks to this merit, these people who sang and played music for us will not fall into the Three Lower Realms but will be reborn in the heavens and the human realm and receive comfort and pleasures for one hundred *kalpa* years. After that, they will all become Hyakushi Buddhas and be called by the name Myōshō, 'Exquisite Voices.'"

So if someone venerates the Three Treasures by playing music, his merits will be countless.

Thus it was told and handed down.

1:36   HOW A BRAHMAN OF SHAE WALKED AROUND THE BUDDHA

Long ago, the Buddha was begging alms in the capital of Shae. Seeing the stately appearance of the Buddha as he released radiances, a joyful Brahman walked around the Buddha, paying him homage, and left.

The Buddha smiled at this and said to Anan, "The Brahman rejoiced to see me and walked around me with a pure mind. Thanks to this merit, he will never fall into the Three Lower Realms, but will be reborn in the heavens and the human realm, and always receive pleasures for the period of twenty-five *kalpa* years. After that he will become Bibashi Buddha and will be called Jishin-nateiri."

Judging by this, circling Buddhas and pagodas will bring one five kinds of merit: First, one will be born handsome or beautiful; second, one will be reborn in exquisite surrounding; third, one will be reborn in the heavens; fourth, one will be reborn into royal families; and fifth, one will enter *nirvana*.

Though it may be easy to do, one is encouraged to circle Buddhas and pagodas respectfully, since countless merits will be earned.

Thus it was told and handed down.

1:37   HOW THE CHILD OF ZAITOKU AVOIDED DANGER BY CALLING OUT THE BUDDHA'S NAME

Long ago in India, Zaitoku, a wealthy man, had a child. Zaitoku cherished his child and always taught him to recite *namo butsu*, "Faith in the Buddha." As instructed by his father, the child recited the phrase constantly.

One day, the child was sleeping. A demon deity suddenly descended and was about to seize and devour him. At that moment, the child uttered the phrase, "Faith in the Buddha." His voice was immediately heard in the Gionshōja. The Buddha instantly came to the child, protected him, and did not allow the demon to take him away.

When the Buddha shouted, "Protectors of the Law, descend!,"

the Kongō deity[118] of all the worlds, the guardian of the Law, appeared, subjugated the demon, and explained the divine incantations to him. Hearing the Kongō deity, the demon vowed, "I will become a guardian of the Law and protect the people."

Repeating the phrase "Faith in the Buddha" is easy, but will guarantee the Buddha's protection. So one should recite the Buddha's name single-mindedly.

Thus it was told and handed down.

1:38   ABOUT THE FIVE HUNDRED BANDITS OF THE COUNTRY OF SHAE

Long ago, there were five hundred bandits in the country of Shae. On account of their serious crimes, King Hashinoku captured them all. He had their eyeballs plucked and their limbs amputated, and expelled them to the foot of Mount Kōzen.[119]

The grieving and tearful bandits said to each other, "Even though we have lost our eyes and limbs, we have continued to live. Yet our hunger pangs are unbearable. How can we obtain food?"

"Five hundred of us are disfigured like non-humans or broken earthenware. We will undergo pain and suffering by being called freaks all our lives, and undoubtedly will fall into the Three Lower Realms. If we had feet, we could visit the Buddha; if we had hands, we could clasp them in prayer; and if we had eyes, we could watch the Buddha. Without all these and with our incorrect views, we have made our present and future lives futile," the bandits mourned.

A wise bandit among them proposed, "The Buddha appears in this life to save all sentient beings from their sufferings. Let's all recite his name in unison and ask his help in releasing us from our sufferings!"

Another bandit said, "When we had our eyes and limbs, we neither worshipped Buddha, nor listened to the Law, nor respected priests. Instead we violated and stole the belongings of the Three Treasures. Why would the Buddha help us now?"

....

118. 執金剛. The *vajra-pāṇi*, or diamond-holder, refers to the various celestial beings in the Diamond Section of the Womb World Mandala who hold the *vajra* or diamond as a symbol of wisdom.

119. Unknown.

Another bandit insisted, "I have heard that the Buddha extends his mercy equally, even to a single child. Although we have violated and stolen the possessions of the Three Treasures, how can he not benefit us? We should continue to recite his name and ask for more benefits."

So the five hundred bandits, raising their voices, recited in unison, "Faith in the Shaka Buddha. Please deliver us from our sufferings." As their voices were heard at the foot of Mount Ryōju,[120] the Buddha, with his radiance, illuminated each of the five hundred bandits. Immediately their eyes and limbs were restored, and all the bandits attained arhatship and became the Buddha's five hundred disciples of Mount Ryōju.

Even those who committed serious sins were benefited by reciting the Buddha's name. Because of their exultation over the restoration of their eyes and limbs, they attained arhatship and became the Buddha's disciples. How can it be futile if one recites the Buddha's name single-mindedly with a pure heart?

Thus it was told and handed down.

....

120. See note 49.

CHAPTER 2

2:1   HOW KING JŌBON, THE FATHER OF THE BUDDHA,
       PASSED AWAY

Long ago, the Buddha's father, King Jōbon of the country of Kabirae, became ill in his old age. The king suffered intensely for days from the pain, which caused such pressure that he felt as if the fat were being squeezed from his body. The king realized that his last moments had arrived. He lamented over dying without seeing his sons, Shaka Buddha and Nanda; his grandson, Ragora; and his nephew, Anan.[121]

The king's people thought that they should inform the Buddha, but they were afraid the king would die while the messengers were traveling the fifty *yujun*[122] from Kabirae to Shae, where the Buddha stayed.

While the queen and ministers were distressed and worried, the Buddha, who was at Mount Ryōju, naturally learned of his father's painful and serious illness and of his people's grief. The Buddha went to lead Nanda, Anan, and Ragora to the king's palace. Suddenly every corner of the palace brilliantly reflected golden rays as if the morning sun were shining on it.

The king and his people marveled greatly. Under the illumination, the king was relieved of his sickness and pain and felt greatly comforted. Soon the Buddha descended from the sky with Nanda, Anan, and Ragora.

Seeing the Buddha, the king pressed his palms together in prayer

121. See note 72.
122. *Yujun* or *yojana*, a unit of distance, has been equated with 120 kilometers and 160 kilometers.

and cried for joy with tears which flowed down his cheeks like rain. As the Buddha explained and preached the *Honjōkyō*[123] by the king's side, the king immediately attained the third stage of enlightenment, *anagonka*.[124]

When the king took the Buddha's hands and drew them to his chest, he received the fourth stage of enlightenment, *arakanka*.[125] After a while, the king passed away.

At that time, all the people in the palace and in the city grieved immensely and their lament echoed throughout the city.

A casket decorated with seven jewels was made immediately. The scented body of the king dressed in brocade was placed in it. The Buddha and Nanda stood by the king's head, while Anan and Ragora stood at his feet.

When the Buddha was going to carry his father's casket at the funeral, in order to warn the people of later generations who would neglect their filial duty, the earth quaked and the world became unsettled. The people were all confused and tumbled about by the sudden quakes as if they were on board a ship tossed by great waves. The Four Deva Kings asked to carry the casket, and the Buddha allowed them to do so.

The Buddha took an incense burner and walked in front of the casket. The burial was on the peak of Mount Ryōju. When they arrived at the mountain, arhats appeared with sandalwood branches which had drifted to the seashore and been gathered. With these branches the arhats cremated the deceased king as the sound of fire roared through the air.

Just then, the Buddha preached about the verses on impermanence. After the incineration, the king's relics were gathered and placed in a golden casket, and a stupa was built for them.

Thus it was told and handed down.

....

123. It refers to the *Honjōkyō* (本生経), the *Jātaka-sūtra*; stories of the Buddha's previous incarnations, one of the twelve classes of sutras.

124. 阿那含果. *Anagonka* refers to the stage of Non-returning (*anāgāmin*), the third of the Four Stages of Enlightenment to be attained by a Hīnayāna follower by avoiding false views and false practices. The one who has attained this stage may be reborn in the *shikikai* (material world) or the *mushikikai* (non-material world), but not in the *yokkai* (World of Desire). Thus the appellation "Non-returning" is applied to the one who attained this stage. Refer to notes 44 and 72.

125. 阿羅漢果. *Arakanka* refers to the stage of *arhat* or saint who is free from all craving and rebirth.

2:2   HOW THE BUDDHA ASCENDED TO THE TŌRI HEAVEN
FOR THE SAKE OF LADY MAYA

Long ago, Lady Maya passed away seven days after giving birth to the Buddha. The Buddha later left his city, went to the mountains, engaged in severe ascetic practices for six years, and attained Buddhahood.

For more than forty years afterward, the Buddha preached about the Law in various ways and cultivated people. After her death, Lady Maya was reborn in the Tōri Heaven.

The Buddha ascended to the Tōri Heaven so he could cultivate his mother. He stood under the Harishitta[126] tala tree in the Garden of Joy. The Buddha sent Bodhisattva Monju to Lady Maya as a messenger and had him say, "Lady Maya, the Buddha wishes you to come to him, listen to the teachings of the Law and respect the Three Treasures."

As Lady Maya heard the Buddha's message, milk flowed from one of her breasts. She said, "If the Buddha is Prince Shidda, to whom I gave birth in Enbudai, this milk should naturally flow into his mouth." Lady Maya squeezed milk from her other breast. The milk entered the Buddha's mouth. Lady Maya rejoiced to see this and the world seemed to rock with her joy.

Lady Maya and Monju went to the Buddha. He was immensely pleased to see Lady Maya. The Buddha said to her, "Please leave the pleasure and suffering of this world and attain enlightenment forever," and preached about the Law.

As Lady Maya listened, she understood the karmic relation of life, left the eighty billion delusions, and immediately attained the first stage of enlightenment, *shudaonka*.[127]

Lady Maya said to the Buddha, "I have already left the karmic cycle of life and death and attained enlightenment." Hearing this, the people present all beseeched the Buddha, "Merciful Buddha, please allow all sentient beings to attain enlightenment like this." The Buddha preached about the Law to all those sentient beings and thus remained in Tōri Heaven for three months.

One day, the Buddha said to Kumara, one of his best disciples,

....

126. It refers to the *paricitra* or coral tree which sheds its leaves about June and has dark red flowers.

127. See note 94.

"Descend to Enbudai and tell the people that I myself will enter nirvana before long." Kumara went down to Endubai and spoke the Buddha's words to the people. Those who heard lamented greatly. "Until this moment, we did not know where the Buddha was. Then we were pleased to learn that he is in the Tōri Heaven. But we also hear that he is going to leave this life and enter nirvana. We wish that the Buddha will descend quickly to Enbudai and extend his mercy to us." Kumara ascended to the Tōri Heaven and reported the wish of the people to the Buddha.

When the Buddha was going to descend to Enbudai, Taishaku learned about the Buddha's descent and had demon deities make three stairways from the Tōri Heaven to Enbudai. The middle way was decorated with the gold dust produced by the river flowing through the great forest of Enbu trees,[128] the left one with lapis lazuli and the right with agate.

The Buddha said to Lady Maya, "Separation is inevitable in life. I will enter nirvana shortly after I descend to Enbudai. This is the only moment for us to see each other." Lady Maya shed countless tears.

After leaving his mother, the Buddha walked down the jeweled stairways. He led many bodhisattvas, including priests and various laymen. Brahmans, Taishaku, and the Four Deva Kings all followed to the left and right of the Buddha. One can hardly imagine how stately and ceremonial it was!

At Enbudai, the people, including King Hashinoku, all waited in line at the foot of the stairways and rejoiced to see the Buddha. After the Buddha descended the stairways, he returned to Gionshoja.

Thus it was told and handed down.

2:3   HOW THE BUDDHA REPAID HIS OBLIGATION TO A SICK PRIEST

Long ago, a priest lived in Gionshōja. He became seriously ill and suffered for five or six years. Since his body was soiled by the mucus and blood which flowed from the abscesses and released a stench of urine and excrement, people shunned him. His dwelling became dilapidated.

....

128. *Enbu* or *jambu* is the name of a tall tree. The continent south of Mount Sumeru, Jambu-dvīpa (Enbudai), has a large grove of *jambus* north of the Himalayas.

The Buddha pitied the priest and went to him after sending away his five hundred disciples, including Anan and Sharihotsu. The Buddha illuminated a distant place with radiance from his five fingers and asked, "Why have you no one to accompany you?" "I am alone because I have been sick for years," replied the priest.

Taishaku appeared at that time and offered the Buddha a jeweled bottle of water. The Buddha received it in his hands, which had a purplish gold radiance. As the Buddha washed the priest's body with his right hand and stroked the abscesses with his left hand, the priest's sickness was completely cured.

The Buddha said to the priest, "Since I became obligated to you in the past, I came here thus to repay you." Then the Buddha spoke about the Law and the priest attained the last stage of enlightenment, *arakanka*.

Taishaku asked, "My lord Buddha, why did you repay this sick priest?" The Buddha replied, "Countless years ago, a king wished to increase his property. He secretly summoned a man called Gohyaku and said, 'If you detect someone stealing public property, we will confiscate and divide his possessions between us.'

"A lay Buddhist embezzled a small amount of the public property. He was reported to Gohyaku for punishment. But Gohyaku did not punish him since he heard that the lay Buddhist had been practicing good deeds. The lay Buddhist joyfully left after being excused from punishment. The Gohyaku of that time was this sick priest, and I was the lay Buddhist. This is why I came here to repay him."

Thus it was told and handed down.

2:4   HOW THE BUDDHA PAID HOMAGE TO A PAGODA

Long ago, the Buddha was in the country of Kabirae. He went under a *dala* palm tree in Yūsen[129] and paid homage to the pagoda there. His disciples, including Anan, Sharihotsu, Kashō,[130] and Mokuren, felt this strange and asked, "Our lord Buddha, why did you treat this pagoda with such respect? The Buddha should be respected by others. Why should anything be regarded as more noble than the Buddha?"

....

129. It refers to the Yūsen palm tree.
130. Makakashō. See note 38.

The Buddha replied, "A great king lived in this country Long ago. Being childless, he prayed to heaven and to the dragon deities for a child. His queen soon became pregnant and gave birth to a prince. The queen cherished and raised him with great care. When the prince was ten years old, the king became ill. Neither prayers to heaven and deities nor medicines cured the king.

"One medicine man said, 'The king will be cured immediately if he takes medicine compounded from the bones and eyes of a person who has never been angry since birth.' Who could this be except the Buddha, who had never become angry? 'This is quite impossible,' said the lamenting people.

"The prince heard this and thought, 'I am the one who has never been angry since birth.' The prince went to his mother and said, 'Those who are born will surely perish, and those who meet will certainly separate. Who can avoid these consequences? I would rather lose my life and save my father than exist vainly in this transient life.' The mother could not speak but shed bitter tears.

"The prince thought again, 'I shall not regret giving my life for the sake of filial piety. If I wish to preserve my life, I will sin by being unfilial to my parents. Even if I have a long life, I will not avoid death. Undoubtedly I will fall into the Three Lower Realms. I would much prefer to die to preserve my father's life, and attain the highest stage of nirvana, and benefit all sentient beings.'

"Vowing thus, the prince secretly spoke with a man of the lowly *sendara* class, which engaged in hunting and slaughtering. The *sendara* man was so frightened that he would not listen to the prince. Yet the prince's wish to fulfill his filial duty was stronger. The prince gave the *sendara* man five hundred swords and forced him to take his eyes and bones.

"The medicine compounded with the prince's eyes and bones was offered to the king, who was instantly cured.

"Unaware of this, the king later inquired, 'The prince should visit me. Why hasn't he come for so long?' One of his ministers replied, 'The prince has passed away. A medicine man said that the king would be cured by the bones and eyes of a person who had never been angry, and the prince declared that he was the only person who had never been angry during his entire life. The prince had a *sendara* man take out his eyes and bones and offered them to the king. You were treated with this medicine, my lord, and your illness is cured.'

"Hearing this, the king wept in his boundless grief and sorrow. After a time, the king said, 'I have heard stories of thrones usurped by killing one's father, but I have never heard of prolonging life by taking the bones and flesh of one's own child. How sad it is that I was ignorant of it and was pleased with my recovery.' The king immediately erected a pagoda at the foot of the *dala* palm of Yūsen.

"The king of that time was my father, King Jōbon, and I was the prince. Since the pagoda was erected for me, I am paying homage to it. Because of this pagoda, I have attained enlightenment and cultivated all sentient beings."

Thus it was told and handed down.

2:5   ABOUT THE BUDDHA'S SIX-DAY STAY AT SOMEONE'S PLACE

Long ago, the Buddha received offerings and veneration during six days spent at a man's house in the country of Shae. On the seventh morning, when the Buddha was about to leave, the sky became suddenly dark, the wind blew, and the rivers flooded.

The master of the house said to the Buddha, "Please stay today because the rain and wind are violent. I will entertain you another seven days." The Buddha's disciples, including Sharihotsu, Mokuren, Anan, and Kashō, urged the Buddha, "Please remain here today."

The Buddha said, "No, you are very foolish. Exchanging one word and creating a relationship by sharing one night's shelter are all due to karmic effects from one's previous lives. Listen to me well, master of the house. When you were born as a human being in your previous life, you were deserted and were about to perish because of the cold. At that time, I held and warmed you for six days and you survived. But on the seventh morning, you were finally overcome by the cold and died. This is why I stayed and received your offerings and venerations just for six days. I should not stay at your place today." The Buddha returned to the Mount Ryōju.

The disciples and the master of the house all felt extremely exalted and truly realized that exchanging one word and receiving one night's shelter were all related to causes from previous lives.

Thus it was told and handed down.

2:6   HOW AN OLD MOTHER WAS REBORN IN THE HEAVEN,
       THANKS TO KASHŌ, AND REPAID HER OBLIGATION

Long ago, Kashō of India went to a village to beg for alms. Kashō
thought, "I am not going to wealthy houses but will visit poor people
and accept their offerings." He meditated single-mindedly, looked for
a poor person, entered the city of Ōsha,[131] and went to an old mother.

The old mother was extremely poor and sick. She lay amid the
droppings and excrement on the street. A broken bowl filled with
spoiled rice water was beside the old mother. Kashō approached and
begged for alms.

The old mother said, "Since I am sick and poor, I have nothing to
offer except this spoiled water. Can you possibly accept?" "This is fine.
Offer it to me quickly, " replied Kashō.

As soon as Kashō had drunk the rice water, he ascended into the
air and revealed the Eighteen Mysterious Changes.[132] The old mother
got up and watched. Kashō asked, "What would you wish, in return
for your good deed? Do you wish the status of the King of the Turning Wheel, Taishaku, one of the Four Deva Kings, a human being,
a Buddha, or a bodhisattva?" "Since I want to avoid poverty and the
sufferings of this world, I would like to be reborn in the heaven," said
the old mother.

Seven days later, the old mother passed away. She was reborn immediately as a Heavenly Lady in the Tōri Heaven, endowed with mysterious powers, and having a stately appearance. At that time heaven
and earth trembled and shed bright lights just as if seven suns appeared together.

Seeing this, Taishaku asked the Heavenly Lady the cause. The
woman explained in detail, "Since I respected Kashō, I was reborn in
the heaven and received joys and pleasures. I will repay him for this."

The Heavenly Lady took incense and flowers. Accompanied by
the heavenly maidens who attended her, she descended to pay her respects to Kashō. As soon as she had venerated Kashō, she returned to
the heaven.

....

131. Rājagṛha.

132. Eighteen Mysterious Changes refers to the eighteen kinds of mysterious changes
     done by bodhisattvas and *arhats*. Such changes described in the *Lotus Sutra* include
     producing fire and water from one's sides, and sitting and walking in space.

At that time, the Buddha explained, "The old mother offered little, but since she did it with a sincere heart, she was blessed greatly. So, in the future, encourage people to make offerings."

Thus it was told and handed down.

2:7 HOW A FEMALE SERVANT WAS REBORN IN HEAVEN, THANKS TO KASENNEN,[133] AND REPAID THE FAVOR

Long ago, there was a wealthy man in the country of Ahandai[134] of India. His large house had many treasures. Yet the man was miserly and merciless. He had a female servant. One day she made a small mistake. The wealthy man hit her and confined her in a storehouse. He gave her no clothes or food, and only a small amount of water. The woman wept loudly.

Kasennen was in that country at the time. He heard the woman weep in the distance, went to her place, and asked, "If you are poor, why don't you sell yourself?"

"Who would buy poverty? If I could sell my poverty, I would. But how can I sell it?" asked the woman.

Kasennen said, "If you wish to sell your poverty, you should make donations as I tell you. In this way you will sell your poverty."

The woman replied, "I am impoverished and have neither clothes nor food to offer, only a small amount of water allowed me by my master. Might I offer you this water?"

"Fine. Quickly offer it to me," said Kasennen.

"Well, just as he says," thought the woman, and she poured the water into his bowl.

As soon as Kasennen received the woman's water, he chanted incantations, offered the woman precepts, and encouraged her to recite the name of the Buddha. Kasennen asked the woman, "At what sort of place do you usually stay?"

"I stay either in the kitchen or the outhouse," replied the woman.

Kasennen told her, "After your master retires to his bed, quickly open the door, enter the house, spread grass over the floor, sit on it, and think of nothing evil, but only the Buddha."

As instructed, the woman opened the door that night. She en-

....

133. 迦旃延. Kātyana, one of the ten great disciples of Buddha, was a skillful debater.
134. 阿槃提. It was one of the sixteen great countries of India at the time of Śākyamuni.

tered, spread the grass on the floor, sat on it, thought only of the Buddha, and passed away. She was reborn immediately in the Tōri Heaven.

In the morning, the wealthy man saw the dead woman. He became very angry. He had his people tie a rope around the feet of the dead woman, drag her into a cold forest, and abandon her.

The woman who had been reborn in the heaven watched how her corpse was treated. She immediately descended to the forest with incense and flowers, leading five hundred Heavenly Persons. The Heavenly Lady venerated her own corpse by burning incense and scattered flowers over it. She also shed bright lights and illuminated the wood.

People from distant and neighboring places, including the wealthy man, saw this and asked, "Why is the corpse of this dead female servant venerated like this?" The Heavenly Lady replied that the corpse was her old body and the reason for her rebirth in the heaven. The wealthy man thought her story most extraordinary.

Later the Heavenly Lady went to Kasennen and repaid her obligation by burning incense and scattering flowers. Kasennen preached the Law to the woman. The five hundred Heavenly Persons listened and all attained the *shudaonka* stage of enlightenment and returned to the heaven.

Thus it was told and handed down.

2:8   ABOUT PRIEST KONTEN OF THE COUNTRY OF SHAE

Long ago, a baby boy was born to a rich man in the country of Shae whose house was filled with countless treasures. The boy was golden-hued and was matchlessly handsome. The parents were delighted and greatly cherished the boy. Since the boy was golden, he was named Konten, Golden Heaven. On his birthday, a well eight feet wide and eight feet deep appeared of its own accord in the house compound. The well produced pure water, food, clothes, gold, silver, and other rare treasures. The family could take and use them as they wished.

The boy grew into a learned man with a superior mind. The father thought, "My son is incomparably fine. I shall find him a wife."

About that time, a baby girl was born to a wealthy man in the country of Shukujō.[135] She was called Konkōmyō, Golden Light.

....

135. It may refer to a small city within the country of Śrāvastī.

Her body was golden-hued and she was matchlessly beautiful. On her birthday, a well eight feet deep appeared of its own accord in the house compound and produced various treasures, including foods and clothes, as was desired.

Her parents thought, "The beauty of our daughter surpasses any girl in the world. We have been looking for a husband for her, and now we know about Konten." Finally Konten and Konkōmyō were married.

Sometime later, Konten invited the Buddha and venerated him with offerings. The Buddha preached to Konten, his wife, and their parents. After listening, all attained the *shudaonka* enlightenment. Konten and his wife wished to enter Buddhahood and asked their parents' permission. With this permission, they went to the Buddha, entered Buddhahood, and attained the final stage of enlightenment, *arakanka*.

Seeing this, Anan addressed the Buddha, "Both the golden-hued Konten and his golden-hued wife were born into wealthy families, were blessed with eight-foot-deep and eight-foot-wide wells which produced various treasures, and finally met the Buddha and immediately attained enlightenment. What sort of good had they practiced in their former lives to deserve all these benefits?"

The Buddha replied, "Long ago, when Buddha Bibashi[136] entered nirvana, various traveling priests arrived at a village. The villagers competed in making offerings to venerate these priests.

"A poor married couple in the village had no rice. Seeing other villagers making offerings to these priests, the husband lamented their own poverty and wept with tears. His tears fell on his wife's arms, and she asked, 'Why are you crying?' The husband answered, 'When my father lived, our storehouse was filled with countless treasures. In my generation, I have become impoverished and cannot make any offerings to these priests. Due to making no offerings I have become poor like this. If I don't make offerings now, my future life will be worse. That is why I cry.'

"The wife suggested, 'Why not go to your father's old house and search about to see if anything is left.' Following his wife's suggestion, the husband went to his father's house and found a gold coin. The wife

....

136. 毗婆尸仏. Bibashi Buddha or Vipaśyin was the first of the seven Buddhas of antiquity, Śākyamuni being the seventh.

brought a mirror and a jar. The couple filled the jar with pure water, put in the coin, placed the mirror over the jar, and they offered it to the priests. After making a vow, the couple left.

"The poor husband and wife of that time were Konten and his wife. Thanks to the merit of their offering, they have not fallen into the Three Lower Realms for the period of ninety-one *kalpa* years. They always have been reborn in the heaven and in the world of human beings as a married couple blessed with golden bodies and great fortunes. Finally they met me, entered Buddhahood, and attained enlightenment."

Thus it was told and handed down.

2:9   ABOUT PRIEST HŌTEN OF THE CITY OF SHAE

Long ago, a wealthy man whose house was filled with countless treasures lived in the city of Shae of India. An incomparably beautiful boy was born to him. When the baby was born, seven kinds of jewels fell from the sky like rain and filled the house. This event made the parents very happy, and they named the boy Hōten, Jeweled Heaven. After Hōten grew up, he met the Buddha, entered Buddhahood, and attained the final stage of enlightenment.

Seeing this, Anan spoke to the Buddha, "Priest Hōten was born into a wealthy family. At his birth, seven kinds of jewels fell like rain, and he has never been poor but always has been blessed with food and clothes. Now he has just met the Buddha, entered Buddhahood, and attained enlightenment. What sort of good deeds had he done in his former life to be deserving?"

The Buddha explained, "Long ago, when Buddha Bibashi appeared, many priests were traveling through villages. The wealthy villagers competed in making offerings to these priests. There was a poor man in the village. Even though his heart was filled with joy to see these priests, he had not even a bit of dust to offer them.

"Being distressed, the poor man took a handful of white sand, scattered it on the priests with his sincere prayer and veneration, made a vow, and left. The poor man who offered the white sand to these priests is this Hōten. Thanks to his merit, he has never fallen into the Three Lower Realms for ninety-one *kalpa* years.

"Whenever he was born, seven kinds of jewels rained down and his house was filled with treasures. He was naturally blessed with food and clothes and was never poor. Just now, he met me, entered Buddhahood and attained enlightenment."

Judging from this, although we are without wealth, if we venerate the Three Treasures with sincere hearts, even offering plants and trees or stones and pebbles, we definitely shall have good results.

Thus it was told and handed down.

2:10   ABOUT PRIEST KONZAI OF THE CITY OF SHAE

Long ago, a wealthy man, whose house was filled with countless treasures, lived in the city of Shae of India. An incomparably beautiful boy was born to him. The baby was born with his two fists clenched. The parents opened his fists and found a gold coin in each hand. The parents took the coins from his hands, but soon discovered that their boy was holding two more coins in his hands. No matter how often the parents removed the coins from their boy's hands, the supply of coins in his hands remained inexhaustible. Soon their storehouse was filled with gold coins. The parents were immensely happy and named their boy Konzai, Golden Treasure.

As Konzai grew older, he wished to enter the priesthood. He finally went to the Buddha and attained the final stage of enlightenment.

Seeing this, Anan inquired of the Buddha, "Priest Konzai was born into a wealthy family holding gold coins, which were inexhaustible. He just met the Buddha and quickly attained enlightenment. What sort of good seeds had he planted in his former life to deserve all this?"

The Buddha explained, "Long ago, when Buddha Bibashi appeared in this world, a very poor man lived by selling firewood. At one time, he had earned two gold coins by selling his firewood. When he saw the Buddha and his priests, he gave them the coins, made a vow, and left. The poor man who donated the coins to the Buddha in those days is this man, Konzai. Thanks to his merit, he has never fallen into the Three Lower Realms, but always is reborn in the heavens and in the human realm. Each time he has been reborn, he has an inexhaustible supply of gold coins. Just now he met me, entered Buddhahood, and attained enlightenment."

Judging by this, although one may be reluctant to give away precious valuables, if one offers them to the Three Treasures, one will surely gain unlimited future blessings. Thus it was told and handed down.

2:11   ABOUT PRIEST HŌSHU OF THE CITY OF SHAE

Long ago, a wealthy man lived in the city of Shae of India. His house was filled with countless treasures and an incomparably beautiful baby boy was born to him. The boy held a gold coin in each hand. The parents took the coins from his hands, but more coins appeared in the boy's hands. The parents were immensely happy and named their boy Hōshu, Treasure Hands.

Hōshu became a merciful man and made donations regularly. Every time someone begged for alms, Hōshu willingly opened his hands and donated his coins. One day Hōshu asked his parents' permission to visit the Buddha in Gionshōja. Hōshu was immensely impressed with the Buddha's appearance. With joy in his heart, Hōshu sincerely venerated the Buddha and his disciples, saying, "Please receive my offerings." Anan said to Hōshu, "If you wish to make offerings to the Buddha you should prepare some treasures."

As soon as Hōshu opened his hands, numerous coins fell to the ground. The Buddha preached the Law to him. After hearing the Buddha, Hōshu attained the *shudaonka* stage of enlightenment.

After Hōshu returned home, he asked his parents' permission to enter Buddhahood. With their permission Hōshu returned to the Buddha, entered Buddhahood, and attained the final stage of enlightenment.

Seeing this, Anan addressed the Buddha, "Priest Hōshu was born into a wealthy family with an inexhaustible supply of gold coins in his hands. He met the Buddha, entered Buddhahood, and quickly attained enlightenment. What good seeds had he planted in his previous life to deserve all this?"

The Buddha explained, "Long ago, after Buddha Bibashi entered nirvana, a king gathered the relics of the Buddha and built a pagoda adorned with four kinds of jewels. Seeing this, a wealthy man was overcome with joy placed a gold coin under the pagoda, made a vow, and left. The wealthy man who placed the coin under the pagoda is Priest Hōshu. Thanks to his merit, he has never fallen into the Three Lower Realms, but has been reborn in the heaven in the human realm holding inexhaustible gold coins in his hands and always being blessed with unlimited fortune."

Judging by this, one always should support joyfully a person who practices good deeds. One surely will gain countless future blessings.

Thus it was told and handed down.

2:12   ABOUT PRIEST TŌSHI OF THE CITY OF ŌSHA

Long ago, a wealthy man lived in the city of Ōsha of India. His house was filled with countless treasures and an incomparably beautiful boy was born to him. When the baby was born, he released a radiance from one of his fingers that illuminated a distance of ten *ri*. The parents rejoiced immensely and named him Tōshi, the Radiant Finger.

One day, King Ajase[137] heard of Tōshi and summoned him. The wealthy man took Tōshi to the palace. When they arrived, the radiance of Tōshi's finger illuminated the palace. Everything in the palace shone with a golden hue. The mystified king wondered, "What sort of light is this that suddenly illuminates my place? I wonder if the Buddha has come?"

The king sent a messenger to the palace gate. The messenger reported, "The light is released from a finger of the boy whom you summoned." The king let Tōshi into the palace, curiously held his hand, and had him remain.

When the night fell, the king had Tōshi ride an elephant and lead the way into a garden. In the dark night, the garden suddenly became illuminated by the radiance from Tōshi's finger, as bright as noon. The rejoicing king gave Tōshi abundant treasures and sent him home.

When Tōshi had grown, his parents passed away. Gradually his household declined. His treasures and properties were stolen by thieves and bandits. His storehouse became empty; his people, including his wife and children, left him, and all his relatives passed away. Those who were close to him in earlier days became distant like enemies. He lost everything on which he had depended and had no means.

Finally Tōshi was almost naked without any clothes. He spent his days begging alms from town to town. "Why have I become so poor

....

137. See note 53.

and why am I suffering like this? I am going to destroy myself." As he thought in this way, Tōshi futilely tried to harm himself.

Distressed and confused, Tōshi went to a graveyard, took a corpse, and carried it to the palace. The guards at the gate refused him entry. They beat him and struck his head. Tōshi cried bitterly, raising his voice.

Tōshi took the corpse to his place and lamented. The corpse changed of its own accord into a golden body. After a while, the golden body was broken into pieces, including the head, and the limbs, and they were piled on the ground. Tōshi's storehouse filled and he became richer than before. His people, including his wife and children, returned to him and his old friends rejoined him. Tōshi was immensely pleased at this.

King Ajase soon heard and had someone take the golden head and limbs from Tōshi. But the golden head and limbs were transformed into those of a deceased man. As soon as the king gave them up, the head and limbs became golden. Tōshi realized that the king wanted gold and offered him the golden head and limbs. He also offered various other treasures to numerous people, left secular life, went to the Buddha, entered Buddhahood, and became an arhat. He always kept the treasures of the golden corpse.

A priest questioned the Buddha, "Why did Tōshi release the lights from his finger and why did he become so poor and finally own a corpse which turned to gold?"

The Buddha said, "Long ago, Tōshi was born to a wealthy man of the country of Harana.[138] Once he went out for pleasure and returned home late at night. He knocked at the gate, but no one answered. After a while his parents came and opened the door for him. At that time, he abused his mother.

"Because of this sin, he fell into the hell and suffered intolerably. Although his term in the hell ended and he was born into the human world, he suffered from poverty due to his remaining guilt. However, ninety-one *kalpa* years ago, after Buddha Bibashi entered nirvana, Tōshi, a wealthy man at that time, saw a clay Buddhist statue whose finger was missing.

"Tōshi repaired the statue's finger, and vowed, 'Due to this merit,

---

138. See note 36.

I shall be born into the heaven and human world blessed with fortune. I shall also meet the Buddha, enter Buddhahood, and attain enlightenment.' Since he had repaired the finger of the Buddhist statue, he released lights from his finger and was blessed with the treasures of the corpse."

Realize from this that one should never abuse one's parents because one will commit countless sins. And if one happens to see a broken Buddhist statue, one should certainly repair the damage with clay and wood, since one will be blessed forever with fortune due to that deed.

Thus it was told and handed down.

2:13 ABOUT THE NUN SHUKURI OF THE CITY OF SHAE

Long ago, a wealthy man lived in the city of Shae of India. His house was filled with countless treasures and an incomparably beautiful baby girl was born to him. At birth, she was covered with a fine white cloth. Seeing this, her parents named her Shukuri, Leaving the World.

When she grew up, she avoided mundane matters and searched for the Buddhist Way. Finally she went to the Buddha and said, "I would like to enter Buddhahood." When the Buddha said, "You are welcome," her hair fell out of its own accord, and her white dress became a nun's robe. The Buddha preached to her. After listening, Shukuri instantly attained the final stage of enlightenment.

Seeing this, Anan asked the Buddha, "This nun was born covered with a white cloth and into a wealthy family. She met the Buddha and immediately attained enlightenment. What sort of good seeds had she planted in her former existence to deserve this?"

The Buddha replied, "Ninety-one *kalpa* years ago, Buddha Bibashi appeared in this world. A priest traveled through the country, encouraged people to listen to the Buddha's preaching, and had them make offerings. A woman named Dankanka and her husband were so poor that the only thing they possessed was one garment. If the husband wore it to go out, the wife remained at home without any clothes. When the wife went out, the husband stayed at home naked.

"One day, the priest came to their house and spoke to the wife, 'The Buddha's appearance in this world is unusual, chances to listen to his preaching are rare, and birth as a human being is difficult to achieve. You should see the Buddha now, listen to him preach, and make a donation.'

"The wife replied, 'My husband is out. When he comes home, I will tell him and make a offering.'

"When the husband returned, the wife said, 'A priest came and encouraged me to make an offering. I think I will do it with you.'

"The husband asked, 'Although we wish to do that, what can we offer since we are so poor?'

"The wife replied, 'Since we made no offerings in our previous lives, we have been born poor into this world. If we don't make a donation in this life, we will be just as poor in our future lives. Please permit it. I would like to make an offering.'

"Hearing this, the husband thought, 'My wife may have secretly accumulated some treasures. I think I will let her do this.' He said, 'Do as you wish. If you have anything to offer, offer it quickly.'

"The wife asked, 'Will you take off the garment that you are wearing? I would like to offer that.'

"'This is the only garment we have. If we offer this now, what shall we wear?' asked the husband.

"'Although we are so poor and have nothing to wear, we shall surely obtain fortune in our later lives, if we offer this now. Don't be reluctant,' said the wife.

"The husband was deeply impressed by his wife's sincere heart and gave his permission. The wife called the priest into the house, took off the garment she was wearing, and offered it to the priest.

"The priest asked, 'Why didn't you offer it outside where I was, rather than discreetly inside the dark house?'

"'This is the only thing for us to wear. My body is soiled and unsightly, so I called you inside our house and made this offer directly,' explained the wife.

"The priest accepted the garment, uttered incantations, and left.

"When the priest brought the garment, the Buddha held it high, and said to the crowd, 'No offering is purer than this.'

"On that occasion, the king and queen had come to hear the Buddha preach. Hearing the priest's story, the queen took off her garment and jewels, and sent them to the poor wife. The king, too, took off his clothes and sent them to the husband. Later the husband also joined the Buddha, who preached to him.

"The wife of that time is Shukuri, the nun. Thanks to her merit, she has not fallen into the Three Lower Realms for ninety-one *kalpa* years and has always been born with fortunes in the heavens and in the human realm. She met me and attained enlightenment."

Thus it was told and handed down.

2:14   ABOUT A WOMAN SERVANT OF KING AIKU[139]

Long ago, when the Buddha was traveling in India with his disciples, including Anan, he entered the city of Ōsha and asked for alms.

At that time, two children were on the street. One was called Toku, Virtue, and the other Shō, Victory. They were amusing themselves by making houses and storehouses out of earth. They piled dirt in the storehouses and called it flour for fun.

As they played, the Buddha came by. The children noticed the Buddha's stately appearance, and watched him illuminate the city gates by shedding golden rays. Deeply impressed and with joy in their hearts, the children offered the dirt they called flour from the warehouse to the Buddha. The children vowed, "In the future, allow us to make offerings widely under heaven." Later these children died.

Thanks to their good deed, one hundred years after the Buddha entered nirvana, they were reborn in Enbudai as a King of the Turning Wheel, who governed the world with the correct Law and was named King Aiku. The king made eighty-four thousand jeweled pagodas to hold the Buddha's relics. Enacting the vow made in his previous life, the king always invited priests to the palace and gave them donations.

At that time a poor woman servant of lowly status lived in the palace. Seeing the king practice good deeds, the woman thought, "Due to good deeds in his previous lives, my lord was born as King Tenrin, a King of the Turning Wheel. Since he is accumulating more merit now, his future blessings may surpass those of the present. On the contrary, I was born poor and received a lowly status due to the sins of my former lives. If I do nothing good now, my future status will be worse." The woman felt sad and lamented her situation.

....

139. 阿育王. King Aiku or Aśoka, the grandson of Chandragupta, the son of Bindusāra, was the third king of Mauryan dynasty, reigning from ca. 269 to ca. 232 B.C. During his reign, Buddhism spread throughout India and Southeast Asia, and into some areas of western Asia due to his conferences, including the third Buddhist Council at the capital Pāṭaliputra (Keshijō), the erection of stupas throughout the country, and sending missionaries abroad.

One day, the woman found a copper coin as she swept the droppings. Rejoicing, she gave the coin to the priests.

Shortly afterward, the woman became ill and died. Immediately she was conceived by the queen of King Aiku. Ten months later, she was born as an incomparably beautiful girl. The girl always clenched her right hand. When the girl became five years old, the queen said to the king, "I don't know why our daughter's right hand is always clenched." The king held the daughter on his lap and opened her right hand. He saw a gold coin in her palm. As he took it out, another coin appeared in her palm. The mystified king took it again, and instantly another coin appeared in her hand. As he took coins, an inexhaustible supply appeared. Soon the king's storehouse was filled with gold coins.

Still puzzled, the king took his daughter to Priest Sha[140] and asked, "What good had my daughter done to deserve inexhaustible gold coins in her hand?"

The priest replied, "In her previous life, she was a poor female servant in the king's palace. She found a copper coin as she swept the droppings and offered it to the priests. Thanks to that merit, she has been born into the king's family, and has been blessed with beauty and an inexhaustible fortune of gold in her hand."

Thus it was told and handed down.

2:15   HOW SOMAN, A DAUGHTER OF A WEALTHY MAN, SHUDATSU, DELIVERED TEN EGGS

Long ago, a wealthy man called Shudatsu lived in the city of Shae of India. His daughter, Soman, was incomparably beautiful, and Shudatsu immensely cherished her and loved her more than his other children. Every time he went out, he took her along. Once Shudatsu visited Gionshōja with Soman. When Soman saw the Buddha, her mind was joyful and she thought, "I will coat the wall of the Buddha's room with incense."

After she returned home, she bought various kinds of incense. She visited Gionshōja, ground and mixed the incense, and painted the Buddha's room.

....

140. Priest Sha or Yaśa, a son of a rich man of Vāraṇasī in central India, met Śākyamuni, entered Buddhahood, and became the sixth disciple.

At about that time, the king of the country of Shari[141] passed away and the prince visited Gionshōja. Seeing the beautiful Soman grind and mix the incense, the prince fell deeply in love and wished to marry her. The prince went to King Hashinoku and said, "I want Soman as my wife."

The king said, "I cannot make any arrangements for you. You should talk to her yourself."

The prince returned to his country and thought, "I will steal her." The prince led his men to Gionshōja when Soman was visiting there. The prince took her to his country on an elephant. Shudatsu sent his people to recover his daughter, but the prince kept her and made her his wife.

Sometime later, Soman delivered ten eggs, each of which hatched a baby boy. They were all handsome, brave, and strong. When they grew up, these ten boys heard that the Buddha was in the country of Shae. With their parents' permission, they visited Shae. First they went to Shudatsu, their maternal grandfather. Shudatsu was delighted to see them, and took them to the Buddha. The Buddha preached to the boys. After hearing the Buddha preach, all the boys attained the *shudaonka* enlightenment.

Seeing this, Anan asked the Buddha, "What sort of merit in their former lives caused these boys to be born handsome to a wealthy family and to meet the Buddha and attain enlightenment?"

The Buddha said, "Long ago, ninety-one *kalpa* years ago, after Buddha Bibashi entered nirvana, the Buddha's relics were divided and many pagodas were erected for them. At that time, an old mother rebuilt a broken pagoda. Ten boys happened to come by, saw the old mother, and helped her reconstruct the pagoda. When they finished, they vowed, 'Due to this merit, we should be reborn as a mother and brothers at the same place in our future lives.'

"The old woman of that time is today's Soman. The ten young boys who helped the old mother repair the pagoda are Soman's ten boys. Thanks to their good deeds in their former lives, they have never fallen into the Three Lower Realms for ninety-one *kalpa* years but have been reborn in the heaven and in the human realm, always bless-

---

141. 德叉始羅. Takṣaśilā, a country of Shari, is located southwest of Kashmir and southeast of Gandhāra of North India. Both King Aśoka and the doctor Jivaka once lived there.

ed with fortune and pleasure. They are also rewarded with the three superior qualities: first, a handsome appearance; second, being loved by others; and third, a long life. Since they have met me, they all have entered Buddhahood and attained enliglitenment."

Judging by this, the merit acquired by repairing a pagoda is immeasurable. So, as is said in the *Sōgiritsu*,[142] "One should repair the Buddhist pagoda in sincerity with a lump of mud rather than make an offering of a hundred thousand gold pieces."

Thus it was told and handed down.

2:16   HOW A MAN WITH A FRAGRANT MOUTH BURNED INCENSE

Long ago, a man and his incomparably beautiful wife lived at a remote place in India. The king of the country wished to have a beautiful woman for his queen regardless of her status. He sent an order throughout the country to search for a beautiful woman, but he had found no one suitable.

Seeing the king lamenting over the situation, a minister said, "In a certain district of this country, there is an incomparably beautiful woman qualified to be your queen." Hearing this, the overjoyed king immediately sent a messenger to the woman.

When the messenger arrived, the husband was surprised and suspicious. "People seldom come to a place like this. Who are you that have come like this?"

"I am the king's messenger. Our king heard of your beautiful woman and wants to summon her. Don't regret it, but offer her immediately."

The husband asked, "I have been living here for a long time but have offended no public official. I am neither farming nor accumulating treasure. Why should the king take my wife away?"

"Even though you have offended no one, you have been living on the king's land. Why should you oppose the royal command?" And the messenger took the woman away as if arresting her. The helpless husband bid farewell to his wife in tears and left his place.

The messenger brought the woman to the palace. Seeing her, the king thought that the woman was as beautiful as he had heard. Loving

---

142. 僧祇律. The *sōgiritsu* or *sānghikāh*, the rules for monks and nuns.

her by day and night, he neglected affairs of state. Soon the king made the woman his queen.

However, the queen, who should have felt very fortunate to be queen after having been a wife of a rural commoner, never seemed happy, even after days and months had passed.

Even though the king tried to please her in every way, the queen never seemed to show any interest. The distressed king made strenuous efforts to entertain her by various kinds of music and dances, but the queen neither enjoyed hearing them nor smiled to see them.

Finally the king asked, "You have obtained the king of the people, but you look as if you were in a palace of poisonous snakes. Why aren't you happy?" The queen replied, "Although you are the lord of all under heaven, you are inferior even to a man of low status like my former husband. My husband's mouth is as fragrant as if it contained sandalwood incense and sweet daphne. Yours is not. This is why I am not pleased with you."

The king was very embarrassed to hear this and ordered the presence of the queen's former husband. The messenger searched for the husband in the east and west, and finally found him. As they were traveling toward the palace, the queen said to the king, "My former husband is coming. I can smell the nice fragrance." The king heard this and waited for the husband. As the husband approached the palace, truly the fragrance of sandalwood and sweet daphne reached the distance of one *ri*. Feeling it strange, the king went to the Buddha and asked, "Merciful Buddha, please explain why this man can exude the fragrance of sandalwood and sweet daphne for a distance of one *ri*?" The Buddha said, "In his former life, this man was a mere woodcutter. On one occasion, when he carried wood out of the mountain, it began to rain. The man rested for a while by leaning on a stick by the gate of a dilapidated temple by the roadside. In the temple, a priest was reciting the sutra and burning incense before a Buddhist statue. For a moment, the woodcutter also wished to burn incense. Due to his insignificant virtuous thought, in this life the man's mouth releases fragrance which carried for a distance of one *ri*. Eventually, he will become a Buddha and be called the Incense Buddha." Hearing this, the king's mind was filled with joy and he left the Buddha.

Judging by this, his inhaling the incense burned by others and wishing for a moment to do so resulted in the Buddha's prediction of

Buddhahood. One can imagine the merit from venerating the Buddha by actually bringing incense.

Thus it was told and handed down.

2:17   ABOUT KONJIKI, A WEALTHY MAN OF KABIRAE

Long ago, in Kabirae of India, a wealthy man lived in a large house filled with countless treasures. A son born to him was incomparably beautiful and had a golden hue, which illuminated everything in the city with a golden glow. The joyful parents named him Konjiki, Golden Hued. After Konjiki grew up, he wished to enter Buddhahood and asked his parents' permission. With their permission, Konjiki went to the Buddha, entered Buddhahood, and attained the final stage of enlightenment.

Seeing this, a priest inquired of the Buddha, "Priest Konjiki was born into a wealthy family, releasing golden rays from his body. He met the Buddha, entered Buddhahood, and attained enlightenment. What sort of good seeds had he planted in his previous lives to deserve this?"

The Buddha said, "Ninety-one *kalpa* years ago, after Bibashi Buddha entered nirvana, King Banzumatai[143] took the Buddha's relics and built a pagoda encrusted with four kinds of jewels. It was as high as one *yujun*.[144] When a dedicatory service was offered for the pagoda, a man noticed some minor damage. He bought gold leaf and repaired the damage, made a vow, and left. The man who repaired the pagoda is the present Konjiki. Thanks to his merit, for the period of ninety-one *kalpa* years, he has never fallen into the Three Lower Realms but has been reborn in the heavens and in the human realm. He has always released golden rays and has been blessed with countless fortunes. He met me, entered Buddhahood, and attained enlightenment."

Judging by this, immeasurable merit is acquired by repairing a pagoda. In the time of Kashō Buddha, King Binsha[145] once told ninety-three thousand people to repair the pagodas. After the repairs, the king made a vow, "In the future, we shall all be reborn in the same

....

143. 槃頭摩帝. King Pāṇḍuma.

144. See note 122.

145. 瓶沙王. King Bimbisāra was a devoted Buddhist who built the Bamboo Grove Monastery but was later dethroned by his son, King Ajase (Ajātaśatru).

place. When our lives end, we shall be reborn in the Tōri Heaven. When Shaka appears in the world, so shall we."

As he vowed, King Binsha and his ninety-three thousand people were born in the same country and all visited the Buddha. The Buddha preached the Law for them and they all attained the *shudaonka* stage of enlightenment.

Thus it was told and handed down.

2:18   HOW THE KING OF THE KONJI COUNTRY[146] VISITED THE BUDDHA

Long ago, a country called Konji existed to the south of India. The king, Makakoreina, was brave, strong, and wise. He governed the country as he liked with a powerful force of thirty-six thousand soldiers. Not a single man was a traitor, and the king feared nothing.

At that time, the Buddha, by his divine power, had the king come to the Buddha. The king immediately led twenty-one thousand lesser kings to the Buddha. The Buddha preached for the king, and the king attained the *shudaonka* stage of enlightenment. Later, the king said that he would like to enter Buddhahood. The Buddha permitted him to do so, and the king attained the final stage of enlightenment after entering Buddhahood.

Seeing this, Anan asked the Buddha, "The king of Konji was born into a wealthy country. With his great virtues, he met the Buddha with his eighteen thousand lesser kings, entered into Buddhahood, and attained the Way." The Buddha said, "Long ago, when Kashō entered nirvana, two wealthy men built a pagoda and offered a dedicatory service for the pagoda.

"Many years later, the pagoda was decayed and ruined. A man encouraged eighteen thousand people to repair the pagoda. After the repairs, the man held a service for the pagoda and invited many priests, offering foods and bedding. He made a vow, 'In the future, I wish to be reborn at a blessed place with this merit, meet the Buddha, listen to his preaching and attain enlightenment.'

"The man who repaired the pagoda, and held a service for the pagoda and the priests, is the present King of Konji. He has never fallen

....

146. The country is said to have been in the area near the west coast of the Malayan Peninsula.

in the Three Lower Realms but has been reborn in the heavens and the human realm, always blessed with fortunes and pleasures. He also met me, entered Buddhahood, and attained enlightenment. Those eighteen thousand lesser kings who followed King of Konji were those who repaired the pagoda. Due to their merits, they achieved enlightenment."

Thus it was told and handed down.

2:19   HOW ANARITSU GAINED HEAVENLY SIGHT[147]

Long ago, Anaritsu, a cousin of the Buddha on his father's side, was a priest among the Buddha's disciples. He possessed the Heavenly Sight, which enabled him to see the things in the three thousand worlds as if reading his own palms.

At that time Anan asked the Buddha, "What kind of cause in his former life has blessed him with such superior Heavenly Sight?"

The Buddha replied, "Ninety-one *kalpa* years ago after Buddha Bibashi entered nirvana, Anaritsu was a poor thief. There was a pagoda which stored treasures. Anaritsu thought, 'At night, I will secretly break into the pagoda, steal the treasures, sell them and live on the proceeds!' When night fell, Anaritsu took his bow and arrows to the pagoda, carefully opened the door, and entered. He saw a lit taper before a Buddhist statue. It was nearly out.

"To see the treasures well enough to steal, he lifted the taper on the point of an arrow. The golden Buddhist statue gleamed, and the rays filled the pagoda. Anaritsu went about looking at the statues and returned to the front. Putting his palms together, Anaritsu thought, 'I wonder who made this statue and pagoda, offering the treasures like these? I am a human being just like the man who did this. How can I steal the things of Buddha? If I do, in the future my poverty may become worse.'

"Thinking thus, Anaritsu left without taking any treasures. Due to his merit in holding the lit taper for the Buddhist statue, he has been reborn in good situations for the period of ninety-one *kalpa* years, finally met me, entered Buddhahood, attained enlightenment, and gained the Heavenly Sight."

So although one did not offer the lit taper to the Buddha inten-

147. It refers to the Buddha Eye. See note 32.

tionally, but held it high in order to steal, yet such merit produced those results. If done sincerely, one can imagine how much merit would accrue.

Thus it was told and handed down.

2:20   HOW HAKURA[148] WAS REWARDED WELL

The Buddha had a disciple called Hakura in India. Ninety-one *kalpa* years ago, after Bibashi Buddha entered nirvana, there was a priest who always had a headache. Hakura, a poor man at that time, pitied the priest and gave him a fruit called *kariroku*[149] to cure his headache. The priest took the fruit and his headache was gone. Due to this merit, Hakura had been born into the heavens and the human realm for the period of ninety-one *kalpa* years. He was always blessed with happiness and good health. Finally he was born as a son of a Brahman.

When Hakura was still small, his mother died and his father remarried. Hakura once watched his stepmother making rice cakes and asked her for one. The stepmother did not like him and put him in the pan. Even though the pan became burning hot, Hakura did not get scorched.

The father came home and saw Hakura in the hot pan. The surprised father took him down. Afterward, the stepmother's hatred for Hakura increased. She threw him into a cauldron of boiling water. But Hakura did not get burned.

Since his father did not see him, his father called his name. Hakura answered from the cauldron. The confused father hastily took Hakura out of the cauldron and found him unharmed as before.

The stepmother became more angry. She took Hakura to a large river and plunged him into the water. A large fish in the bottom of the river swallowed Hakura, but with his good luck, Hakura survived inside the fish.

A fisherman was fishing by the river and caught the fish. Pleased by the large fish, the fisherman immediately took it to the fish market

....

148. 薄拘羅. Hakura or Vakula, a disciple who never had a moment's illness or pain during his eighty years of life.

149. The *kariroku* (呵梨勒菓) tree in India bears oval fruit with a tart taste that is effective for colds and diseases of the eye.

to sell. But nobody bought it. Toward the evening, the fish became spoiled and stank.

Just at that time, Hakura's father came by and bought the fish. He took it home and was about to cut open the belly of the fish with a knife. He heard a voice saying, "Oh, please, father, don't harm me." The surprised father cut open the fish and found Hakura inside. The father removed him from the fish and found him safe.

When Hakura was grown, he visited the Buddha, entered Buddhahood, attained the final stage of enlightenment, was endowed with the Six Mysterious Powers,[150] and became the Buddha's disciple. He was never sick and lived until he became one hundred and sixty years old. The Buddha explained that this was all due to his good deed in offering the medicinal fruit to the priest in his former existence.

Thus it was told and handed down.

2:21　HOW A HEAVENLY LADY OBTAINED CORRECT VIEWS[151] AFTER HEARING ABOUT THE LAW

Long ago, when the Buddha was in Gionshōja, a Heavenly Lady descended. The Buddha preached about the Law of the Four Noble Truths for her.

Anan asked the Buddha, "Why did you let this woman hear your preaching about the Law of the Four Noble Truths and let her maintain correct views?" The Buddha said, "When Shudatsu, a wealthy man, built this pagoda, he had a female servant sweep the temple yard. Thanks to that good deed, the female servant was reborn in the Tōri Heaven. This Heavenly Lady was that female servant. She came down to see me, listened to my preaching, and maintained correct views."

So the woman involuntarily heard the words of another, swept the temple yard, and was rewarded this much for her merit. One can easily imagine how much merit would accrue if someone with a sincere mind swept the temple yard.

Thus it was told and handed down.

....

150. The six kinds of supernatural powers gained by Buddhas and *arhats* through meditation and wisdom. The Six Powers include seeing and hearing everything, insight into others, thinking of and remembering one's former existence, and perfect freedom.

151. It refers to ability or insight in perceiving the truth.

2:22   HOW A MAN WAS ALWAYS COVERED WITH A CANOPY

Long ago in India lived a man who was always covered by a canopy. The people who saw thought it strange and asked the Buddha, "Why does he always have a canopy over his head?" The Buddha explained, "This man was born into a lowly and poor family in his former life. He lived by the roadside to help passersby. One time when it rained, the man saw a traveler passing in front of his house. The man offered the traveler his broken umbrella, and the traveler went on without becoming wet. Due to this merit, he became permanently equipped with a canopy."

Judging by this, one can imagine how much merit will accrue if one offers a good umbrella to a priest.

Thus it was told and handed down.

2:23   HOW A WEALTHY MAN, JUDAIKA,[152] WAS REWARDED BY FORTUNE

Long ago, in India, a flower as large as a wheel and a cloth fell from the sky before a king's palace. The king, nobles, and ministers were all pleased, and said, "This is because the heaven was impressed with our country and lowered the heavenly flower and cloth for us."

In the country was a wealthy man called Judaika who was not pleased about this. The king inquired of Judaika, "You are the only person in this country who is not pleased about this. Why?"

Judaika replied, "I have many flowers blooming in my back garden. This is one of my flowers, which withered and was brought here by the wind. The cloth is of low quality compared to my other treasures."

The king, the ministers, and the nobles all felt this most extraordinary. The king thought that he would go to Judaika's house together with his ministers and noblemen and see these unusual things. He said to Judaika, "I am going to visit your place. You return to your place first and prepare for me."

Judaika said, "I have already clothes, treasures, and palaces, and don't need to go ahead to prepare for your visit." The king felt more amazed.

----

152. 樹重提伽. See note 63.

When the king arrived at Judaika's place, he saw four beautiful women standing by the gates. "Who are you?" asked the king. The women said, "We are the female servants guarding the gates." The king passed through three gates and came to the middle of the garden. There the ground was covered with mercury. The king thought it water and did not advance, wondering, "How should I go into the water?" "This looks like water but is actually mercury which covers the ground," said Judaika. He preceded the king and the king followed him.

Seeing the king approach, the wife of Judaika came out of one hundred and twenty layers of gold and silver hangings with tears in her eyes. The king thought that the wife was shedding tears of joy at seeing him, but it was the smoke which made her shed tears.

The king and his followers were entertained with natural foods and drinks. At night, glistening balls were hung to illuminate the place with their natural light, and no other lights were used. The king spent several days looking about Judaika's house. Finally, a messenger was sent from the palace to warn the king that he was staying too long. When the king was about to return hurriedly, Judaika opened his storehouses and offered the king various treasures. The king took the treasures with him to the palace.

At the palace, the king talked to his ministers, "Judaika is one of my countrymen. Why is he superior to me in every respect? We should attack him," and decided to raise an army of forty thousand soldiers. When the army surrounded Judaika's house, one strong guard left the house and struck the forty thousand soldiers with an iron spear.

The defeated soldiers all lay prone on the ground. Judaika came from the sky riding on a jeweled carriage and asked, "Why have you soldiers come to my place?" "We came at the king's order," said the soldiers. Judaika pitied them. Thanks to this, the strong guard revived each soldier. After the soldiers returned to the palace, they reported this to the king.

When the king heard of the virtuous deed of Judaika, he sent the messenger to summon him and apologized, "Being ignorant of your virtue, I foolishly tried to attack you. Please forgive me."

Judaika and the king rode in a jeweled carriage and visited the Buddha. The king asked the Buddha, "What kind of good deeds did Judaika plant in his former life to be rewarded with such blessings?"

The Buddha explained, "Judaika was rewarded for his merit in making offerings in his former existence. Once he passed through a mountain with five hundred merchants. There was a sick man in the mountain. Judaika pitied the sick man, built a grass hut, fixed the floor, gave him food, prepared the lights, and took care of him. Due to these merits, he was rewarded like this in his present life. The virtuous man who made offerings was the present Judaika." Hearing this, the king felt very noble.

Thus it was told and handed down.

2:24 ABOUT ZENKŌNYO,[153] A DAUGHTER OF KING HASHINOKU

Long ago, in the country of Shae of India, King Hashinoku had a daughter called Zenkōnyo. Her beauty surpassed that of others and illuminated her surroundings. Her parents cherished her immensely. The king especially loved her and once asked, "Do you know that I cherish you very much?" Zenkōnyo replied, "I am not particularly pleased. Reward and retribution for good and evil all result from causes and relations in one's former lives. So I was naturally born in this way." The king became very angry to hear this and said, "If the results of good and bad, as you say, are all due to one's previous lives, I will not cherish you any longer. Leave the palace immediately and go elsewhere!"

The king summoned the most ugly of beggars and said, "This is my daughter. Take her as your wife. Since she says that my care and love are simply due to causes from her previous lives, her becoming your wife should also be due to her former life." So the king gave Zenkōnyo to the beggar.

The beggar felt awkward with Zenkōnyo, but since it was the king's order, he left the palace with her. After they had married, they went to an unknown distant place. The husband thought, "I have been living alone as a beggar for years and I have stayed anywhere. Now that I have the king's daughter with me, how can I use such shelter?"

Seeing her husband distressed, Zenkōnyo asked, "Do you have parents?"

....

153. Unknown.

"I had, but they are dead now and I don't know anyone. Since I had no one on whom to rely, I became a beggar," said her husband.

"Who were your parents?" asked Zenkōnyo.

"I was a son of the most wealthy man of a neighboring country. My parents were incomparably wealthy, and their place was no different from the king's palace," replied the husband.

Zenkōnyo asked him, "Do you still know the place where you lived?" "Yes I do. But it has become a wilderness and only the ruins remain. But how can I forget it?" "Then take me there," said Zenkōnyo.

The husband took her to his old place. Zenkōnyo saw the ruins of the enclosed earthen walls spreading wide in the distance. Many cornerstones for various structures in the compound revealed the wealth of her husband's parents.

The couple built a grass hut in the compound and lived there. Later, when Zenkōnyo looked at the ruins of the storehouses, she saw many treasures, including buried gold and silver, releasing radiance from the earth. She thought it most extraordinary, hired someone, and had him dig.

Countless treasures of gold and silver were uncovered. These treasures made the couple richer daily. Many people, including their relatives, joined the couple, who now owned innumerable horses and cows. The couple rebuilt various rooms in a stately fashion and decorated them as before. Their place became equal to the king's palace. The appearance of the husband naturally improved until he was very handsome.

Meanwhile, the king felt pity and regretted that he had given Zenkōnyo to a beggar and had driven her out from the palace. He dispatched a messenger to look for his daughter. Finally the messenger found her, and saw that her place was no different from the king's palace.

The astonished messenger returned to the palace and reported this to the king. The king felt it most extraordinary, immediately visited the Buddha, and asked, "Why was Zenkōnyo born into a royal family releasing radiance from her body? Why, after being driven from the palace and married to a beggar, does she with undeclining fortune still live in a place comparable to that of a king?"

The Buddha said, "Listen to me well. Once, ninety-one *kalpa* years ago, after Bibashi Buddha entered nirvana, King Banzuma built a pagoda adorned with seven kinds of jewels and placed the relics of the Buddha inside. At that time, the king's queen placed a *mani*[154] jewel ball in her crown, placed it inside the pagoda, and vowed, 'On being reborn with this merit, I will live long and will not be born into the Eight Realms,[155] including the Three Lower Ones.' The queen of these old days is Zenkōnyo. As she vowed, she was born to a royal family, shedding radiance from her body. Even though she was driven from the palace, her fortune endured. King Banzuma of the old days is the present husband of Zenkōnyo. Due to their close relationship from previous lives, she has become his wife in this life and is thus rewarded."

King Hashinoku paid his respects, bowing to the Buddha, and returned to the palace. "Truly the reward and retribution of good and evil all depends on one's previous lives, " thought the king. He went to Zenkōnyo's residence and found it like king's palace. The king and Zenkōnyo exchanged visits and lived happily thereafter.

Thus it was told and handed down.

2:25 HOW A MINISTER OF THE COUNTRY OF HARANA WISHED FOR A CHILD

Long ago, a minister in the country of Harana was rich with abundant treasures, but childless. He lamented and wished for a child both morning and evening, but had no way to obtain one.

The country had a deity called Manibatsuda.[156] People visited his shrine to pray for the granting of their wishes. The distressed minister went there and prayed, "I am childless. Please grant my desire and bless me with a child. If you give me one, I will adorn your shrine with gold and silver treasures and coat your statue with fragrant incense. If

....

154. *Mani* jewel ball or *nyoishu*, a fabulous gem gotten from the head of the huge fish, Makara; or the dragon king of the seas; or the relics of the Buddha. This gem is capable of granting wishes to its holder.

155. Eight Realms refers to *aṣṭākṣaṇāḥ*, the eight circumstances, which make one unable to see the Buddha or to hear the Law. Such states include being in hell, being animals, being hungry spirits, being in the heaven of long life, being in remote places, blindness or deafness, having secular prejudice, and during the period of the Buddha's absence.

156. 摩尼抜胎. Manibhadra was one of the eight great generals and a king of the Yakshas, the tutelary deity of travelers and merchants.

not, I will destroy your shrine and throw it into a cesspool." Thus the minister prayed single-mindedly.

The deity was surprised to hear this and looked for a child for the minister. Since the minister was of noble birth and so wealthy, finding him a suitable child was difficult. The distressed deity went to another deity, Bishamon,[157] and discussed the problem.

Bishamon said, "I, too, would not be able to find a child qualified to be the son of the minister. I will talk with Taishaku," Bishamon immediately ascended to the Tōri Heaven and told Taishaku, "A childless minister of the country of Harana of Enbudai has prayed for a child to Manibatsuda, who is unable to give him one. Manibatsuda came to see me, but I, too, cannot grant the wish. So I am asking you, Taishaku."

Taishaku carefully listened and summoned a Heavenly Person who had already shown the Five Deteriorations[158] and was about to die. "Your life is almost at an end. Be the son of the minister to grant his wish."

"The minister is incomparably wealthy. If I am born to him, I may lose my pious mind," said the Heavenly Person.

"Even if you were born into his family, I would help you to maintain your pious mind," promised Taishaku. Taishaku encouraged the Heavenly Person, and he was finally born into the minister's family.

A son who looked like a Buddha was born to the minister. The rejoicing parents cherished their son and raised him with great care. He grew up and was very pious. The son asked his parents, "Please allow me to enter Buddhahood. This is my sincere intention."

"No, you should not enter Buddhahood since you are our only child and our family heir," said his parents and refused him permission.

The son became more pious and thought, "I should die soon, be reborn into a pious family, and enter Buddhahood as I originally wished. Now I have no recourse other than to leave this life quickly." The son stealthily left his parents, climbed the summit of a mountain, and threw himself into a deep valley. Yet he was not at all injured. He went to a large river and plunged into the deep water, but could not die. Even though he ate poison, it had no effect. He futilely tried to kill himself in various ways.

....

157. See note 12.
158. Refer to 1:1.

Finally he thought, "I will steal from the king and be captured and executed."

King Ajase had led many court ladies to a pond in his garden and was amusing himself. The son secretly entered the garden and took some valuable robes of the ladies. The guard saw this, caught him, and took him to the king.

The king became angry and shot at the son with an arrow. Instead of hitting the son, the arrow's flight was reversed toward the king, and it fell on the ground. The king attempted to shoot him three more times and the arrows' flight was reversed three times.

The frightened king threw away his bow and arrows and questioned the son, "Are you a dragon deity or a demon deity?"

The son explained, "I am neither a dragon nor a demon deity, but am the son of the minister of the country of Harana. Since I wished to enter Buddhahood, I asked my parents' permission but could not obtain it. So I thought I had no other recourse than to die soon, be reborn into a pious family, and realize my original wish. I flung myself from a high mountain, I threw myself into deep water, and I took poison, but I could not terminate my life. Finally I thought of being executed for a crime and stole these ladies' robes."

Hearing this, the king was deeply moved and allowed him to enter Buddhahood. The king took him to the Buddha and had him enter Buddhahood. After engaging in many ascetic practices, the son finally became an arhat.

The king asked the Buddha, "The son flung himself from the summit, plunged into water, took poison, was shot by arrows but was never injured, and was finally so fortunate as to meet the Buddha. What sort of good seeds had he planted in his former life to deserve all this?"

The Buddha said to the king, "Listen well to me. Numberless years ago, King Hofumada[159] of the country of Harana led many officials and attendants to the forest to amuse himself. In the forest, the court ladies entertained the king by singing, dancing, and playing musical instruments. In the choir was a man who sang in a very high voice. The king was very disturbed and displeased with this man, and had him taken to be executed.

"A minister came from outside the forest, saw the arrested man,

---

159. 梵摩達. King Hofumada or Brahmadatta, a king of Vārāṇaśī.

and asked the people, 'Why was he arrested?' After hearing the explanation, the minister said to the king, 'This man committed no serious crime. Please don't kill him.'

"The king pardoned the man and halted the execution. Since the man was saved by the minister, he served the minister for many months. One day, the man thought, 'Because I was ambitious, I sang higher than any of these court ladies and was almost going to be executed.' The man explained his thought to the minister and asked if he could enter Buddhahood.

"The minister said, 'I won't disagree with you. Quickly enter Buddhahood as you originally wished and learn about the Law. When you return, come and see me.'

"The man immediately went to a mountain, concentrated on the wonderful Law, mastered the correct teachings, and became Hyakushi Buddha. After he returned to the capital he went to see the minister.

"The rejoicing minister offered service of veneration for the Buddha. Hyakushi Buddha ascended into the air and revealed the Eighteen Mysterious Changes.[160]

"Seeing this, the minister vowed, 'Because of my help, the man prolonged his life. Just like a Buddha, I will be reborn for generations after generations with blessings and long lives. I will widely cultivate and deliver the sentient beings.'

"The minister who had saved the man's life is this son. Due to the karmic relation from his previous lives, he learned the Law and quickly attained the Way."

Thus it was told and handed down.

2:26   HOW THE MAN WHO KEPT THE PRECEPT AGAINST KILLING WAS BORN TO BE THE KING OF TWO COUNTRIES

Long ago, a childless king in India prayed to the Buddhas and gods for a child. His queen became pregnant and gave birth to a handsome baby boy. The king was immensely pleased and carefully cherished the baby.

The king, the queen, and the prince went on a trip. While crossing a large river, the prince was dropped in the water by mistake. The

....

160. See note 132.

king and his people searched for the prince in confusion, but since the river was bottomlessly deep, there was no way to rescue the prince. The helpless king returned to his palace, but his grieving and lamenting did not cease even for a moment.

After falling into the river, the prince was swallowed by a large fish. The fish left the depths, swam downstream, and entered the boundaries of a neighboring country. A fisherman caught the fish, was pleased at its size, and placed it on a cutting board. When the fisherman began to cut the fish's belly, he heard a voice. "I am inside the fish. Don't plunge the knife deeply, but cut it open carefully."

The shocked fisherman told this to the people around him and carefully cut open the fish. A handsome boy tumbled from its belly. Though thinking it most extraordinary, they were happy to see such a attractive boy, and bathed him. The boy did not look like a child of common birth, and all the excited villagers gathered to see him.

Soon the news reached the king of the country, who immediately summoned the boy. The king was very much impressed by the boy's appearance and thought, "I am childless and have no way to obtain an heir. I have been praying for a child to the Buddhas and gods. Now I have found a boy in my country. Surely the Buddhas and gods must have sent him as my heir. Certainly the boy does not have the appearance of a common man." The king immediately took the boy as his prince and greatly cherished him.

Later, the first king who had lost his prince heard the news and thought, "That must be my son who fell into the river by mistake and was swallowed by a fish." The first king sent a message to the second king in the neighboring country, and asked for the boy. The second king replied, "Heaven gave me this child. I cannot send him to you." After that, the two kings fought over the boy.

These two kings had respect for another great and noble king who governed another country. Finally, these two kings decided to appeal to the great king, and agreed, "We will accept the great king's decision." They went to see the great king and told their stories. The great king evaluated the situation, "It is difficult to decide since each of you has his own reasons. I suggest that the two of you create another capital at the boundary of your countries, place the boy there, and raise him as your own prince representing both kingdoms." The two kings accepted this suggestion and happily raised the boy as their prince. Finally the prince became the king of both countries.

Seeing this, the Buddha explained, "The prince, in his previous life, when he was born as a man, had wished to keep the Five Precepts[161] but could keep only one, not to kill. Due to this merit, he prolonged his life, finally became the king of the two countries and inherited the treasures of his two fathers."

One can be blessed this much by keeping only a single precept. If one keeps the Five Precepts, his blessings should be limitless.

Thus it was told and handed down.

2:27   HOW AN INDIAN GOD GAVE KURU, A WEALTHY MAN, SWEET DEWS

Long ago, Kuru, a wealthy man in India, led five hundred merchants to a distant country to trade. On the way, their food was exhausted and they all collapsed with fatigue and hunger. The distressed Kuru looked about and saw a distant house beside a dense forest at the foot of a mountain.

Thinking that someone might live there, Kuru approached and found that the house was the shrine of a god. Kuru said to the god, "I have traveled a considerable distance leading five hundred merchants. Now our food is exhausted and we are about to die of hunger. O, merciful god, please help us."

The god stretched out his arms toward Kuru. Sweet dew dropped in his hands. As soon as he drank it, his hunger disappeared and he felt very full.

Kuru again made a request, "Thanks to your sweet dew, I am no longer starving. But the five hundred merchants are dying from hunger. Please release them from their sufferings."

The god invited the merchants to his shrine and had them take his sweet dew. The five hundred merchants were all relieved from hunger, regained their strength, and asked together, "Dear god, with what sort of merit do you produce such sweet dew from your finger?"

The god explained, "Long ago, when I was born as a man in the time of Kashō Buddha, I made my living by polishing mirrors. Once a begging priest asked me on the street, 'Where is a wealthy man's place?' I showed him the way by pointing my finger saying, 'That is

....

161. See note 75.

the house.' Due to this merit, I am presently rewarded with the sweet dew produced from my finger."

Kuru rejoiced to hear this. After he returned home, he invited one thousand priests to a service of veneration. The Buddha explained that the events of the story had occurred when he was still in this life.

Thus it was told and handed down.

2:28   HOW KING RURI[162] KILLED THE SHAKA PEOPLE

Long ago, the Buddha was born in a country of India. His people were all called the Shaka. They were very prestigious and were regarded as nobles by the five countries of India. A wealthy man, Shakumanan of the Shaka was known for his intelligence and wisdom, and taught his people as the master of the state.

At that time, King Hashinoku of the country of Shae had many queens but wished to have another chosen from the Shaka. The king sent a messenger to the king of Kabirae to say, "All of my queens are inferior. I would like to choose another queen from the Shaka."

The king of Kabirae gathered many ministers and wise men for consultation and said in distress, "King Hashinoku of Shae wished a queen from the Shaka. His country is inferior to ours. How can we send one of our women to that country, even if she would become a queen? Yet if we don't send any, they will attack us in force and we won't be able to defend ourselves."

A wise minister said, "Shakumanan has a very attractive female servant. How about sending her as one of our women?" The king and other ministers all agreed, "That is a good idea." So they decorated and dressed the female servant of Shakumanan and sent her to Shae with a message saying, "This is a Shaka woman." King Hashinoku found her extremely beautiful and incomparably superior to any of his queens in his country. The king called her Lady Mari[163] and greatly cherished her.

Soon Mari gave birth to two boys, the sons of King Hashinoku. One of the sons grew up intelligent and brilliant. When he became

162. 琉璃王. Virūdhaka, the son of King Prasenajit.
163. Mallikā was born in Kapilavastu in central India and married King Prasenajīt of Śrāvastī.

eight years old, he was told, "You have a relationship to Kabirae, which is your mother's country. That country surpasses others in its men of intelligence and wisdom. Shakumanan is especially blessed with virtue and wisdom. We hear that even pebbles become gold and silver in his hands. So the king made him the master of the state and many Shaka people learn from him. We do not have any one comparable to him. Since you are of the same Shaka, go and learn from him." So the son was sent to Kabirae with a companion of the same age who was a son of a minister.

When they arrived in Kabirae, they saw a large new hall in the city. In the hall was a high and wide seat for Shakumanan, seats on the opposite side where the Shaka people sat to learn, and seats for those other than the Shaka in a separate location.

Prince Ruri, the son of King Hashinoku, climbed into a seat for the Shaka, thinking that he was one of them. Seeing this, the Shaka people rejected him: "That seat is reserved for a Shaka person who learns from the Great Master Shakumanan. Though you are a prince of King Hashimoku, you are a child of a mere female servant. How dare you degrade such a noble seat!" And they drove him from the seat.

The prince thought this extremely shameful and said to his minister's son, "We should let no one of Shae know that I was driven from the seat. When I become the king of Shae, I will attack the Shaka. But before that, don't let any one know about this." Making a firm promise to each other, Prince Ruri and the minister's son returned home.

Later King Hashinoku died and Prince Ruri inherited the throne. The son of the minister now became a minister and was called Kōku. King Ruri said to Kōku, "I have not forgotten what I said about the country of Kabirae. We should go there and attack the Shaka." King Ruri led countless soldiers toward the country of Kabirae.

Mokuren heard of this, hastened to the Buddha, and said, "King Ruri of Shae is coming to this country with countless soldiers to attack the Shaka. Many Shaka will be killed."

"How can I alter the course of their karma?" asked the Buddha. "It is beyond my power." He went where King Ruri would pass and sat under a withered tree by the roadside.

King Ruri and his troops were about to enter the city of Kabirae. They saw the Buddha sitting alone at a distance. The king quickly descended from his carriage, went to the Buddha, and respectfully asked, "My lord Buddha, why do you sit under this withered tree?"

The Buddha said, "I am sitting under this withered tree because the Shaka will be destroyed." Hearing this, the king felt hesitant and led his forces home. The Buddha returned to Mount Ryōju.

Sometime later, Kōku said to King Ruri, "We still should attack the Shaka." The king again led his troops to the city of Kabirae.

Mokuren went to the Buddha again, "King Ruri's forces have returned. I think I will place King Ruri and his forces in another world."

The Buddha asked, "Are you really going to divert the karmic result of the Shaka people by putting King Ruri and his soldiers into another world?"

Mokuren said, "Truly, the karmic result cannot be placed in another world." Mokuren continued, "I will move the city of Kabirae and place it in an open space."

"Can the karmic result of the Shaka be put in an open space?" asked the Buddha.

"The karmic result cannot be put in an open space. I will place an iron basket over the city of Kabirae," said Mokuren.

"Can the karmic result be covered by an iron basket?" the Buddha asked.

"The karmic result cannot be covered by the iron basket. I will take some Shaka people, put them in a bowl and hide them in an open space," said Mokuren.

"Even though you hide them they cannot escape their karmic destiny," said the Buddha and lay down with a headache.

When King Ruri and his soldiers reached the city of Kabirae, the Shaka people defended the city by shooting arrows. The king's soldiers fell when struck by arrows, but none died. The king's army hesitated and no longer advanced.

Seeing this, Kōku said to the king, "Although the Shaka people have attained the way of warriors, since they all observe the precepts, they will not harm even an insect. How dare they harm people? They will never kill us. So we should attack them without hesitation."

So, without hesitating, the king's army attacked the city. The Shaka had no way to defend themselves and all retired into the city. King Ruri, who stayed outside the city, said to the Shaka, "Quickly open the city gate. Otherwise we will kill many of you."

In the Kabirae city was a fifteen-year-old Shaka boy called Shama. When he heard that King Ruri was outside the city, he put on his armor, took his bows and arrows, left the city, and fought alone against the king's army. Many soldiers were killed by him and others fled. The king was immensely frightened.

When the Shaka people heard this, they called the boy into the city and scolded him, "You are still young. Why did you act contrary to our precepts? Don't you know that we Shakas have been practicing the correct Law and would not harm a single insect? How dare we harm people? For this reason, leave us immediately." Shama left the city and departed. King Ruri was still calling, "Open the gate quickly."

At that time, a demon deity transformed himself into a Shaka man and said to the Shaka people, "Quickly open the city gates, but don't fight." When the gates were opened, the king said to his subjects, "We see too many Shaka people to kill them by bows and arrows. Have elephants stamp them to death." So the subjects did as the king ordered.

The king also ordered his subjects, "Bring me five hundred attractive Shaka women." The subjects brought the king five hundred beautiful women. "Don't be reluctant. I will be your husband and you will be my wives," said the king to the women and approached one and fondled her.

The woman asked the king, "Great king, why do you do this?" "I am going to have intercourse with you," said the king.

The woman rejected him saying, "Why am I, a Shaka woman, to have intercourse with the king born to a female servant?" The enraged king ordered his subjects to cut off the women's limbs and throw her into a deep pit. Other Shaka women, too, abused the king saying, "Who would sleep with the king born to a female servant?" The infuriated king had the limbs of all five hundred Shaka women amputated, and threw them into a big hole.

In that occasion, Makao,[164] a grandfather of King Ruri, said to the king, "Please grant my wish."

"What do you wish?" asked the king.

"I am going to dive. If I don't come back to the surface of the water, release the Shaka people," said Makao.

"Fine. Your wish is granted," said the king.

When Makao reached the bottom of the pond, he tied his hair to the roots of a tree and drowned. Meanwhile many Shaka people were

....

164. It refers to Shakumanan.

released. Because of this confusion, some ran out through the eastern gate, some through the western gate, some through the southern gate, and others entered the city through the northern gate. The king asked, "Why is Makao staying at the bottom of the water so long and why doesn't he come up?" "He drowned at the bottom of the water," said the subjects. The king greatly regretted Makao's death and said, "My grandfather is already dead. This is because he loved his Shaka people."

The Shaka people who were killed by King Ruri numbered nine thousand, nine hundred and ninety-nine. Some were buried in the ground and others were trampled to death by elephants. Their blood formed a pool. The palace buildings in the city were completely burned. King Ruri led his army home to his country.

Mokuren found the Shaka people all dead whom he had placed in the bowl for concealment in the open space. So there was no error when the Buddha said, "No one can escape his karmic fate."

The Buddha said, "King Ruri and his soldiers will die in seven days." The frightened king heard this and told his soldiers. Kōku said, "Don't be frightened, great king. There will be no difficulties and misfortunes outside." To alleviate his worry, the king led his soldiers and court ladies to the River Ashira.[165] While they were entertained by music and games, a great storm suddenly brought a heavy rain with rolling thunder and flashing lightning. The king and all his people were blown to their death in the river. It was just as though they were in the Abi Hell.[166] A fire from the sky burned down all the palace buildings in the city. All the Shaka people killed at that time were reborn in the heavens since they had kept the precepts during their present life.

Many of the Buddha's disciples asked the Buddha, "Why were these Shaka people killed by King Ruri?" The Buddha explained, "Once there was a fishing village in Raetsu.[167] In a time of drought and famine, people from the city came and fished in the pond in the village. Two fish, one called Kusa and the other Tazetsu, spoke to-

----

165. The Rapti River in Nepal and North India.
166. 阿鼻地獄. The Hell of No-Interval is the lowest of the Eight Hells in the Buddhist cosmology, which include the Hell of Repetition, the Hell of the Black Rope, the Hell of All Living Beings, the Hell of Lamentations, the Hell of Great Lamentations, the Hell of Scorching Heat, and the Hell of Great Scorching Heat.
167. Raetsu refers to Rājagṛha.

gether. 'Although we did nothing wrong in our previous lives, we are about to be eaten by these people. Since we accumulated merit in our previous lives, we will surely be rewarded and have a chance to avenge ourselves.'

"At that time, an eight-year-old boy in the village did not catch any fish, but amused himself by watching the fish from the riverbank. So now we know that the people of Raetsu city are the present Shaka people. The fish called Kusa is King Ruri and the fish Tazetsu is Kōku. I am the boy who amused himself by watching the fish. Since I hit the head of a fish, I now have a headache in my present life. The Shaka people, due to their sin in catching fish, fell into the hell and suffered a long time. Although they were reborn as human beings and met me, their reward is limited to this extent. King Ruri, Kōku, and other soldiers of the king fell into the Abi Hell because they killed many Shaka people."

Thus it was told and handed down.

2:29   HOW A BANDIT OF THE COUNTRY OF SHAE KILLED KARUDAI[168]

Long ago, a pious Brahman in the country of Shae always venerated Arhat Karudai. The Brahman had a son. On his deathbed, the father said to his son, "If you intend to be filial, venerate this arhat as I have, even after my death. Don't ever neglect him." As soon as the father uttered his last words, he passed away.

Afterward, the son firmly believed his father's words and sincerely venerated the arhat in the morning and in the evening. Once the son was making a business trip to a distant place. The son said to his wife, "While I am away, venerate this great arhat and don't ever neglect him." The son left for a distant place.

The wife was attractive and very lustful. One of the five hundred bandits in that country saw the wife and was attracted by her. He secretly communicated with her and attained his wish. The great arhat naturally learned about this. Being afraid that the arhat might tell her husband, the wife incited the bandit and had him kill the arhat.

King Hashinoku heard about this and greatly lamented, "A most noble and enlightened man of our country, the great arhat, was killed

....

168. It refers to Udai. See note 17.

by the wife of a Brahman." The enraged king caught the five hundred bandits and killed them, together with the Brahman's wife, by cutting off their limbs and heads.

More than eight thousand houses in the wife's neighborhood were completely destroyed.

Seeing this, many disciples of the Buddha asked, "Due to what sort of evil committed in his previous life was he killed by the Brahman's wife, causing so much trouble?" The Buddha answered, "Countless years ago, when Karudai was born as a master to worship Great Jizaiten, he caught a lamb with his five hundred people, cut off its limbs, and offered it to Jizaiten as a sacrifice. Due to that sin, he fell into the hells and suffered incessantly. The lamb killed at that time was the Brahman's wife, and the master who venerated the great Jizaiten was present Karudai, and his five hundred people were the five hundred bandits.

"The sin of killing does not dissipate for generations, and its effect is repeated by a killing like this. Even though the arhat was fortunately reborn as a human being in this life, and attained the final stage of enlightenment, he could not escape his karmic relation to his past sin."

This it was told and handed down.

2:30   HOW KING HASHINOKU KILLED THE THIRTY-TWO SONS OF BISHARI

Long ago in India, a wealthy man called Rikimi had seven children. All were married except for the seventh child, Bishari. Bishari was a brilliant girl. King Hashinoku heard of her, wished to marry her, and finally invited her to be his queen.

Bishari became pregnant. After some months had passed, she delivered thirty-two eggs, which each hatched a baby.

Each boy was immensely good-looking, brave, and blessed with the strength of a thousand men. When these boys matured, they all married daughters of noble families in the countries.

When Bishari once invited the Buddha and his disciples to her place, the Buddha preached the Law, and all of her people, including her sons, attained the *shudaonka* enlightenment except the youngest son. The youngest son was out riding an elephant.

When the youngest son was crossing a bridge, he met a minister's son riding in a carriage. The youngest son pushed the carriage and threw it into the ditch under the bridge. The carriage was broken and the minister's son was injured.

On being informed, the minister said to his son, "He is too strong and wild for you. If you want revenge, make thirty-two whips, each with seven kinds of jewels and containing a sword. Give these thirty-two whips to these thirty-two men without revealing any antagonism."

The minister's son did as his father suggested. The thirty-two men were very pleased to receive the whips.

It was a custom of the country that people did not wear swords before the king. The minister slanderously remarked to the king, "The thirty-two sons of Bishari are strong and in their prime. Each has the strength of a thousand men and is immensely bold and brave. Now they are treacherous; they have made whips containing swords and are plotting to harm the king."

The king believed his minister and killed all thirty-two men. The heads of the thirty-two sons were placed in sealed boxes and sent to Bishari. At that time, Bishari was receiving the Buddha and his priests.

Seeing the boxes, Bishari was about to open them, thinking that they might be offerings from the king for the Buddha and his disciples. But the Buddha did not allow her to do this.

When the meal was finished, the Buddha preached the Law and the transciency of this life. Hearing this, Bishari attained the *anagonka* enlightenment. After the Buddha left, Bishari opened the boxes and saw the thirty-two heads of her sons.

Since Bishari had already attained enlightenment and had abandoned worldly feelings of attachment, she neither grieved nor lamented. She only said, "No one can escape the cycle of birth and death. Being together is impossible."

However, the wives and the relatives of the thirty-two men grieved, saying, "The king killed good men for no reason. We should definitely have revenge."

They gathered many soldiers and were about to attack the king. Hearing this, the frightened king left to visit the Buddha in the Gion-shōja. The soldiers heard of this, went to the Gionshōja, surrounded it, and waited for the king.

Anan saw these soldiers. Joining his palms in the attitude of prayer, he asked the Buddha, "What sort of deeds in their previous lives caused these thirty-two sons of Bishari to be killed by the king?"

The Buddha explained, "Long ago, these thirty-two men stole a cow and took it to an old woman. The old woman gave the men weapons to slaughter the cow. Kneeling on the ground under their swords, the cow begged for her life.

"Yet these cruel men would not release her. Just before the cow was killed, she vowed, 'You are going to kill me now but I will surely have revenge in the future.'

"The thirty-two men ate the cow. The old woman also ate until she was tired and said, pleased, 'I am so happy today to have guests like you.'

"The cow of that time is the present King Hashinoku. The thirty-two men who killed the cow are the thirty-two sons of Bishari. The old woman of the past is Bishari. Since these thirty-two men killed the cow, they always have been killed for five hundred generations. Since the old woman rejoiced at the slaughtering of the cow, she has been the mother of the thirty-two men for five hundred generations and always has suffered by seeing each of her children killed. Since she has met me now, she has finally attained the *anagonka* enlightenment."

Listening to the Buddha preach, the relatives of the thirty-two men lost their desire for vengence and said, "Killing a cow results in this much suffering. Just imagine how the king who killed all these thirty-two men for no cause will suffer! Since we have heard the Buddha preach, we have given up our desires for vengeance. Besides, the king is the head of our country, we will not harm him." The king regretted what he had done and remained silent.

Anan again asked the Buddha, "What sort of good causes in her previous lives resulted in Bishari meeting the Buddha and attaining the Way?"

The Buddha replied, "An old woman once mixed ointment with various kinds of incense and coated a pagoda. She also encouraged the thirty-two men on the street to coat the pagoda. After coating the pagoda, the old woman vowed. 'We will be reborn in a noble status, always as mother and children, will meet the Buddha, and will attain the Way.'

"Later the old woman and the thirty-two men always were reborn in a noble status as a mother and her children for five hundred generations. She had met the Buddha and attained the Way."

Thus it was told and handed down.

2:31 ABOUT THE NUN MIMYŌ

Long ago in India, a nun called Mimyō had attained arhatship. She told the other nuns how she had experienced the karmic relation of good and evil.

"Long ago, there was a very wealthy man with abundant treasures but no children. Later he took a mistress, whom he had loved very much. He finally had a son by this mistress. The wealthy man and his mistress cherished their son immensely.

"The formal wife of the man became jealous and thought, 'When this boy matures, he will succeed to the family occupation and I will be neglected. Why should I work hard to maintain the household and family occupation? There is no recourse other than to kill this boy.'

"The formal wife secretly took an iron needle. At a convenient time she thrust it through the boy's head. The boy died. The boy's mother, the mistress, grieved and thought, 'Surely my son has been killed by the jealous wife.'

"The mistress went to the wife and accused her, 'You killed my child.'

"The wife said, 'I did not kill your child. By reciting incantations, you can learn whether I am guilty. If I killed your child, and if I have a husband in my future life, may he will be bitten to death by a snake; if I have children, may they be drowned and eaten by a wolf!' With this oath, the formal wife died.

"Because the wife killed the child, she fell into the hell and underwent great suffering. After her period of expiation in the hells was ended, she was reborn as a Brahman's daughter. When she had grown, she married a man and bore a child. Soon she became pregnant again.

"On a day near the end of her pregnancy, she and her husband were going to her parents. Since her husband was poor, no attendants accompanied them. While traveling, she had pains in her abdomen and delivered a baby. At night, they took shelter under some trees. The husband was lying at a separate place from his wife and children.

"Suddenly a poisonous snake appeared and bit the husband to

death. The wife, seeing her husband die, fainted from grief. She revived as dawn broke.

"The grieving woman started on her way to her parents, carrying the older child on her shoulder and holding the newborn baby. Soon she came to a large river. She left the older child on the riverbank and crossed holding the baby. Leaving the baby on the far bank, she returned for the older child. Seeing the mother cross the river, the excited older child stepped into the water. The distraught mother tried to grasp the older child, who was carried downstream. The woman did her best to rescue the child, who was drowned in a few short moments.

"The grieving woman returned to the other bank, where she looked for her baby. She only found blood and a wolf, which had just eaten the baby. The mother fainted from shock. After a while, she revived and started on her way alone. She met a Brahman who was a close friend of her father's.

"The woman told him the details about her husband and children. The Brahman, too, grieved and lamented. 'Is my parents' house safe?' asked the woman. 'No. Unfortunately, there was a fire at your parents' house yesterday and all of your people, including your parents were burned to death,' replied the Brahman. At this bad news, the overwhelmed woman fainted on the spot. She was revived and taken to the Brahman's house. He pitied and took care of her.

"Soon the woman married again and became pregnant. When she was in the final stages of her pregnancy, her husband went out, got drunk, and was returning home about sunset. Since darkness was falling, the wife had barred the gates. Just as the husband stood knocking outside the gates, the wife's labor pains began. There was no one to go out and open the gates for her husband.

"Meanwhile, the wife finished her labor and delivered the baby by herself. Finally, the angry husband broke open the gates. He came into the house and hit his wife. The wife explained to him about the birth of her child. However, the enraged husband took the baby, killed it, boiled it in oil, and forced his wife to eat it.

" 'Since I was born with bad fortune, I have a husband like this. I should leave him,' thought the woman and quickly ran away.

"The woman reached the country of Harana and was resting under a tree. A son of a wealthy man in the country had just lost his beloved wife and was mourning. When the son saw the woman resting under the tree, he questioned her. The woman replied and told the details of her story. The son took her as his wife.

"Several days later, the husband suddenly died. The country had a custom that a wife should be buried alive when her husband died. Bandits came to take the wife. The chief of the bandits kidnapped her and made her his wife.

"Several days passed. Her husband, the chief of the bandits, broke into a house to steal and was killed by the master. The corpse of her husband was brought to the wife, and the wife was buried alive according to the custom of the country.

"Three days later, foxes and wolves ravaged the house compound and the woman managed to crawl out of her grave. The woman thought, 'What sort of sins in my past have caused me to encounter so many misfortunes, to die, and to be revived so many times? Where am I going now? If I continue to live, I would like to visit Shaka Buddha in the Gionshōja and enter Buddhahood.'

"In the past, the woman had offered food to Hyakushi Buddha[169] and had made a vow. Due to these merits, she could meet the Buddha. She entered Buddhahood, practiced the Way, and attained arhatship. Yet she had fallen into the hells due to her sin of killing in her previous life. She is now having bad consequences due to her faults in uttering incantations. I am the formal wife of the past. Even though I have attained the *arakanka* enlightenment, I have been undergoing unbearable pain and suffering for days and nights, since a hot iron needle is thrust through me from head to foot."

Thus Mimyō told her story. So the results and rewards of sins and merits recur and never cease.

Thus it was told and handed down.

2:32   ABOUT SHISHITSU, A MINISTER OF THE COUNTRY OF SHAE

Long ago, Sharihotsu always kept his wise eyes on the sentient beings. When he noticed someone who should become an ascetic, he had the person immediately practice the Way.

At that time a very wealthy man was in the country. Shishitsu, a minister of King Hashinoku, owned countless treasures. Sharihotsu

....

169. See note 88.

thought the minister should practice the Way and went to his house to beg alms.

The minister venerated Sharihotsu, invited him in, and prepared a meal as an offering. After having received the offerings, Sharihotsu preached the Law to the minister, saying, "Wealth and prosperity cause all suffering. Remaining in secular life and loving one's wife and children is like incarceration in a prison. All that exists is transient."

Hearing this, the minister rejoiced and immediately developed a pious mind. The minister entrusted his younger brother with his family occupation and his household, including his wife and children. The minister entered Buddhahood and went to a mountain.

Later the wife of the minister missed him and was displeased with his younger brother. Being aware of this, the younger brother said, "I think that you regret living with me as man and wife. Why are you always so sad?" The wife replied, "I am sad because I miss my former husband, the minister."

The younger brother hired a bandit to go to the mountain and kill his older brother. The bandit understood the younger brother's request, went to the mountain, and found the priest, the older brother. "At your brother's request, I have come here to take your life," said the bandit. The frightened priest appealed to the bandit, "Although I have entered the priesthood, I have not met the Buddha, nor do I understand the Law. Don't kill me now, but wait until I have met the Buddha and have listened to him preach the Law. That should not be long."

"No, I cannot let you do that," said the bandit. The priest raised his arm and said, "Cut off and take my arm. But preserve my life for a while. I still wish to see the Buddha." So the bandit, instead of killing him, cut off his arm and took it away.

The priest immediately went to the Buddha and venerated him. The Buddha preached the Law for the priest, who immediately attained the *arakanka* enlightenment and entered *nirvana*.

Meanwhile the bandit took the arm to the younger brother. The younger brother took it and placed it before the wife and said, "This is the arm of your former husband." The wife could not speak, but was choked by her tears. Later the wife went to the palace of King Hashinoku and told the king the details of her story. The enraged king caught and killed the younger brother.

At that time, priests asked the Buddha, "Due to what sort of evil causes in his previous lives, did this priest have his arm severed, meet the Buddha, and attain the Way?"

The Buddha replied, "Long ago, King Tatsu[170] of the contry of Harana went hunting and lost his way in a mountain. While standing under a tree and looking for the right way, the king saw Hyakushi Buddha in the mountain. The king asked Hyakushi to tell him the right way. Hyakushi indicated the way to the king by using his elbow. He could not raise his hand because of his bad arm. The king became angry at him, drew his sword, and slashed him. 'King, unless you repent of your sin now, you will be severely punished!' said Hyakushi. He jumped in front of the king, ascended into the air, and revealed Mysterious Changes.

"The impressed king thought, 'I have met an enlightened person.' He crouched on the ground and raised his voice, 'Hyakushi Buddha, please descend and listen to my repentance!' Hyakushi Buddha descended. The king paid his respects to Hyakushi with his face touching the ground and said, 'Please accept my repentance with pity and mercy and release me from the painful consequences of my sins.' Hyakushi heard this and immediately entered *nirvana*.

"The king built a pagoda on that spot and worshipped it. Even afterward, the king went to the pagoda and constantly repented for his sins, and was finally delivered.

"The priest of today was King Tatsu. Since he struck off the arm of Hyakushi in his former life, he had his arm cut off in return in this life. Thanks to his repentance, he avoided falling into the hells and attained the Way."

Thus it was told and handed down.

2:33 HOW THE DAUGHTERS IN A COUNTRY OF INDIA COULD NOT INHERIT THEIR FATHER'S TREASURES

Long ago, a country in India had a custom that only sons could inherit their father's treasures. Daughters could not. If there was no son as the heir, treasures were confiscated as public property after the father's death.

There was a wealthy man in that country who had abundant trea-

---

170. 婆羅達. He was a king of Vārāṇasī, which was an ancient kingdom and city on the Ganges, present-day Benares.

sures and five daughters but no sons. All his treasures would become public property if the man died. His wife became pregnant and all his household anxiously hoped that his next child would be a boy. However, the wealthy man suddenly died before his new baby was born.

The official messengers came to the house and sealed all the storehouses containing the treasures. The first daughter had the messenger report to the king, "If the newborn baby is a boy, he can inherit our father's treasures. However, he will not be able to inherit them if the treasures are confiscated as public property. Please keep the treasures sealed until the baby is born. If it is a girl, the treasures can be confiscated. If it is a boy, he can inherit them."

The king agreed, "What she says is reasonable. We should wait till the baby is born." Soon a baby boy was born, and the household, including the five daughters, all rejoiced. But the baby had no eyes, no ears, and no tongue. They thought this most extraordinary and had mixed emotions of joy and sorrow because the baby was a boy but defective.

The first daughter suggested, "We should first report this to the king and comply with his decision." The other four daughters agreed and explained to the king about the baby.

The king said, "Although abnormal, he is a boy and should inherit his father's treasures." So the official messengers came, removed the seals from the storehouses, and left, saying, "The newborn boy should look after his father's treasures." The five daughters were immensely pleased and used the treasures as they wished.

Since the treasures were inherited by the boy, even though he was a freak, he was appreciated by the people, including the household family and others in that country.

One day, the first daughter said to her husband, "Thanks to the virtue of our defective brother, we can keep the treasures at our place and use them as we wish. I would like to know why this brother has become the owner of the treasures." She invited the Buddha and asked, "This child was born as a boy and inherited his father's treasures, but he is without eyes, ears, and tongue. What did he do in his former lives to deserve this?"

The Buddha said, "Listen to me well. Long ago, two brothers lived in a country. The older brother was a wise man who was respected and trusted by the high and humble for his true words and honesty. The younger brother possessed abundant treasures, made loans, increased his property, and greatly prospered in his business.

"A merchant made his living by importing treasures from other countries by ship. This merchant was going to sea to search for treasures. Since he needed more capital, he went to the wealthy younger brother to borrow money.

"The younger brother said, 'I will lend you the money you need. However, if I die before you return, you should repay the exact amount of the loan to my son. My older brother is highly respected for his intelligence and integrity. I will make the loan in his presence,' and the younger brother took his son and the merchant to his older brother.

" 'I am going to make a loan to this merchant. But I am not sure of his integrity. If I die, the loan should be repaid to my son. Since he is still young, my son may have difficulty in recovering the money from the merchant. I am going to make this merchant a loan in front of you. If something happens to me, take care of the matter for my son. The people of our world use you as their witness on an occasion like this. Why shouldn't I, your younger brother, rely on you? Be sure to take care of the matter reasonably,' said the younger brother to his older brother and made a considerable loan to the merchant.

"Shortly afterward, the younger brother passed away. Seven years later, the merchant returned with numerous treasures. The son of the younger brother had been waiting to hear from the merchant, but had had no contact from him.

"One day, the son went to a marketplace to shop and saw the merchant. The son said, 'I heard that you returned from the sea a long time ago. You have not contacted me. Why don't you return the money that you borrowed from my father?'

"The merchant thought, 'I should certainly return the correct amount. Yet it is a great sum. Seeking treasures by going to sea is not easy. I even had to risk my life. It is very difficult for me to pay back so much of what I obtained at the risk of my life.' He said, 'I am not very much sure of the amount of the loan. I will check and tell you.'

"The son replied, 'What an extraordinary thing to say! You and my father made a contract, a mutual promise before my uncle, the wise man of the country. We should go together to see my uncle, and ask him to judge.' 'You are right. Well go there in three or four days,' said the merchant. He set a time with the son and left.

"After returning home, the merchant took a fine radiant jewel which would shine at night to the wife of the older brother. The merchant said to the wife, 'Once when I went to sea to obtain treasures,

I was short of money. I borrowed money from the younger brother of your husband with your husband as our witness. After I returned from overseas, the son of the younger brother quite reasonably demanded the return of the loan. Yet, since the sum is so large, I regretted the return of the sum and said that I did not remember. The son of the younger brother said, "This is quite outrageous. My father feared a situation like this, and made you the loan with my uncle as the witness. So, we should go to see my uncle and follow his judgment!" We agreed on a time to see his uncle, the wise man. Now this is an unusual jewel which lights up the darkness of the night and can't be compared to other jewels. Please take this jewel and have your husband arrange that I don't have to repay the loan when the son and I bring up the matter.' The merchant pressed the wife to accept the jewel and left.

"The older brother returned home toward evening after settling some lawsuits. The wife took the jewel to her husband and told him what the merchant had discreetly said. The enraged older brother said, 'Don't you know my mind after being with me for all these years? Why do you talk as if you don't know me at all! Quickly return the jewel.'

"The wife called the merchant and returned the jewel, slipping it into one of his sleeves. The merchant went home. He took two jewels which were superior to the first and went to see the wife again. At a proper time, the merchant secretly slipped the jewels into the wife's sleeves.

"When her husband returned home, the wife showed the two jewels and said, sobbing, 'It is hard for me to return these two jewels this time. If you insist, I will throw myself into a river with my only son.' The older brother's resolve weakened. He said, 'Well, I don't know. Do as you wish,' and was gone.

"The joyful wife secretly sent a message to the merchant, who was also pleased with his plot. When the day came, he and the son of the younger brother went to see the older brother. The son mentioned the details such as the date and the amount of the loan made by his father.

"'All this did not happen,' said the merchant, lying unreservedly. The older brother said, 'I have listened to you both. Though I would tell the truth, I remember nothing of this.'

"The younger brother's son thought the statement most extraordinary and felt enraged but tearfully said, 'Since you are known as a wise man who speaks the truth, my father made a deal before you as he wished. Now you speak with a double tongue and betray us!' His uncle left without a word, the merchant with joy and the son with bitter sadness.

"Shortly after, the older brother died of a serious illness. He fell into the hell and underwent countless sufferings due to his sin. He was reborn as a man but was eyeless, earless, and tongueless due to the sin of his tongue in his former life. However, thanks to his assistance to others as a virtuous man of the country, and since he had been highly respected as a wise man of the country by the people, including the king, he was able to inherit treasures in this life." The first daughter thought this most noble, worshipped the Buddha, and left.

Thus it was told and handed down.

2:34   ABOUT A FISH WITH A HUNDRED HEADS

Long ago in India, the Buddha went to the Riotsu River[171] with his priests. Many people had gathered by the river to fish. They netted a fish with a hundred heads of animals, such as a donkey, horse, cow, wild boar, and dog. Five hundred people tried to draw up the net, but the fish was not raised out of the water.

By the river were another five hundred men herding their cows. They let their cows come to the riverbank and pulled up the net together with the other five hundred men. With the power of one thousand men, the fish was finally raised out of the water. The people gathered and looked at this most extraordinary fish.

The Buddha went with his priests to see the fish and asked, "Where is your mother?" "In the Mugen Hell,"[172] replied the fish.

Seeing this, Anan asked the Buddha the cause. The Buddha explained, "Long ago at the time of Kashō Buddha,[173] a Brahman had an incomparably brilliant and intelligent boy called Kabiri.

"After his father died, the mother said to her son, 'You are brilliant boy. Is there anyone superior to you in this world?'

" 'Ascetics are superior to me. When I ask them about my doubts, they take pleasure in enabling me to understand my problems. When they ask me a question, I am unable to answer,' said the boy.

....

171. The Revata River is said to be in Kashmir.
172. Hell of No-Interval. See note 166.
173. Makakashō. See note 38.

" 'Why don't you, too, learn about the Law?' asked the mother.

" 'If I want to learn about the Law, I should become a priest. I am a layman and they don't teach the laity,' said the boy.

" 'Well then, pretend that you intend to become a priest, learn about the Law, and return home,' suggested the mother. The boy followed her suggestion. He became a false priest, went to an ascetic, learned about the Law, and returned home.

"The mother asked her son, 'Have you learned about the Law or not?'

" 'No, I have not yet finished learning,' answered the son.

" 'If you are not learning anything more, go and insult your master. Then he may teach you something better!' said his mother.

"Following her suggestion, the son went to his master and abused him, saying, 'You are a fool with no knowledge and have the head of animal,' and left.

"Due to these sins, the mother fell into the Mugen Hell, while her son was reborn as a fish with a hundred animal heads."

Anan asked the Buddha, "Could the fish leave his status as a fish?" The Buddha answered "Even in this generation when a thousand Buddhas appear after a long period of countless *kalpa* years, he could not escape from the body of the fish. So one should be careful about one's body, mouth, and intentions. If one insults and abuses others, one will receive results according to one's words."

Thus it was told and handed down.

2:35   HOW A HEAVENLY PERSON OF UNUSUAL FORM DESCENDED IN INDIA

Long ago a Heavenly Person descended in India. It had a golden-hued body and the head of a wild boar. It ate filth in dirty places, such as gutters and toilets.

The watching people thought this most extraordinary and asked the Buddha, "Due to what karmic relation from its previous life was this Heavenly Person born with a golden-hued body, an animal head, and eating things in dirty places?"

The Buddha explained, "Ninety-one *kalpa* years ago, when Bibashi Buddha appeared in the world, this Heavenly Person was born as a woman and became the wife of a man. At one time a priest came to her place to beg alms. Her husband was going to offer the priest gold, but the greedy wife became angry and stopped her husband from offering the gold to the priest. She has received this status for ninety-one *kalpa* years as the result of that sin.

"On one occasion, she paid her respects to the Buddha by bowing. Thanks to that, she now has a golden-hued body which releases radiance. As you see, even if she was born in heaven, this is still her bad *karma*."

Thus it was told and handed down.

2:36   THE STORY OF ENBARA,[174] A SON OF A WEALTHY MAN, SHARA, IN INDIA

Long ago in India, a wealthy man called Shara lived in the city of Bishari.[175] After his wife became pregnant, her body became soiled and released a bad odor. People did not come near her. Ten months later, a baby boy was born. The baby was born covered with excrement and was so skinny that his skin was attached to his bones. The parents did not even want to see him. As he grew, he would not obey his parents and ate only excrement. His parents and relatives detested him, sent him away, and did not come near him. In other places, too, he always ate excrement, and the people hated him, calling him Enbara.

A heretic once saw Enbara while traveling on his way. The heretic encouraged Enbara, saying, "Come and be my disciple," and taught him ascetic practices. Even when Enbara was practicing ascetic ways, he still ate excrement. Seeing this, the heretic abused him and chased him away. Enbara ran off, went to the riverbank, and remained there, lamenting sadly.

At that time, the Buddha saw Enbara, went to his place, and delivered him. Seeing the Buddha, Enbara rejoiced and threw his body on the ground. He wished to enter Buddhahood. "You are welcome," said the Buddha. As soon as Enbara heard the Buddha's words, his hair fell out of its own accord, he became dressed naturally in a priestly robe, and he became a priest.

As the Buddha preached the Law to him, Enbara got rid of his filth and attained the *arakanka* enlightenment.

Seeing this, the Buddha's priests asked, "Due to what sort of

....

174. Unknown.

175. 毗舍離. Vaiśālī was one of the sixteen great countries in the Buddha's time.

seeds planted in his former lives did Enbara receive such punishment, and thanks to what karmic relation did he meet the Buddha and attain the Way?"

The Buddha replied, "Long ago, Kuruson Buddha[176] appeared in this world. The king of the country invited the Buddha and other priests to his jeweled palace. He built a temple and appointed one of the priests as its master.

"Once, when many temple patrons gave baths to the priests, the priests' bodies were anointed afterward with scented oil. Seeing this, the master of the temple became angry and abused a priest who held the status of an arhat, 'You priest, oiling your body is just like putting excrement over it!' The priest pitied the master of the temple and revealed Mysterious Powers, such as ascending in the air and showing the Eighteen Mysterious Changes.

"Overwhelmed by this, the master of the temple repented and futilely asked to be rid of his sins. Due to his sins, the master was reborn with a soiled body for five hundred generations, and was shunned by the people. But thanks to his entering into Buddhahood and repentance toward the arhat, he met me, became a priest, and attained the Way."

Thus it was told and handed down.

2:37   HOW ARHAT MANZOKU WENT TO THE REALM OF THE HUNGRY GHOSTS[177]

Long ago, Arhat Manzoku, a disciple of the Buddha with Mysterious Power, went to the Realm of the Hungry Ghosts.

He saw a formidable hungry ghost, several tens of *jō*[178] tall, emitting flames from its eyes, nose, limbs, and other parts of its body. It had a pendulous lip like that of a wild boar. Clutching its own hand, it ran east and west, crying loudly. Seeing this, Manzoku asked the hungry ghost, "What kind of sins in your former life cause you to suffer this much?"

The hungry ghost explained, "When I was born as a priest, I was attached to a temple and was avaricious. Being proud of my power-

176. 拘留孫仏. Kuruson Buddha, Krakucchonda, the first of the Buddhas of the present: Bhadrakalpa, the fourth of the seven ancient Buddhas.
177. See note 62.
178. One *jō* equals ten feet.

ful family, I spoke evil words. Whenever I saw a priest who kept the precepts and was devoted in ascetic ways, I abused, embarrassed, and despised him. Due to these sins, I am undergoing these sufferings. Now I would like to cut off my tongue with a knife so that I will neither abuse nor slander devoted priests. If you return to the Enbudai world, use me as an example; tell many priests to watch their speech and not to speak evil words. When they see a person obeying the precepts, they should respect him. Since I was born in the form of a hungry ghost, I have been suffering for several ten thousands of years. After my life here is ended, I am supposed to fall into the hells." After saying this, he threw himself onto the ground and groaned. His voice resounded as if a great mountain were collasping, and shook the heavens and rocked the earth.

This was all due to sins caused by speech. Manzoku told this story to his people after he returned to the Enbudai.

Thus it was told and handed down.

2:38   HOW TWO WEALTHY MEN OF INDIA, A FATHER AND HIS SON, BECAME AVARICIOUS

Long ago, two wealthy men, a father and his son, lived in India. Both were prosperous and had abundant treasures. Yet they were avaricious and had no inclination to make offerings. Naturally, when begging priests came to their gates, they drove them away and never let them enter.

The father became ill and soon passed away. After his death, he was conceived by a blind female beggar of the country. After the months passed, the blind woman gave birth to a blind child. The months and years passed, and the blind child became seven years old. Both the mother and the son lived by begging alms.

The blind child happened to come to the house of the wealthy man, the son of the deceased father. Since the gatekeeper was absent for a short while, nobody chased him away and the child entered and stood in the southern part of the house.

Seeing him, the angry wealthy man chased him from the house. Just then the gatekeeper returned, took one of the child's arms and threw him to the ground. The child landed with his hand and head broken. Hearing his loud cry, his beggar mother came in confusion, took him in her arms, and grieved.

Pitying them, the Buddha came near the beggar child and said, "Listen well to me. You were the father of this wealthy man here. In your previous life, you were very avaricious and never offered anything to any one, but forcefully drove away the beggars. Due to such sins, you are getting these results. You are suffering mildly. After this, you will suffer in the hells for countless years. What a pity."

The Buddha approached the child and stroked his head. The beggar child's eyes opened. After hearing the Buddha preach, he knew that he had been the avaricious father of this wealthy man, and had had no intention of making offerings. He knew that due to the sins he committed by chasing out beggars, he had come there to his child but had suffered like this. The beggar repented. Since he confessed his sins and venerated the Buddha, he fortunately avoided further punishment.

Thus it was told and handed down.

2:39   ABOUT PRIEST RIGUSHI OF INDIA

Long ago a priest called Rigushi lived in India. When he was a layman, his food and clothes were insufficient. After he became a priest, his food and clothes were still insufficient.

On one occasion, he took shelter in a hall. The food was scanty, and what he received was not enough. He spent seven days in the hall without food and was about to starve.

Pitying him, the Buddha's disciples, including Shubodai, Mokuren, and Anan, brought food for the priest every day. They always missed him, and the priest did not get any food. The priest had not eaten for ten days.

When Mokuren brought him food in a bowl, the doors of the hall were tightly closed and did not open. Mokuren used his Mysterious Powers to bring the bowl into the hall through an aperture. He offered the bowl of food to the priest.

When the overjoyed priest accepted the bowl in his hands, it slipped from his fingers and fell into a hole five hundred *yujun* deep in the ground. Again using his mysterious power, Mokuren stretched out his arm, grasped the bowl and offered it to the priest. When the priest accepted it and was about to eat the food from the bowl, his mouth suddenly closed and would not open. So the priest again could not eat.

Mokuren took Priest Rigushi to the Buddha and asked, "Why can't Rigushi take his food?" The Buddha said, "You really should know that as a child in his previous life, he became greedy while watching his mother make offerings to a priest, and begrudged him the offered treasures. The child confined his mother in an earthen storehouse and starved her to death.

"This child is the present Rigushi. Due to his sin, he cannot obtain any food in this life. However, thanks to the merits accumulated by his parents, he joined me and attained the Way."

Thus it was told and handed down.

2:40   ABOUT FUNAKI, A SERVANT OF DONMAMI, A WEALTHY MAN

Long ago, India contained a country called Hōhachi.[179] Donmami was the most wealthy man in that country. Donmami had two sons; Mina was the older and Shōgun was the younger. A female servant cared for the wealthy man and assisted him in his occupation. The female servant had a son called Funaki.[180]

The wealthy man had died, and Funaki now belonged to the older brother, Mina, who became rich and finally more prosperous than his father.

Funaki wished to enter Buddhahood and asked Mina's permission. His wish was granted and he entered Buddhahood, practiced the Way, and finally attained the *arakanka* enlightenment.

Later Funaki returned and recommended that Mina build a hall for the Buddha. Mina followed Funaki's suggestion and constructed a hall of sandalwood.

Afterward, Funaki made another suggestion, "Invite the Buddha with his priests and venerate them with offerings." Mina answered, "I will invite them. But when shall I invite them? Since they are at a distant place, they will not be able to come so soon."

Funaki took Mina to a building, burned incense, and had the incense blown toward the Buddha to invite him.

The Buddha somehow knew their intention. He used his Mys-

....

179. 放鉢国. The country may refer to an ancient city, Parvata, otherwise unknown.

180. 富楼那. Funaki, Pūrṇa, one of the ten great disciples of the Buddha, was known as the most eloquent of the Buddha's disciples.

terious Powers, brought many of his disciples to Mina's place, and took his seat on the golden floor. Mina venerated the Buddha and his numerous priests with various foods and drinks. After the meal, the Buddha preached the Law. The high and humble men and women of the household and the country listened to him preach and attained the Way.

Seeing this, Anan asked the Buddha, "What sins had Funaki committed to be born as a servant, and what good seeds did he plant so that he met the Buddha and attained the Way?"

The Buddha said to Anan, "Long ago, in the time of Kashō Buddha, a wealthy man built a temple for priests and venerated them by offering food, clothes, bedding, and medicine so they would never be poor. After the wealthy man died, the temple became dilapidated. The priests left and no one lived there.

"A son of the wealthy man entered the priesthood, learned about the Way, and was called Jizai. Seeing the dilapidated temple, the son encouraged many people to repair the temple. The priests returned and lived in the temple as before.

"An arhat was among the residing priests of the temple. One day, when Jizai was sweeping the temple yard, he abused the arhat for no reason. Jizai, son of the wealthy man of the old days, is the present Funaki. Because he abused the arhat, he has been born as a servant for five hundred generations. Yet, thanks to his merit in encouraging the people to repair the temple, he finished expiating his sins, met me, and attained the Way. The high and humble people of the country were those encouraged to repair the temple."

Thus it was told and handed down.

2:41 ABOUT BADAI,[181] A WEALTHY MAN OF INDIA

Long ago, a wealthy man called Badai lived in the capital of Shae in India. He was extremely rich and prosperous, with countless properties, including gold, silver, and other precious treasures as well as food and clothes, which filled his storehouses.

Yet he was very greedy and miserable. He economized so much even on his food and clothes that he always appeared shabby. He would not offer even a handful of dust to his people, including his wife, chil-

---

181. See note 40.

dren, brothers, and relatives. Needless to say, he made offerings to priests and Brahmans.

After Badai passed away, his treasures became government property. King Hashinoku of the country came himself and took all the treasures and stored them.

The king went to the Buddha and said, "Badai, the wealthy man, passed away today. He was very greedy when he was alive. Do you know where he has been reborn?" The Buddha replied, "Badai's good karma is already exhausted and enough new merits are not yet accumulated. Since he had nothing but an evil mind with no good source of merits, he has fallen into the Abi Hell[182] after his death."

Hearing this, the king cried bitterly with tears and again asked the Buddha, "What kind of karma did Badai have to be reborn in a family with innumerable treasures and what sort of evil deserts caused him to be born with avarice and to fall into the hell?"

The Buddha answered, "Long ago, after Kashō Buddha entered nirvana, Badai was born as a son of a rural family in the country of Shae. Once Hyakushi Buddha came and begged alms. Badai offered the Buddha food, and vowed, 'With this good deed, I shall not fall into the Three Lower Realms but always shall be blessed with treasures and make offerings.'

"However, he later regretted making the offerings and thought, 'From now on, I shall give food to my servants, but not to a priest.' Since Badai offered food to a Hyakushi Buddha, he always was born in places with abundant treasures. Yet, since he regretted having made offerings, he always appeared shabby and did not like food and clothes even though he owned so much treasure.

"Since he had not given anything to his people, including his wife and children, brothers, and relatives, he finally fell into the hell because of his avarice and greed."

Judging by this, one should never regret making offerings to priests, but do it with pleasure.

Thus it was told and handed down.

....

182. See note 166.

CHAPTER 3

3:1 ABOUT JŌMYŌKOJI[183] OF THE CITY OF BISHARI OF
INDIA

Long ago, an old ascetic called Jōmyō lived in the city of Bishari of
India. His place was only ten feet square. Yet ten thousand of the various Buddhas led countless bodhisattvas and other sentient beings to
gather in this small place and listen to the Law. Thirty-two thousand
Buddhas who were respectively followed by innumerable people seated themselves on the delicately decorated floor in the ten-foot-square
room and preached the Law.

Jōmyō also listened to the Law there. Even with so many peo-
ple, Jōmyō's place had space for more listeners. This was due to the
Jōmyō's unusual and mysterious influence. His place was called "A
Most Marvelous Pure Land Superior to Those in the Ten Thousand
Directions."

Jōmyō always lay on a straw mat and suffered from illness. Monju
once visited Jōmyō and inquired, "I hear that you always lie on a straw
mat. From what kind of illness do you suffer?"

Jōmyō replied, "I am ill because I suffer from all the delusions of
various other sentient beings for them. I have no other illness." Hearing this, Monju rejoiced and returned to his place.

When Jōmyō became more than eighty years old, he walked with
difficulty. Once he wished to hear the Buddha preach and walked forty
ri.[184] When he met the Buddha, he said, "Bring an old man, I walk

....

183. 浄名居士. Jōmyōkoji, Vimalakirti, a rich man of Vaisali, appears in the *Vimalakī-
tinirdeśa-sūtra*.

184. A Japanese league, approximately 2.44 miles.

with difficulty. Yet I walked forty *ri* to listen to the Law here. How much is this merit worth?"

The Buddha answered, "You came here to hear the Law. Your merit cannot be measured. The dirt under each step will be measured and a single particle of dirt will equal one *kalpa* of years. The number of the *kalpa*[185] years will atone for that many sins. Your life will last as long as the number of dirt particles. You will certainly become a Buddha. Your merit is inmeasurable."

Hearing this, Jōmyō rejoiced and returned. Listening to the Law offers this much merit.

Thus it was told and handed down.

3:2   HOW MONJU WAS BORN IN THE WORLD OF HUMAN BEINGS

Long ago, Monju became the son of the Brahman called Bondoku of Tarajuraku[186] in the country of Shae[187] of central India. He was born from the right side of his mother. At his birth, his house and the gate were transformed into lotus blossoms. He had a golden-hued body like a Heavenly Boy and a canopy decorated with seven kinds of jewels.

Ten kinds of auspicious signs appeared in the garden. For example, sweet dew covered the heavens, hidden treasure of the earth was revealed, millet grains became gold pieces, lotus bloomed in the garden, a radiance filled the house, hens gave birth to phoenixes, horses delivered giraffes, cows delivered white camel-like animals, wild boars produced domestic pigs, and tusked elephants appeared.

Because of these good omens, people named the baby Monju. When he grew up, he became a disciple of the Buddha and was endowed with the Mysterious Powers and wisdom of the future Buddha of the universe.

Monju was the ninth master of Shaka Buddha. However, since Shaka Buddha had already appeared and two Buddhas usually did not appear in this world at the same time, Monju appeared as a bodhisattva and converted numerous sentient beings. The Buddha preached about

....

185. *Kalpa* refers to a long duration of time. See note 102.
186. 多羅聚落. Tāla village.
187. 舍衛国. It refers to Śrāvasti, the capital of Kośala. It is present-day Sāhetmāhet.

the *Shukuyōkyō*[188] for the sentient beings of the Degenerated Age[189] and entrusted the teachings to Monju. Monju listened to the Buddha, and for a hundred and fifty years after the Buddha entered nirvana, Monju preached for the hermits at the summit of a high mountain.

The influence of Monju caused Buddhist and non-Buddhist writings to be widely diffused and the people of the Degenerate Age learned the results of good and evil.

Thus it was told and handed down.

3:3   HOW MOKUREN WENT INTO THE WORLD TO LISTEN TO
       THE BUDDHA'S VOICE

Long ago, Mokuren, a disciple of the Buddha, was well-endowed with Mysterious Powers. He said to other disciples of the Buddha, "No matter where we hear the Buddha's voice, it always seems to come from the same place. I am going to a distant place with my Mysterious Power to listen to the high and low tones of his voice."

Mokuren flew over all the worlds where the Buddhist teachings were diffused and passed innumerable lands to the west. The Buddha's voice still sounded as if it came from the same place.

Finally Mokuren became weak and fell into the world of Buddhas. At that time, priests of that country were sitting and receiving alms. Mokuren flew down and rested on the edge of the bowl of one of the priests. Seeing this, the priest said, "A bug which resembles a priest is resting on the edge of my bowl. I wonder what kind of bug fell out of my clothes?" Other priests gathered and watched Mokuren with amusement.

A cultured Buddha explained to the priests, "You don't know this since you are ignorant. It is not a bug on the edge of the bowl. Countless miles from this Buddha Land is another world to the east called Shaba, the secular world. A Buddha called Shaka appeared in

....

188. 宿暉経. The *Shukuyōkyō*, translated by Amoghavajra (705–774), deals with the teaching about foretelling one's life.

189. It refers to one of the three periods after the Buddha's decease. The three periods include the Period of the Righteous Law (*shōbō*), when Buddhist doctrines, practices, and enlightenment exist; the Period of the Imitative Law (*zōbō*), when both doctrine and practices still exist, but without enlightenment; and the Period of the Last Law (*mappō*), when the doctrines alone are alive without practices and enlightenment. After these three periods, the doctrine itself vanishes.

that country. Shaka has a disciple called Mokuren whose Mysterious Powers are superior to that of any other disciple. Mokuren became suspicious because his master's voice sounded the same wherever it was heard, and came to this land passing through distant worlds innumerable miles away."

The priests who heard this all rejoiced and Mokuren returned happily to his land. Afterward he respected and believed even more the mysterious voice of the Buddha.

Thus it was told and handed down.

Shariputra

3:4   HOW SHARIHOTSU BECAME DISTRESSED AND CONFINED HIMSELF

Long ago, in India, the Buddha's disciples gathered before him after their rainy season retreat.[190] Sharihotsu and Ragora sat to the left and the right of the Buddha. The Buddha asked Ragora, "Whom among my disciples shall I choose to be the senior priest?" "Sharihotsu should be the one," said Ragora.

The Buddha looked at both Sharihotsu and Ragora and saw that Sharihotsu was fat and white while Ragora was bony and dark. The Buddha asked, "Why is Sharihotsu, among my disciples, so fat?"

Ragora replied, "Since Sharihotsu is brilliant and intelligent, both the nobles and the commoners of this country respect him as their master and bring him rare and tasty foods. This is why he is fat. But this is not so in Ragora's case, and he is thin."

The Buddha asked again, "Eating fatty foods violates my teachings. I wonder why Sharihotsu is fat?" Hearing this, Sharihotsu was disturbed. He hid, confining himself.

Afterward, Sharihotsu would not accept gifts, even from the king, ministers, or wealthy men of the country. The king, ministers, wealthy men, and officials all went to the Buddha and proposed, "My lord Buddha, please call Sharihotsu back and tell him to accept our invitations. If the great masters, including Sharihotsu, do not accept the people's invitations, who shall be the master at the Buddhist service?" The Buddha explained to the people, "In his former life, Sharihotsu

....

190. Buddhist priests observe the Rain Retreat or *vārṣika* by not crushing insects and young grasses, and sequester themselves in mountain caves or their temples to practice the Way.

was a snake. Since he had the spiteful mind of the snake from his previous existence, he felt antagonistic toward what I said."

The Buddha immediately called Sharihotsu and said, "Quickly accept the people's invitation and become their master for the sake of the Law." So Sharihotsu, following the Buddha's words, accepted various people's invitations and served in the Buddhist service as before.

Thus it was told and handed down.

3:5   HOW SHARIHOTSU AND MOKUREN COMPETED WITH THEIR MYSTERIOUS POWERS

Long ago, when the Buddha was in Gionshōja and many of his disciples had gathered, Sharihotsu did not appear. The Buddha said to Mokuren, "Quickly go and bring Sharihotsu." Mokuren obediently went to Sharihotsu and delivered the Buddha's message. Sharihotsu was repairing his clothes. He untied his sash, placed it on the ground, and said to Mokuren, "You have the strongest Mysterious Powers among us. Use your powers and move this sash from the ground."

Mokuren used his powers and attempted to raise the sash. It did not move at all. Even Mount Shumi trembled and the great earth rocked, but the sash did not move at all. Sharihotsu said to Mokuren, "Quickly return to the Buddha. I will come later." So Mokuren went back to the Buddha.

Soon Sharihotsu appeared before the Buddha appearing as stately as previously. Now Mokuren knew and reflected, "I thought that my Mysterious Powers were the strongest of all, but Sharihotsu's powers are superior." So Sharihotsu was superior in wisdom and Mysterious Powers among the Buddha's disciples.

Even the disciples of the Buddha challenged each other in matters like this. It is quite natural that priests of later generations compete in their wisdom and power.

Thus it was told and handed down.

3:6   HOW SHARIHOTSU DESPISED ANAN

Long ago in India, Sharihotsu was regarded as having the deepest wisdom among the disciples of the Buddha. Anan was a well-learned man, but his wisdom was rather shallow. Sharihotsu always despised Anan. Anan thought, "How can I overcome Sharihotsu?" Just at that time, Anan had caught a cold and lay in bed with a bowl of rice gruel by his pillow.

Sharihotsu visited Anan. Sharihotsu was dressed in the white robe of a layman, not in a priestly robe. Since Anan had not taken the rice gruel, he offered it to Sharihotsu. As Sharihotsu finished the rice gruel, Anan took grass from under his bed, gave it to Sharihotsu, and said, "Quickly take this grass to our master." With the grass, Sharihotsu started back to the Buddha. On his way, Sharihotsu found that his fingernails and toenails had become those of a cow.

The shocked Sharihotsu hurried to the Buddha and asked the explanation. The Buddha said, "Your body has already become that of a cow. The grass that you brought here is for your food. But I know nothing of this. Go back to Anan quickly and ask him the reason."

Sharihotsu was more surprised at the Buddha's words and ran back to Anan and asked him. Anan said to Sharihotsu, "You should know that if a priest accepts offerings without wearing a priestly robe and uttering incantations, he will receive the body of an animal. You accepted my offering without shame. Your deed is having the proper result."

As Sharihotsu sincerely repented and wished to alter the result, his nails became as before. Judging by this, priests should always wear their robes of office when receiving alms, and should always utter incantations. The priests of later generations heard this and have always worn priestly robes to take alms and have recited incantations.

Thus it was told and handed down.

3:7   HOW THE NEW DRAGON OVERCAME THE OLD DRAGON

Long ago, a dragon lived in a pond on the summit of the Great Snow Mountain of India. Every day an invited priest flew to the dragon's place on a chair of woven rope to receive the dragon's veneration.

A novice, the priest's disciple, watched his master fly to the dragon and asked if he could accompany him. The priest said, "No. Since you are still young, something evil may happen. I cannot take you with me."

However, this novice secretly hid himself under the chair and flew to the dragon's place when his master was invited again. When they arrived at the dragon's place, the priest was amazed to see the novice.

The dragon offered especially tasty and piquant dishes to the priest. The novice was given ordinary food. The novice thought both his master and he were eating the same food. When the novice washed the dishes, he tasted a portion of the leftover food in his master's bowl. It was more delicious than his food. The novice became angry and hated both his master and the dragon. He thought, "I wish I were a wicked dragon, then I would kill this dragon, live in this place and become king of the dragons!"

After the novice returned with his master, his mind became evil. He single-mindedly wished to become a wicked dragon. Before dawn, he passed away. He was immediately reborn as a wicked dragon as he had wished. The new dragon went to the old dragon, overcame him, and lived in his place.

Learning of this, the lamenting priest went to the king, Kanishika,[191] and told the story in detail. The surprised king immediately filled the pond. At that time, the enraged wicked dragon caused various evil incidents. He rained pebbles and stones as though from dust clouds, uprooted trees with violent winds, and made the day dark like a moonless night with clouds and mists. The furious king emitted great clouds of smoke from between his eyebrows. The frightened evil dragon stopped doing evil.

Afterward, the king built a temple on the site of the old pond. The wicked dragon still exerted his evil influence and burned down the temple. Again the king built a temple together with a pagoda and a stupa which contained relics and bones of the Buddha.

On that occasion, the wicked dragon changed himself into the form of a Brahman, came to the king, and said, "I am going to discard my wicked mind." At the sound of striking the pillars of the temple, the dragon said, "I just gave up my evil mind!" However, even then, from time to time, this place was covered by clouds.

Thus it was told and handed down.

3:8 ABOUT KUBARA, THE DRAGON

Long ago, a cowherd in India had the duty of providing the king with condensed milk. Once when his cow became dry unexpectedly, he

....

191. 迦膩色迦王. Kaniṣka was a devout Buddhist ruler of northern India and Central Asia. He lived in the latter half of the first century or in the first half of the second century and is regarded as the third great king of the Kuṣāṇa dynasty. He established a country called Gandhāra and became a great patron of Buddhism.

could not offer milk to the king. The king became furious. He sent a messenger to the cowherd. The messenger abused him greatly. Feeling that such abuse was unbearable, the cowherd became indignant.

The cowherd bought some flowers with his money, offered them to a stupa, and vowed, "Although guiltless, I have been unbearably abused. I will become a wicked dragon, destroy this country, and harm the king." The cowherd climbed to the top of a steep rock, threw himself down, and died. As he wished, he was reborn as a wicked dragon.

Southwest of a temple was deep valley with an immensely frightening atmosphere surrounded by high steep cliffs. East of the valley was a tall wall-like rock which had a large cave. The opening into the cave was small. The interior was dark and always damp with dripping moisture. The wicked dragon made this cave his dwelling. Still recalling his original evil vow, the dragon intended to destroy the country and harm the king.

With his Mysterious Powers, Shaka Buddha naturally knew the dragon's intention and came to the cave from the central part of India. When the dragon saw the Buddha, he immediately abandoned his evil plans, accepted the principle of preserving life, and promised to protect the Law. The dragon said, "Oh Lord Buddha, please always stay in this cave. Also encourage your many disciples to accept my veneration."

The Buddha said to the dragon, "I will soon enter nirvana, but I will leave my image for you. I will also send five arhats and have them always accept your veneration. You should never even dream of ignoring this. If evil thoughts ever return, you should look at my image. Your evil ideas will naturally disappear. And hereafter, the Buddhas who will appear in this world will have pity for you." The Buddha gave this promise and left.

The Buddha's image still remains in the cave. The name of the dragon was Kubara. Genshō Sanzō[192] of Tang China came to India, visited this cave, saw the image of the Buddha, and recorded this.

Thus it was told and handed down.

....

192. 玄奘三蔵. Xuan-zhuang (600–664), a Chinese priest of the Tang dynasty, traveled to India via Central Asia and Afghanistan to obtain original Sanskrit texts. He brought to China 657 Sanskrit texts and translated more than a thousand fascicles of scriptures into Chinese. He also wrote an extensive record of his travels to India titled *Da-tang-xi-yu-ji*. He is sometimes regarded as the founder of the Fa-Xiang (Hossō) sect.

3:9   HOW THE DRAGON OFFSPRING ESCAPED FROM THE
        DANGER OF THE GOLDEN WINGED BIRD[193]

Long ago in India, various dragon kings lived at the bottom of a great
sea. They were always menaced by the attack of the Golden Winged
Bird. The dragon kings also had a pond called Munecchi[194] where
there was no danger from the bird. The Golden Winged Bird fanned
the surface of the great sea with its wings until the water had dried,
took the children of the dragon kings and ate them.

The dragon kings lamented, went to the Buddha, and appealed,
"Our children were taken by the Golden Winged Bird but we could
not prevent it. How can we avoid this predicament?" "Take a piece
from the corner of a priestly robe and place it over your children," said
the Buddha. So the dragon kings, as suggested by the Buddha, took a
corner piece from a priestly robe to put over their children.

With its wings, the Golden Winged Bird fanned the great sea
dry and searched for the dragon children, but could not find them.
Finally the bird left without the children.

This bird was also called Karura. If one knows that its spread
wings measured three hundred and sixty thousand *ri*, then one can
imagine how large the bird was. One also should respect the priestly
robe. Just using a piece of it prevented danger from the bird. Certainly
one should respect the priest who wears his robe. Even if the priest
violates precepts, one should not despise him.

Thus it was told and handed down.

3:10   HOW THE CHICKS OF THE GOLDEN WINGED BIRD
        AVOIDED ASHURA[195]

Long ago, a Golden Winged Bird made a nest in the cave on Mount
Shumi and gave birth to its chicks. The height of Mount Shumi was a
hundred thousand and sixty *yujun*. Eighty thousand *yujun* were above

....

193. The Golden Winged Bird (金翅鳥) is identified with Jarunda in the Indian myth
      and feeds on dragons. See note 23.
194. 无熱池. It refers to Anavatapta, which is identified as an imaginary lake located to
      the north of the Himalaya Mountains and irrigates the soil of Jambu-dvipa.
195. 阿修羅. Ashura (Asura) in Buddhism are regarded as demons who like fighting.
      See note 103.

the water level, and the remaining eighty thousand *yujun* were below the water level. The bird's nest was forty thousand *yujun* above the water level.

At that time the tremendously gigantic Ashura lived in two places. One was by the sea, and other was at the bottom of the sea. The Ashura's dwelling by the sea was on the bend of the sea in the valley of Mount Shumi on which the Golden Winged Bird made its nest. Ashura often rocked the mountain, shook the chicks from their nest, took them, and ate them.

The lamenting Golden Winged Bird visited the Buddha and said, "Ashura ate my children by the sea, but I could not prevent it. How should I avoid this danger? Please tell me, my lord." The Buddha said, "If you wish to avoid this danger, do as I say. There are places where Buddhist services are performed during the forty-nine days after one's death. On these occasions, priests are venerated, recite incantations, and accept offerings. You take some rice from the offerings and place it by the corner of the mountain. Then you can avoid this danger." The bird listened to the Buddha carefully and returned.

As instructed by the Buddha, the bird placed the offered food by the side of the mountain. Later Ashura came and tried to rock the mountain. But the mountain did not move. Increasing his power, Ashura again attempted to rock the mountain, but not even a speck of dust shifted. Finally, Ashura's strength was exhausted and he left. Since the mountain did not rock, the chicks were not shaken from the nest and were raised in peace.

Judging by this, the offerings for the period of forty-nine days are a very serious matter. Unless invited, one should not go to the Buddhist service for the forty-nine days and eat the offered food.

Thus it was told and handed down.

3:11   HOW A SHAKA MAN BECAME A DRAGON KING'S SON-IN-LAW

Long ago, men of four classes[196] became kings of India. No one from other classes could become king. Shaka Buddha was of the Shaka peo-

....

196. The four castes in India include the priestly caste; the warrior caste; the caste of peasants, artisans, and merchants; and the slave caste.

ple. Only those who had not taken life could be born as Shaka men since the Shaka were related to the Buddha.

King Ruri[197] of the country of Shae killed five hundred Shaka people of the country of Kabirae. Although well trained in military skills, the Shaka refused to kill others even if it cost their own lives. Because of this custom, they would not kill their enemies. As a result, they lost their lives without fighting in battle.

However, four Shaka men fought against King Ruri at that time. Later these four Shaka men were forced to sever their relationship to the Shaka and were exiled.

As one of the four Shaka men wandered, he became tired and rested on the way. He saw a huge wild goose nearby who showed no fear at his sight. Since the wild goose did not run when the Shaka man approached, he rode on its back. The wild goose flew to an unknown distant place where there was a pond. The Shaka man went to a shady place by a tree, lay down, and fell asleep.

At that time, a daughter of the dragon who lived in the pond had come out of the water and was playing by the pond. She saw the sleeping Shaka man and wished to have him as her husband. Yet she thought, "This must be a human being. I am a strange creature living below the surface. He must certainly think me a weird creature and despise me." The dragon's daughter assumed human form and calmly amused herself by the pond. The Shaka man soon noticed her, spoke to her, and became friends with her.

Still puzzled, the Shaka man said, "Since I am traveling, I must look terrible. My clothes are soiled and I am thin from hunger. How could you be so friendly? You certainly must be afraid of me." "My parents have instructed me to do this. Thanks to you, we have become so close like this. Will you listen to me?" asked the daughter.

"Why, of course, whatever you say. Since we are so intimate, it would be hard for me to leave you," said the Shaka man.

"You are a noble Shaka man while I am of low status," said the daughter.

"How can you be low? I am in a lowly state wandering around like this. This place is deep in the mountains and this pond is very large, but I see no houses for people. Where do you live?" asked the Shaka man.

"I will tell you, but you may think it distasteful. However, I have

---

197. 琉璃王. Virūdhaka, the son of King Prasenajit.

reason to hide it, since we have become friends. The truth is that I am a daughter of the dragon who lives in this pond. We heard that some noble Shaka people were wandering. Fortunately, when I saw you resting by the pond, I became intimate with you and have entertained you in your boredom. Due to sins in our family's lives, we have received bodies with these scales. Human beings and animals are naturally in different realms. We have restricted ourselves in every way and our place is in the pond," said the dragon's daughter. "Since we have already become so intimate, let's remain as we are," said the Shaka man.

"No, I cannot allow the situation to remain as is. I will tell my parents about us," and the woman went to see her parents.

When she saw them, she said, "Today, as I was amusing myself by the pond, I met a Shaka man. Thanks to his virtue, I could became a person. We developed an intimate relationship." The dragon king was very pleased for his daughter to become a person and felt respect for the Shaka man.

The dragon king left the pond, changed himself into a man, knelt before the Shaka man, and said, "It is very gracious of you, a man of the Shaka, to accept us in spite of our lowly status. Will you please come to our place?"

Following the dragon king, the Shaka man entered the dragon palace. The palace was radiant like the Pure Land of the Buddha. It was adorned with the seven kinds of jewels and had golden ridges and eaves, silver walls, emerald tiles, mouldings decorated with *mani* balls, and pillars of sandalwood. The interior decorations were dazzling. The hangings were ornamented with the seven kinds of jewels. One wondered how much treasure was in the palace. There were also beautiful multi-storied palaces, from which noble and stately looking people appeared, wearing decorated crowns. They welcomed the Shaka man and had him sit on the floor, which was ornamented with seven kinds of jewels.

Jeweled decorations hung from various kinds of trees, and various musical compositions were played on the decorated boats floating on a large pond. Many ministers and noblemen and hundreds and thousands of people of various kinds were there. There was nothing that they could not enjoy for their pleasure.

However, the Shaka man always felt frightened and thought, "In spite of all these decorations and treasures, they are actually nothing but many snakes coiling and crawling about. How can I leave this place and return to the world of people?"

The dragon king perceived the Shaka man's anxiety, and said, "Please stay in this world as a king." The Shaka man said, "This is not what I wish. I wish to be king of my own country."

"That is easy. It seems better in this world with countless treasures as one wishes, living in a palace decorated with the seven kinds of jewels, and with a long life in a wider country without boundaries. However, all you wish is to return to your own country and it is quite natural. If so, please look at this," and the dragon king showed the Shaka man a sword wrapped in a delicately woven brocade in a box decorated with the seven kinds of jewels.

The king gave the sword to the Shaka man and said, "The king of India always examines things brought from distant countries by taking them in his own hands. Taking advantage of this, go near him, and stab him."

Following the dragon king's instructions, the Shaka man returned to his own country, went to the king, and offered him the box. When the king took the box in his hands, the Shaka man took the king's sleeves and stabbed him to death.

When the confused ministers and noblemen caught him and were about to kill him, the Shaka man stood, drew the sword, and said, "I killed the king at the order of the god who gave me this sword and said, 'Kill the king and take his throne.'" The ministers and noblemen said, "In that case, there is no reason for us to oppose you," and they enthroned him. Since the Shaka man governed the country wisely, the people respected and obeyed him.

Later the Shaka man visited the dragon palace, leading ministers, noblemen, and a hundred officials. He returned to his country with his wife from the dragon palace. Both the king and the queen were very much in love. The queen, although dainty and beautiful, revealed her original dragon nature from time to time. When she was asleep or having intercourse, nine snake heads with flickering red tongues appeared from her head. The watching king considered this weird.

When she was sleeping, he cut off all the wriggling snake heads. At that moment, the queen awoke and said, "This will cause no harm to you. But your children as well as your people in this country will have headaches for generation after generation." Since then, as the queen had said, all the people in the country had headaches.

Thus it was told and handed down.

3:12 ABOUT THE PARROTS OF THE WEALTHY SHUDATSU[198]

Long ago, a wealthy man called Shudatsu lived in India. He respected the Law and was a patron of priests, whom he venerated with offerings.

Shudatsu had two parrots called Ritsudai and Sharitsudai. Though animals, these birds had minds and wisdom. When priests visited Shudatsu, these birds first came out, saw them, told Shudatsu about them, and welcomed them.

Anan once visited Shudatsu, saw these intelligent birds, and preached to them about the Four Noble Truths. The birds flew to a tree in front of the house and listened to the preaching. They rejoiced to listen. While the birds perched in the tree at night, they were killed and eaten by a badger.

It is said, "The two birds should be reborn in the heaven of the Four Deva Kings since they rejoiced at the Law. After their lives end, they will be reborn in the heaven of Takejizai.[199] They will be reborn seven times, and when their life in the heavens is terminated, they will be reborn in the human realm, become priests, practice the Way, and finally attain the stage of Hyakushi Buddha. One of them will be called Donma and the other Shudonma."

Judging by this, listening to the Law with joy endows one with immeasurable merits.

Thus it was told and handed down.

3:13 HOW THE BUDDHA EXPLAINED THE KARMIC RELATION OF YASHUDARA

Long ago, when the Buddha was still called Prince Shidda, he had three wives. One of them was Yashudara. Although the prince treated Yashudara with sincere care, she was never appreciative. Although the prince gave Yashudara countless rare treasures, she was never pleased.

After the prince became the Buddha, he explained the karmic relation of Yashudara: "In her former life, there was a country called Kara. The queen of the country was called Haranaba. The king was a very violent man with an evil mind and attitudes. The king had a

---

198. 須達. Sudatta, a rich man of Śrāvastī. See note 56.
199. 他化自在天. It is the sixth and the highest heaven in the World of Desire. See note 86.

prince who was later driven from the country because of minor errors. Accompanied by his wife, the prince passed the frontier and remained at a shrine.

Since they had no food, the prince shot animals with his arrows and ate them. They spent some days in this way. There was a famine, and hunting and fishing provided no food. Everybody wept because of the starvation.

One day, the royal couple saw a large tortoise crawling. They caught it, killed it, separated it from its shell, put it in a pan, and cooked it. The prince said to his wife, "You go and bring some water. We will cook this well and eat it together." Following her husband's suggestion, the wife went farther away carrying a bucket to get water.

Meanwhile, the prince was unable to resist his hunger. He ate a piece of half-cooked tortoise meat. Soon all the tortoise meat was gone! Then the prince was in distress, wondering, "What shall I say when she returns with water?"

The completely exhausted wife returned with water. She looked inside the pan and saw no tortoise. "Where is it?" Unable to think of a better excuse, the husband said, "While I slept, the tortoise went into the sea since it was half-cooked. People say that the tortoise has a long life!"

"No, you are telling me a lie. How in the world could a half-cooked tortoise separated from its shell run into the sea? You should have said that you ate it because of hunger. You deliberately sent me to a distant place when I was hungry and exhausted, and ate it all by yourself. Even if I had been with you, probably you would not have stopped eating," and the wife reproached him immensely.

The king, the father of the prince, suddenly died of illness and the prince was received as a new king, and his wife, too, was invited to be the queen. The king governed the country and gave his wife abundant treasures. Yet the queen was not pleased. The king asked the queen, "I have given you everything you wished. Why aren't you happy?"

"Although I now have everything I wish, I am not pleased. If I had died of hunger in the past, I would neither get the treasure nor own all these things as I wish. But since we now govern our country, we naturally own its treasures. So owning them does not make me especially happy. At the most difficult time in our past, you ate the tortoise meat all by yourself and did not let me have even a piece," said the queen, and she remained unhappy.

"I am the prince who ate the tortoise meat. Yashudara is my wife who went to bring water. Due to our karmic relationship in our previous lives, we do not get along well when reborn as man and wife for generation after generation. A mere piece of tortoise meat could cause anger and falsehood."

Thus it was told and handed down.

3:14   ABOUT KONGŌSHŪNYO, A DAUGHTER OF KING HASHINOKU

Long ago, King Hashinoku lived in the country of Shae in India. The queen, Lady Mari, was incomparably beautiful when matched against any women in the sixteen great countries of India. Lady Mari delivered a baby girl whose skin looked like that of a poisonous snake and whom people shunned because of her bad odor. Her coarse hair was wound to the left like a demon, and since everything in her appearance was inhuman, only the king, queen, and wet nurse knew about the girl.

The king said to the queen, "Your girl is the frightening Kongōshūnyo, the Ugly Diamond Woman. We should quickly move her to another place." So the king had a ten-foot-square room made two *ri* north from the palace and confined their daughter in the room with her wet nurse and a lady-in-waiting.

When Kongōshūnyo became twelve or thirteen years old, each of the kings of the sixteen great countries of India, judging by the beauty of her mother, Lady Mari, asked for Kongōshūnyo as his wife. However, King Hashinoku, instead of accepting any of these offers, immediately made one of his men a minister and made him the bridegroom of Kongōshūnyo. The new minister grieved for days and nights over the frightening arrangement which was forced upon him. But since he could not disobey the king's order, he stayed in the room with Kongōshūnyo.

Meanwhile, the king held a Buddhist service fulfilling the great vow in his life. Although she was the first daughter of the king, Kongōshūnyo was not invited because of her ugly appearance. Various ministers, unaware of her appearance, felt it odd and became suspicious because of her absence from the great service. They plotted together and made the bridegroom of Kongōshūnyo drunk, stole the key that he wore on his hip, and sent a royal officer to the room to see Kongōshūnyo.

Before the officer arrived, Kongōshūnyo remained alone in her room and prayed, lamenting, "Oh Lord Shaka Buddha, please make my appearance beautiful and let me attend my father's Buddhist service!" Suddenly the Buddha appeared in her yard.

The surprised Kongōshūnyo watched the Buddha appear with tremendous joy. Due to this, the noble appearance of the Buddha was immediately transferred to Kongōshūnyo. Just at the moment when she was going out to tell this to her husband, the officer who had just arrived stealthily peeped inside the room and saw a woman with an appearance as noble as the Buddha standing there. The officer returned to the other ministers and reported, "She is indescribable. I have never seen any woman as noble as she."

When the bridegroom awoke in his room, he saw a strange yet beautiful woman there. The suspicious bridegroom kept at a distance from her and asked, "Who are you?"

"I am your wife, Kongōshūnyo." "No, you cannot be," said the husband.

"I am immediately going to my father's Buddhist service. Due to the Buddha's mercy, I have changed my appearance in this present life."

Hearing this, the minister ran to the king and told him. The surprised king, queen, and ministers immediately went to the room, riding in carriages. As they had been told, they found Kongōshūnyo incomparably beautiful. They immediately invited her to the palace and let her attend the service as she had wished.

The king took her to the Buddha and asked him for a detailed explanation. The Buddha said, "Long ago she was a cooking woman in your palace in her previous life. One day a priest came to your palace to beg alms. Since you had vowed to practice good, you prepared a sack of rice, gave all the people of high and low degree in your palace a handful of rice, and had them offer that to the begging priest. This cooking woman, while offering her rice, insulted the ugly appearance of the priest. The priest went before you, the king, revealed Mysterious Changes, ascended into the air, and entered nirvana. Seeing this, the woman greatly regretted what she had done, repented for her sin in tears, and venerated the priest.

"So now even though she was reborn as a daughter of the king, due to her sin in abusing the priest, she was born in the form of a demon. However, thanks to her sincere repentance, I used my influence and changed her demonic appearance to a noble one, and she has entered Buddhahood forever. So one should never abuse a priest. And should one commit a sin, one should repent with a sincere heart. Repentance is the first step toward good causes."

Thus it was told and handed down.

3:15   ABOUT PRINCE JINKŌ[200] OF THE COUNTRY OF MAKADA

Long ago, the king of the country of Makada in India had five hundred princes. When they grew up, all became strong and prosperous, controlling their lives as they wished. The first of them, Prince Jinkō, had a body as dark as soot and hair as red as flames, and his appearance was as ugly as a demon king. Disliking the prince, both the king and the queen had a ten-foot-square room made and confined the prince so no one could see him.

Meanwhile, another country raised an army to attack Makada. The king of Makada intended to fight the enemy and prepared several ten thousands of soldiers. However, the king's army was inferior in quantity and quality, and the kingdom was almost taken by the enemy. The distressed people of the palace greatly lamented and grieved over their retreat from the palace.

At that time, Prince Jinkō in his room heard about the confusion in the palace. He called his wet nurse and said, "The palace is in unusual confusion. What is the matter?"

The wet nurse answered, "Don't you know that a foreign army has attacked our country? Everybody, including the king, queen, and princes, is fleeing. You should also leave."

"This is nothing. Why didn't they tell me earlier? I will go right now and chase the enemy out," and the prince stood up to go.

The wet nurse reported this to the king, who would not believe it. The prince came before the king and said, "I will drive out the enemy." The prince called someone and said, "The bow of my grandfather, King Tenrin,[201] is in the loft. Bring it to me."

The bow was brought. The prince took the bow and twanged the bowstring. The sound echoed like rolling thunder for forty *ri*. The

....

200. Unknown.
201. 轉輪王. Cakravartin, a king who rules the world by rolling the wheel given to him by heaven at his enthronement. See note 253.

prince took one arrow for the bow, hung a trumpet shell at his waist, and began to leave the palace alone.

His mother, the queen, tried to stop him. She wailed, "Of ten thousands, only one would return safely from the battlefield. Although you have a terrible appearance, you are still my son. Quickly give up this idea and stay." However, the prince did not remain in the palace but hurried to the battlefront. First, he blew his trumpet shell. Many enemy soldiers were frightened at the sound and collapsed on the ground. Second, the prince twanged his bowstring, and the entire enemy army fled.

"They ran like this when I only twanged the bowstring. If I shoot an arrow, what will happen to the army of hundreds of thousands of soldiers?" the prince asked as he returned to the palace. The king was immensely pleased and said, "I have raised five hundred princes, but none of the others is strong enough to cope with the enemy. You are my only son!"

At the age of fifty, the prince for the first time decided to take a wife. "I will not take any woman of low birth but someone from a higher status," said the prince to the king.

The king thought, "Even a lowly women would not come near the prince, fearing his appearance. How can we think a woman of higher status would accept him? Since all the people in this country already know about his appearance, I will make an arrangement for the daughter of another king. But the arrangement should be completed at night since the darkness will conceal his appearance." So the marriage was performed at night.

Days and months passed. One day the king thought, "Even though I have five hundred wives, I have not seen them all. I think I will hold a flower-viewing party and see my wives one by one." The king decided on the date and circulated the notice.

All the ladies prepared their best clothes and dressed in thin and twilled silk garments in various dark and light colors, including blue, yellow, red, and white. When the day arrived, these ladies strolled around the pond in the center of the garden before the southern palace. Some held oars and poles as they rode aboard boats and rafts. Others toyed with flowers in the garden, recited poems, or listened to the insects. They were all amusing themselves. The king and queen rolled up the hangings of their room and watched. Numerous people of high and low degree in the palace gathered like clouds and watched the party. For sightseeing, there was nothing under heaven better than this.

The wife of Prince Jinkō, too, though unaccompanied by her husband, was out in the garden amusing herself. Seeing this, one of the king's ladies laughed and said, "Why are you amusing yourself alone?" "Is it because your husband is so handsome?" asked another lady. The wife of Prince Jinkō was very embarrassed to hear this and withdrew as if into hiding. She secretly called the wet nurse and said, "People talked about my husband. I would like to see my husband. When he comes to me at night, light the torch so I can look at him."

As instructed, the wet nurse suddenly lighted a torch when the prince visited his wife at night. The wife looked at the demonic appearance of her husband, fled, and hid herself. The embarrassed prince retired to his quarters. The wife returned to her own country that night.

The prince lamented greatly. He went deep into a mountain at dawn, climbed to a high place, and threw himself down. Just at that moment, a guardian deity of the tree saved him and placed him on the ground.

At that time, Taishaku descended and gave the prince a jeweled ball. The prince asked, "Who are you who gave me this jewel? Since I am ignorant, I don't know. If you are a Buddha, tell me about my karmic relation to my former life." Taishaku explained, "You were born as a son of a poor man in your former life. When a priest came to beg for some oil, your father told you to give him clear oil. But you saved the clear oil and gave the priest soiled oil. Due to your merit in offering the oil, your father was born to be a king and you his son. However, you received an ugly appearance since you gave soiled oil. I am Taishaku who pitied you and put the jewel in your hair," and Taishaku left.

Later the prince's appearance was changed and he became radiantly handsome. A messenger from the palace who was searching for the prince came and asked, "Are you a Buddha or the prince for whom I am looking?" The prince said, "I am your master, Prince Jinkō. I suddenly changed my appearance into a radiant one. I wonder if this is due to the jewel given to me." When the prince removed the jewel and put it aside, the prince resumed his original appearance. When he wore the jewel, he again became as radiant as a light.

The prince returned to the palace and made a detailed report to the king. Both the king and queen were immensely pleased about this. Several days later, the prince went to his wife's country. His wife rejoiced to see her handsome husband. The king of the country, the prince's father-in-law, gladly gave the throne to the prince. The prince returned to his own country with his wife. His father also resigned and gave his throne to the prince. So the prince became king of two countries and governed them as he wished.

The merit gained by offering a cup of oil amounted to this much. No one can imagine how much more it will be if one offers a Buddhist service with ten thousand lanterns.

Thus it was told and handed down.

3:16   HOW A POOR WOMAN BECAME A QUEEN IN HER
        PRESENT LIFE

Long ago, a poor woman some eighty years old lived in the country of Makada. She had a very filial daughter who was twenty-four years old.

The king of the country made an official visit. All the people in the country, including nobles and commoners, wished to see the king on that occasion. The old mother said to her daughter, "I heard that the king will take an outing tomorrow. I wonder if you will go to see him. If you do go, I will be left unfed." "Then I will not go," said the daughter.

When the day arrived, the daughter went out for a short while to pick greens for her mother and happened to be near the king's party. Yet the daughter did not look at the king, but crouched on the ground as she picked the greens. Seeing the daughter at a distance, the king asked his people, "When everybody wishes to see me, that lowly woman over there pays me no attention. Does she have a reason? Is she ugly or blind?"

The king stopped his carriage and sent his messenger to the daughter to ask the reason. The daughter replied, "Nothing is wrong with my eyes, hands, or feet. I would very much like to watch the king. But since I have a poor old mother at home whom I care for by myself, I have no time to spare. If I went to see the king, I would have to neglect my filial duty. I did not come to see the king's visit, but I just happened to be nearby as I gathered greens for my mother."

The king heard her reason and said, "This woman has an unusually good mind. Summon her immediately." The woman said to the king, "It is a pleasure to receive the king's order. But I am the only person at home to look after my old mother, and I have no time to spare. I will go home and discuss this with my mother. If she permits me, I will return. So allow me a day or so." The king gave her permission to return to her mother.

When the daughter was home, she said to her mother, "You must have thought that I would not come home for a long time." "Yes, I did," said the mother. The daughter told about the king's request for her.

After listening, the pleased mother said, "When I was raising you, I wished that my daughter would become a queen some day. I am so glad that my wish is finally realized and you received the invitation from the king today. All the Buddhas in the ten directions, please protect my daughter. She has been very filial to me. Due to this merit, make the king remember her and invite her."

The day passed. The king, who had returned to his palace, did not forget the daughter. He sent thirty carriages to her place on the following day. In the morning the rumbling clamor of many carriages was heard unexpectedly in front of the poor household of the daughter and her mother. Wondering if some people were passing, they strained their ears and heard someone ask, "Is this the house?" Soon people brought in a carriage decorated with the seven kinds of jewels. They called the daughter, dressed her in beautiful clothes, placed her in the carriage and took her to the palace. Seeing this, the old mother tearfully rejoiced.

The king received the daughter and thought that three thousand of his favorite wives were inferior to her. The king never tired of her even after seeing her for days and nights. He even neglected state affairs for her.

This was due only to her virtue in being filial to her own mother. Thanks to her merit, her status in life was changed and she became a queen.

Thus it was told and handed down.

3:17   HOW AN ARHAT PRIEST WAS IMPRISONED

Long ago, a priest practiced the Buddhist Way deep in the mountains of the country of Keihin[202] and finally attained the status of an arhat.

....

202. 罽賓国. It is a Han name for Kashmir.

At that time a layman of the village lost his cow and came to the arhat on his way to search for his cow.

When the layman looked at the arhat, his black robe became a cowhide, his books and writings on the floor became pieces of meat, and the greens placed to the side became the cow's bones. The layman thought, "My cow was stolen by this priest," and reported this to the king. The king ordered the priest seized and imprisoned.

Meanwhile, the disciples of the priest did not know this since they were in other places. When they returned, they found that their master was absent. Thinking that their master had gone elsewhere, the disciples searched for him, but could not find him for twelve years.

Finally, the disciples found their master in prison. They lamented greatly over his detention and petitioned the king, "We don't know of what our master is guilty, but he has been imprisoned for twelve years. He has attained arhat status and is no different than Sharihotsu, Kasho, Mokuren, and Anan. We, his disciples, have been searching for him for the past twelve years and finally found him imprisoned. Please, great king, pardon him!"

The surprised king sent a messenger to the prison to investigate the master. The messenger went to the prison and saw only a layman but no priest. That was quite natural. Since the priest had not shaved his head for twelve years, his hair had become long and his appearance had become that of a layman. The messenger called out four or five times, asking, "Is there a priest who has been in prison here for twelve years?" A layman responded, came out, immediately revealed the Eighteen Mysterious Changes,[203] and ascended in the air, releasing radiance.

The king's messenger asked the priest, "Why has a holy man, an arhat like you, been imprisoned?"

The priest replied, "In my previous life, I accused an innocent man of guilt. Even though I was born to be an arhat, I could not avoid the consequence of that sin. Yet now my sin is expiated." Saying this, the priest released a radiance as he ascended into the air and disappeared.

The messenger returned to the place and reported this to the king. The king became very frightened of commiting sins at this re-

203. "Eighteen Mysterious Changes" refers to the eighteen kinds of mysterious changes done by bodhisattvas and *arhats*. See note 132.

port. Just after a flower blooms, it bears fruit, so if one sins, one will surely take the consequence. This is why the *Agonkyō* explains actions and their results. Those who are conscientious should be aware of this and not sin. Also one should never accuse the innocent.

Thus it was told and handed down.

3:18   HOW TWO ARHATS SERVED A PRIEST IN THE CITIES OF INDIA

Long ago, in the cities of India, one was not supposed to venerate the Three Treasures unless one offered concentrated honey. A patron went to a mountain temple to venerate a priest but forgot to bring honey. The priest had two novices; they were devoted to their master and served him by picking greens, carrying water, and gathering firewood. They diligently cared for their master in the mornings and in the evenings. However, their priestly master was a spoiled and an evil man who abused these two novices, giving them no rest.

The two novices were sent for the honey which the patron had forgotten. Time passed, yet the two novices had not returned. The anxious patron went out to see if the novices were late. As he waited for them, sitting by a bush alongside the road, he saw the two novices approach.

On their way, the two novices suddenly showed the Eighteen Mysterious Changes and the supernatural power of the Bodhisattva Fugen. They released radiance as they preached the Law, and revealed what had happened to them in their previous lives. Seeing all this from the roadside, the impresed patron felt uplifted, thinking, "These two novices are holy men or arhats!"

The patron hurried to the priest and told him what he had seen by the roadside. The priest was impressed and thought it extraordinary. Just at that time the two novices returned with the honey. The priest said to them "Being ignorant, I have not realized until now that you are arhats. I have been rude to you for the past ten years. Please forgive me." "We are sorry that we suddenly revealed the Mysterious Powers on our way. Now that you, Master, already know about us, how can we serve you?" and the novices lamented over the situation.

They continued, "Without serving a master, it will take a long time for us to attain Buddhahood." They preached the Law, releasing radiance. Listening to them preach, both the priest and patron became very pious. The novices said again, "We are going to ascend to the beginning stage of the bodhisattvahood."

So these two novices were bodhisattvas of a higher rank who had appeared as common laymen and served someone. There are various ways to attain Buddhahood. Those who are aware should realize this.

Thus it was told and handed down.

3:19   HOW AN OLD FEMALE SERVANT ATTAINED THE WAY

Long ago, a wealthy man, Shudatsu, lived in the capital of Shae of India. An old woman servant called Biteira looked after his household affairs. Shudatsu invited the Buddha and priests to venerate them. Seeing this, the greedy old woman servant said hatefully, "My master foolishly believes in these priests' cults. I will never listen to the names of either the Buddha or the priests!"

Lady Mari, the queen of the country, heard this and wondered, "Shudatsu is as good as a lotus flower and is praised by many people. Why does he keep a poisonous snake as a guard?"

Lady Mari said to Shudatsu's wife, "Your old female servant is slandering the Three Treasures. Why don't you drive her away?"

The wife replied, "Even an evil man, Aukutsumara,[204] was overcome by the Buddha. Why not our old woman?"

Lady Mari was pleased to hear that and said, "Tomorrow, I will invite the Buddha to our place. You send your old woman." The wife agreed and returned home.

On the following day, the old female servant of Shudatsu was sent to the palace with a jar containing some gold pieces. Seeing the old woman coming, Lady Mari invited the Buddha.

The Buddha arrived at the palace and entered the front gate accompanied by Nanda on his left, Anan on his right, and Ragora behind him. When the old woman saw the Buddha, she became distressed with surprise and confusion as if her body hair were standing on end, and tried to run away, saying, "This wicked man is already after me. I will leave immediately."

Since the Buddha was standing before the front gate, instead of heading that way, the old woman tried to escape by the side doors. The side doors shut of their own accord. The old woman covered her

----

204. 央崛魔羅. Añgulimālya was a disciple of manibhadra.

face with her fan, but she saw the Buddha before her. The Buddha made the fan like a mirror and prevented her from covering her face. The confused old woman looked toward the east, she saw the Buddha there. When she looked toward the south, west, and north, she saw the Buddha. Looking up and down, she still saw the Buddha. When she covered her face with her hand, she saw various Buddhas on each of her fingertips. When she looked in the open spaces, Buddhas filled the ten directions.

At that time, there were twenty-five *sendara* women and fifty Brahman women in the city and five hundred women in the palace who did not believe in the Buddha. Seeing the Buddha assume innumerable forms for the sake of the old woman, these women abandoned their wrong views and paid homage to the Buddha for the first time, reciting his name and immediately developing pious minds.

However, the old woman, tenacious in her wrong views, still did not believe in the Buddha. Yet, since she actually saw the Buddha, her various sins were expiated.

After the old woman went home, she said to Shudatsu's wife, "Today, when I went to the palace on your errand, I saw the Buddha creating various illusions and fantasies by the palace gate. His body was like a gold mountain releasing limitless radiance, and his eyes were as big as blue lotus blossoms." And the old woman made a basketlike container of wood in which she confined herself.

When the Buddha was about to return to Gionshōja, Lady Mari said, "Please return to Gionshōja after you have cultivated this old woman."

The Buddha returned and said, "This old woman is too sinful and has no relation to me. Ragora has a relationship to her. Let him cultivate her."

So Ragora was sent to Shudatsu. To help the old woman, Ragora changed himself into King Tenrin. He transformed one thousand two hundred and fifty priests into a thousand children and led them to Shudatsu's house. Ragora also changed the old woman into a beautiful woman.

The joyful woman paid homage to King Tenrin, who preached to her about the ten goodnesses. She overcame her evil mind after hearing him preach.

Later, Ragora and the priests changed themselves into their original forms. Seeing this, the old woman said, "The Buddhist Law is pure and clear. It does not discard any sentient beings. Being ignorant, I did not believe during past years. Please correct my shortcomings and enhance them into merits." She received the Five Precepts and attained the *shudaonka* enlightenment.[205] She also went to the Buddha, repented of her sins, and wished to enter Buddhahood. Finally she attained the *arakanka* enlightenment, ascended into the air, and revealed the Eighteen Mysterious Changes.

King Hashinoku saw this and said to the Buddha, "What sins in her previous life caused her to become a servant and serve others? Thanks to what merit has she met the Buddha and attained the Way?"

The Buddha said to the king, "A long time ago, Hōkaitōō Buddha appeared in this world. After he entered nirvana in the Period of the Reflected Law,[206] King Zōhōkakō ruled. The king had a prince, Keken, who later entered Buddhahood and learned the Way. Taking advantage of his rank, he became very arrogant. His master, a priest, explained the doctrine of *śūnyatā* of profound wisdom[207] to the prince. The prince listened and thought it a false theory. After his master had passed away, the prince said, 'My master preached the *śūnyatā* doctrine without much wisdom. I will never see him in a future life.'

"Later, the prince had another master of the *ajari*[208] status. The prince said, 'My master is talented. His wisdom is brilliant. I wish him to be my good leader in my future lives.'

"The prince cultivated his disciples and made them believe that the *śūnyatā* doctrine was a false theory. Although he kept the precepts, he fell into the Abi Hell[209] after his life ended. He suffered immensely because he had doubted the *śūnyatā* theory of wisdom. After he left the hell, he was born poor, deaf, and blind for a hundred generations and as a servant for twelve hundred generations.

"I was the priest, the first master is the prince of that time. *Ajari*, the prince's second master, was Ragora. The prince is this old female

----

205. One of the four stages of enlightenment. See note 316.
206. 像法. The Period of the Reflected Law, see note 212.
207. *Śūnyatā*, the doctrine of nothingness, was explained by Subhati, one of the Buddha's ten disciples.
208. *Ajari*, *ācārya* or teacher, refers to eminent priests who guided and set standards of model conduct for the disciples.
209. It refers to Avīci, the hell of incessant suffering where the sinners are always crying out because of the hot fires. Refer to note 166.

servant. This is why she has no relation with me, but with Ragora who finally cultivated her.

"Besides, thanks to her past merit in learning the Law and leading many disciples, she has attained the Way. The various women with wrong views in the palace were the disciples of the prince."

Thus it was told and handed down.

3:20   HOW THE BUDDHA WENT TO THE HOUSE OF ŌMU

Long ago, in India, the Buddha went to a house to beg for alms. Ōmu, the master of the house, saw the Buddha and came out with a bowl of mixed rice and fish to feed his dog. The Buddha saw the dog and said, "You wished to be born in the heaven of Bonten in your previous life. Why are you here like this?" This insult made the dog angry. He didn't eat the food but remained beside it. The Buddha returned to Mount Ryōju.

Later Ōmu left his house again and saw that his dog hadn't eaten the food but was angry because the Buddha had embarrassed him. Ōmu became furious and abused the Buddha. The Buddha in Mount Ryōju said to his disciples, "It is sad that Ōmu will fall into the hells and suffer greatly because he is angry." The angry Ōmu came to the Buddha and demanded, "Why did you embarrass my dog so that he didn't eat?" The Buddha explained, "Don't you know that your father Tōchō venerated the Fire Deity and wished to be reborn in the heaven of Bonten, but now has been born as a dog and has been raised by you?"

Hearing this, Ōmu became more furious and asked, "Buddha, how do you know that my father has become this dog, and how can you be sure of it?"

The Buddha replied, "After you return home, prepare a brocade seat and a gold bowl filled with tasty food for your dog and say to him, 'If you are my real father, Tōchō, take this seat and eat the food in this bowl. Also teach me the place of the stored treasures.' You should observe what your dog will do."

Although Ōmu was still angry, he did exactly what the Buddha had said after he returned home. When he said to his dog, "If you are my father, take this seat and eat the food in the bowl and tell me the whereabouts of the stored treasures," the dog immediately took the seat and ate the food. After eating, the dog touched the ground near the floor with his nose and began to dig at the spot with his paws.

Feeling strange, Ōmu had someone dig there and found many treasures deeply buried.

Ōmu realized that the dog was really his father and felt pity. He visited the Buddha in Mount Ryōju and said respectfully, "Buddha, you never speak falsely. I will never doubt your words for generations." Ōmu made a vow and asked the Buddha, "Why do some who accumulate merit still fall into hells, and why are sinners reborn in the pure land of Buddha? Why are there rich and poor men? Why do you think some are blessed with prosperity and offspring while others are poor and alone? Why do some live long and others die young? Why are some handsome and others ugly? Why are some harmed, killed, and abused by others?"

The Buddha replied to each question. "Listen well. Some accumulate merit yet fall into hells because they become angry at their last moment due to a bad karma. Others sin, but are reborn in heaven because they meet good teachers and think of Buddhas at their last moments. The rich in this life made offerings in their former lives, while those presently poor did not. Those blessed with offspring regarded others as their own children in their previous existences, while the childless ones did wrong to others in their former lives. Those who live long released captured animals, while the short-lived preferred to kill animals in their former lives. The handsome people were amicable to their parents, while the ugly people bore anger toward their parents in their previous lives.

"Those who are respected now respected others in their former lives, and others who are now despised had looked down upon others in their former lives."

Ōmu heard the Buddha's explanation and felt immensely noble. Thanks to this, he ceased the sins that could have caused him to fall into the hells and followed the Buddhist Way for a long time.

Thus it was told and handed down.

3:21   HOW A WEALTHY MAN'S SERVANT REMOVED MANURE AND ATTAINED THE WAY

Long ago in India, a wealthy man had a woman servant who removed the human wastes from the house both morning and evening for many years. The people of the house despised her. They spat when they saw her on the street, covered their noses, and never went near her.

The Buddha pitied this woman. He once saw the woman on a road carrying a bucket filled with excrement on her head. Embarrassed at seeing the Buddha, the woman hid herself in the roadside bushes. Since her clothes were spotted with excrement, the woman felt shy and went farther into the bushes. The Buddha came closer to help her. He took her to Mount Ryōju and preached to her. The woman immediately attained *arakanka* enlightenment.

The wealthy man was amazed to hear this and intended to embarrass the woman before the Buddha. He hurried to Mount Ryōju. On his way, he saw a woman washing her clothes on a rock in a large river. As the wealthy man watched, she displayed Mysterious Powers such as shedding radiance, disappearing into the rock, appearing under the rock, ascending into the air, and descending to the ground.

The wealthy man thought this most extraordinary. When he saw the Buddha, he said, "I understand that the Buddha is pure and is never affected by dirt and impurity. But you have done something most unusual. Why did you accept one of my women who removed human waste?"

The Buddha responded to the wealthy man's scornful remark: "Did you recognize the woman washing clothes in the river in front of my place?"

"No, I didn't," answered the wealthy man. "Did you see her releasing radiance and revealing the Mysterious Powers?" "Surely I did," replied the wealthy man.

The Buddha explained, "She was the woman of your house who was spattered with excrement. Even though you own as much treasure as you wish, including seven kinds of jewels, your merit is inferior to hers. Thanks to her merit gained by removing the wastes during past years, she has already attained the *arakanka* enlightenment and releases radiance from her body. Due to your error, which always causes you to become angry and sin, you will fall into the hells and suffer many pains."

Hearing this, the wealthy man was ashamed, returned home, and repented.

Thus it was told and handed down.

3:22 ABOUT RUSHI, A WEALTHY MAN

Long ago a wealthy man, Rushi, lived in India. He was so greedy that he grudged giving things even to his wife and his relatives. Once, when he thought, "I would like to eat alone in a quiet place," birds and animals came to watch him eating. He did not like the place, so he looked for another place without people, birds, or animals. He ate his food there. He was so happy that he danced and sang, "Now I can celebrate, and drink as I wish. I am happier than Bishamon and Taishaku." He kicked the jar and jumped for joy.

Taishaku was visiting the Buddha. He heard the wealthy man mocking him and became angry. Taishaku immediately assumed Rushi's form to punish him. He went to Rushi's house, opened the storeroom, removed all the treasures, and gave them to one hundred thousand people. The people of Rushi's house, including his wife and children, thought this extraordinary.

Soon the real Rushi came home and knocked at the door. The people of the house came out and saw the same Rushi. When they were going to drive him out, saying, "This one is the transformed one," the true Rushi said, "I am the real Rushi."

The people of the house did not know which was the real Rushi, so they had a witness judge the situation. The witness asked Rushi's wife which was the true and which the false Rushi. The wife, pointing to the Rushi who was the transformation of Taishaku, said, "This is real Rushi." The people also reported this to the king. The king summoned the two Rushis. Seeing two identical Rushis, the king could not detect any difference. So the king took the two Rushis to the Buddha.

At that time, Taishaku resumed his original form and mentioned Rushi's wrongdoing. The Buddha encouraged Rushi to practice good and preached the Law to him. Hearing the preaching, Rushi attained the Way and rejoiced.

Thus it was told and handed down.

3:23 ABOUT KENDONNYO, THE WIFE OF BADAI, A WEALTHY MAN

Long ago, a wealthy man named Badai[210] lived in India. Thanks to the help of the Buddha's disciples, such as Kashō, Mokuren, and Anaritsu, Badai gave up his delusions and wrong views and believed in the correct Way. Badai had a wife called Kendonnyo, who grudged giving things to others so much that she even guarded her eyeballs so that no

----

210. 跋提. Bhadrika, a son of king Amṛtodana.

one could take them. She always remained behind the gold and silver screen, made rice crackers, and loved to eat them.

At that time, the Buddha had a most intelligent disciple, Binzuru,[211] who was a cousin on his father's side. Binzuru went to correct Kendonnyo from her wrong views. Since the gate was closed, he flew over the gate with his Mysterious Powers to alight with a begging bowl where Kendonnyo was eating rice crackers. He begged for some. She was very selfish and would not offer him any. Binzuru stood there begging from the morning until the Hour of the Sheep.[212] Finally Kendonnyo said, "Even if you die standing there, I will not offer you any." Binzuru collapsed and passed away.

A stench immediately filled the house and distressed everyone. To remove the body, Kendonnyo had three persons drag it from her place, but it did not move. She added several more people, but they could not move the body. Finally she had hundreds and thousands of people pull the body, but it became heavier and did not move at all. The stench became unbearable.

Kendonnyo faced the body of Binzuru, uttered an incantation, and said, "Respected master, if you revive, I will not be selfish but will offer you my rice crackers." As soon as she had spoken, Binzuru immediately revived, stood up, and begged again. Afraid that he might pass away again unless he received a donation, Kendonnyo took her bowl and gave him two rice crackers of five in the bowl. While she was trying to get the three for herself, she and Binzuru fought for the bowl. Binzuru suddenly released his hand from the bowl. The bowl immediately stuck to her nose as tightly as if welded on and she could not remove it.

Now Kendonnyo, facing Binzuru, rubbed her palms and said, "Please relieve me from this pain." Binzuru replied, "This is beyond my ability. You should quickly go to my master, the Buddha, and ask his help. I will take you to the Buddha." Kendonnyo agreed to go. "You should also take various treasures," suggested Binzuru. Following his suggestion, Kendonnyo piled all kinds of treasures in five hundred carriages, had one thousand porters carry additional treasures, and visited the Buddha.

....

211. 宾頭盧. Piṇḍola-bhāradvāja, the first of the sixteen *arhats*, formerly served King Udayana of Kaṇśāmbī and in later years lived on Mt. Malaya in South India.

212. It corresponds with the time between one and three o'clock in the afternoon.

Seeing Kendonnyo, the Buddha preached to her and cultivated her. As soon as she listened to the preaching, the woman attained the *arakanka* enlightenment and ceased being greedy for a long time. Binzuru's way of cultivating her was marvelous!

Thus it was told and handed down.

3:24   ABOUT MOKUREN'S BROTHER

Long ago, Mokuren, the Buddha's disciple, had a younger brother. Although the younger brother was wealthy with abundant treasures, he did not practice good, but was deeply attached to mundane affairs.

Mokuren went to his younger brother and suggested, "You should practice good, otherwise you will fall into the Three Lower Realms and endure limitless sufferings. After all, you will not retain your treasures after your life ends. Those who accumulate merit will not fall into the Three Lower Realms, but undoubtedly will be reborn in the Two Higher Realms.[213]"

The brother said, "My parents told me to remain a layman and live as I wish. There is nothing as regrettable as being a priest. Begging alms is especially shameful. What do you mean by accumulating merit?"

Mokuren replied, "Accumulating merit means to obtain returns by the virtue of giving things to others."

"In that case, I will give things to others as you say." The younger brother opened his storehouses, took out his treasures, and gave them away. He immediately built five or six more storehouses. Someone asked him, "Why have you so quickly built more storehouses?" "Because I am going to accumulate merit," replied the brother.

Thus the brother offered his treasures to others for ninety days and asked Mokuren, "You say that the Buddha never speaks false words. But why haven't I accumulated any merits in my storehouses?" "Catch my priestly robe," said Mokuren to his younger brother and had him catch it. With that robe, Mokuren had his younger brother ascend to the heaven of the Four Deva Kings and to the Tōri, Yomi, Tosotsu, Rakuhenge,[214] and Takejizai Heavens. The brother observed countless

....

213. "Two Higher Realms" refers to the two higher worlds of the Six Worlds in which the souls transmigrate, those of heaven and of men.

214. *Rakuhenge* (楽変化) refers to Keraku Heaven. See note 85.

pleasures and wonders. When he ascended to the sixth heaven, Take-jizai, he saw forty-nine succesive fences. A woman sat within each. A woman of emerald sat on an emerald seat, hanging emerald threads and stitching emerald garment, and a woman of *shako* shell sat on the *shako* shell floor, hanging *shako* shell threads and stitching a *shako* shell robe. By the gate of the last fence was a woman of gold sitting on a golden floor, hanging golden threads and stitching a gold robe.

Seeing each of these, the brother thought, "Even King Tenrin does not have a woman like these in his pleasure houses, neither does the Kiken city[215] of Tōri Heaven, nor the place of our king Hashinoku. This is truly marvelous!"

The brother stooped and asked the women, "Who are you and why are you hanging the threads and what sort of robes are you sewing?" These Heavenly Ladies answered, "We are stitching robes with these threads for the younger brother of the Shaka Buddha's disciple, Mokuren, because he is going to be born into this heaven thanks to his good deeds in the human world. We are supposed to serve him as his people."

Hearing this, the brother almost jumped for joy and said, "Mokuren, my older brother, certainly does not speak false words. He will be my good teacher for life after life and generation after generation." After the younger brother returned to his world, he devoted himself to the practice of good deeds.

The Buddha preached, "Surely the younger brother of Mokuren will be reborn into the sixth heaven and enjoy surpassing pleasures. The life span in that heaven is sixteen thousand years since one day and night there correspond to sixteen hundred years of this world. After his life in that heaven is terminated, he will enter the Buddhist Way."

Thus it was told and handed down.

3:25   HOW A QUEEN DISOBEYED THE KING'S ORDER AND VISITED THE BUDDHA

Long ago, a great king in India had five hundred queens. The king ordered, "Court ladies of the palace, including the queens and ladies-in-waiting, may not practice the Buddhist Way. Anyone violat-

---

215. 善見城. Kiken City refers to the Palace of Correct Views at the top of Mt. Sumeru in the Tuṣita Heaven where Śakro Devānām Indraḥ lives.

ing this decree will be killed with weapons." Many years passed with no ladies of the palace practicing the Way.

However, one day, a favorite queen of the king thought, "I have been loved by the great king and I have never heard the Buddha's teachings. Although I have pleasures as I wish in this world, I may fall into the Three Lower Realms in my future life and never leave. Just as all streams flow into the sea, everyone who is born dies. Even though I am the favorite among his five hundred queens, I will surely fall into a bottomless hell. Sooner or later, one encounters death. No one escapes this. Dying sooner does not concern me. My body will eventually become dust. I might as well visit the Buddha, hear him preach the Law, and die."

The queen stealthily left the palace and went to the Buddha. First she met a priest, the Buddha's disciple, and asked, "Please preach the Law to me. I will listen." The disciple said, "I heard that the people of the palace are prohibited from practicing the Way. If you learn the teachings, what will become of you?"

"I have come here against the king's order. As soon as I return, I undoubtedly will be killed. However, those who live inevitably perish. What flourishes always declines. I will not survive for thousands of years no matter how much the king loves me. To fall into the Three Lower Realms due to a momentary attachment to love and desire is foolish. Please teach me the noble doctrines."

The priest spoke of belief in the Three Treasures. The queen asked, "I wonder if the Buddha preached anything else." The priest spoke about the Twelve Causations and the Four Noble Truths, including sufferings, their causes, enlightenment, and practices to gain enlightenment.

After listening, the queen said, "I have met you and listened. I shall die when I return to the palace. However, I will avoid the sufferings of the Three Lower Realms and plant the seeds for rebirth into the Pure Land of the Buddha. I hope that, due to my good deeds, I will finally become a Buddha in my future existence and benefit all sentient beings." She made this vow, paid her respects to the priest, and left.

The queen reached the palace. Just as she entered her room stealthily, lifting the curtain, the king saw her, took his bow and arrows, and shot her. One of the arrows ascended in the air. Another circled around the queen three times, and finally fell to the ground. The third one was turned toward the king and burned fiercely.

The king said, "You are not a human being. Are you a Deva king, a dragon, a Yasha[216] deity, or a Kendappa deity?"[217] The queen replied, "I am neither a Deva, a dragon, a Yasha, nor a Kendappa. I visited the Buddha and heard his teaching about the Law. Thanks to my good deeds, the deity Shūkongō[218] saved me."

The impressed king threw away his bow and arrows and ordered, "The people in this country, including those in the palace, should believe in the Buddhist Way. Those who oppose this shall be killed as a punishment."

Thus it was told and handed down.

3:26   HOW THE BUDDHA SENT KASENNEN TO THE COUNTRY OF KEIHIN

Long ago, in India, the Buddha sent his five hundred disciples, including Mokuren, Kashō, and Anan, to various countries to convert the people. Kasennen was assigned to the country of Keihin. Kasennen said to the Buddha, "That is the country where they traditionally believe in their deities, and the people have enjoyed hunting and fishing for many years. How am I going to convert them?" "Just go immediately," said the Buddha. Obeying the Buddha's order, Kasennen went to the country.

When he arrived there, he thought, "Branches and leaves will not grow if the tree's roots are cut. I think I will go first to the king of this country and convert him." Kasennen went to the palace.

The king was about to lead many ten thousands of horsemen on a hunting trip. Kasennen carried a stick on his shoulder and held a robe on his arm and a bowl in his hand as he stood before the king.

Seeing this, the surprised people said suspiciously to the king, "A stranger has come. Who is he?"

"Kill him immediately," ordered the king. When the king's people were about to cut off Kasennen's head, he pleaded, "Please

216. 夜叉. It refers to *yaksha*, a female demon.

217. 乾闥婆. Kendappa and Gandharva are the spirits of Gandha-mādana, Incense Mouatains, so called because they do not drink wine or eat meat but feed on incense or fragrance. As musicians of Indrah, they are said to be the same as Kinnaras.

218. 執金剛 (金剛蜜迹). The *vajra-pāni* or diamond holders hold the *vajra* or diamond as a symbol of wisdom. See note 118.

wait a moment. I have something to tell the king," and advanced to the king.

"Who are you? I have never seen you before. It's foolish of you to come here like this," said the king.

"King, you look very splendid while I look very shabby. I will be a herald on your hunting trip," said Kasennen modestly. The king was amused to hear this. He took him on the hunting trip and returned to the palace with him.

"Feed him tasty food," said the king to his people. Kasennen ate it all well. "Was it delicious?" asked the king.

"It was delicious," replied Kasennen.

Next, the king gave Kasennen tasteless food and asked him, "How about it?"

"This too is delicious," answered Kasennen.

"Why did you call both tasty and untasty foods delicious?" the king asked.

"A priest's mouth is like a cauldron. Whether tasty or not, food is the same in one's stomach," said Kasennen. The king was deeply impressed to hear this.

One day, Kasennen left the palace, saying, "A woman invited me to preach to her for ninety days." Kasennen went to the woman, who cut and sold her hair to make gifts to Kasennen. When ninety days had passed, Kasennen returned to the king's palace.

The king spoke to Kasennen, "I have not seen you lately. Where have you been and how did you eat?"

Kasennen said, "I preached ninety days for a woman who sold her hair and offered me food."

"I would like to see the woman," said the king, and he sent a messenger to summon the woman. But the woman did not come. The messenger reported to the king, "The woman is a matchless beauty whose body releases radiance!" The king immediately had a carriage made of flowers sent with thousand of horsemen to welcome the woman.

The woman finally arrived at the palace, riding on the flower carriage and shedding radiance. Seeing her, the king thought that all his five hundred queens were like fireflies in comparison to this woman whose radiant appearance was like the moon and the sun. The king immediately made her one of his queens and immensely cherished her. He attended her in the mornings and in the evenings, during the days and during the nights.

One day, the new queen said to the king, "If you love me so much, beginning with you, all the people in this country should believe the Buddhist teachings." The king followed her suggestion and had faith in the Law for the first time. His people all followed the Buddhist Law.

This was all possible due to Kasennen's powerful preaching, which made a woman into a radiant queen who captured the king's heart. Afterward, the Buddhist Law was spread in that country for the first time, thanks to Kasennen's influence.

Thus it was told and handed down.

3:27   HOW KING AJASE KILLED HIS FATHER

Long ago, in India, King Ajase became very close to Daibadatta, believed him, and thought his words as precious as gold. Daibadatta, noticing the king's devotion, suggested, "You will become a new king by killing the great king, your father, and I will become a new Buddha by killing the Buddha."

At this suggestion, King Ajase caught his father, King Binbashara, and confined him in a remote and strongly made cell with seven series of walls. The doors of the cell were securely closed and the guards were strictly warned several times by the king not to allow any one into the room. Since the order was given even to the ministers and noblemen, none of them approached the room. The plan was to kill the great king within seven days.

The mother of King Ajase, Lady Idiake,[219] was greatly distressed because she had given birth to such an evil son who intended to kill his own father. She secretly prepared a concentrated honey mixed with flour, took it to the room, and rubbed it on the body of the great king. She also made a neck ornament which contained thin rice gruel and stealthily offered it to the great king.

The great king ate the flour, washed his hands, cleansed his mouth, clasped his hands in prayer, faced Mount Ryōju, bowed in tears, and said respectfully, "O, merciful Shaka Buddha, greatest teacher of the generation, please release me from this suffering. Although I am familiar with the Buddhist Law, I am going to be killed because of

....

219. 韋提希夫人. Lady Idaike, Vaidehī, the wife of King Bimbisāra, was the mother of Ajātaśatru (Ajase).

my precepts by my evil son. Where is Mokuren? Show me mercy and grant me the Eight Precepts[220] for my future deliverance!" Hearing this, the Buddha felt pity and sent Mokuren and Furuna to the great king. These two arhats, Mokuren and Furuna, flew to the great king as swiftly as birds, granted the precepts, and preached the Law for him. The two arhats visited the great king every day.

Meanwhile, King Ajase asked one of his guards if his father was still alive. The guard reported, "The great king is still very much alive, his complexion is fine, and his splendid appearance shows no sign of death. This is because the queen, Lady Idaike, applied flour mixed with pure honey to his body and offered him rice gruel contained in a neck ornament. Moreover, the two great arhats Mokuren and Furuna flew to him and preached to him. This is inevitable."

Hearing this, the king became angry. "My mother, Lady Idaike, is a companion of outlaws. Having talked to the evil priests Furuna and Mokuren, she has kept the evil great king alive." The king drew his sword, caught his mother, and was about to cut off her head.

At that time, the minister Giba,[221] the son of Anraenyo, advanced before the king and said, "Since ancient times, there have been eighteen thousand evil kings who killed their fathers to usurp their thrones. But I have not heard of a single king who cruelly harmed his own mother. Now, your highness, please reflect and refrain from this evil act."

The king listened, became very frightened, threw down his sword, and refrained from harming his mother. However, his father, the great king, finally died.

The Buddha later preached about nirvana in the Sala Forest[222] by the River Badai in Kushina. The minister Giba suggested, "King, you sinned and you will surely fall into the hells. Recently, I hear that the Buddha is preaching the Law benefiting all the people in the Sala Forest by the River Badai in Kushina. Please go there quickly and repent."

....

220. The Eight Precepts include not adorning oneself, not participating in singing and dancing, and not sleeping in a comfortable place, in addition to the Five Precepts. See note 75.
221. 耆婆. Giba, Jīvaka, was a physician in Rājagrha in the time of the Buddha.
222. 沙羅林. The forest refers to the Śāla Grove near the bank of the Hiraṇyavatī River in the suburb of Kuśinagara, where the Buddha died.

King Ajase said, "I have already killed my father. The Buddha will not think well of me. Besides, he may not even see me."

"The Buddha will see both those who practice good and those who commit evil. He equally extends his mercy to all. So please go immediately," encouraged the minister.

Yet the king was reluctant, saying, "I am certain to fall into bottomless hells due to my sins. Even if I see the Buddha, it will be difficult to expiate my sins. Besides, I am already old and I think it useless to visit the Buddha now and be embarrassed."

The minister continued to insist, "Unless you see the Buddha now and expiate your sin of killing your father, what are you going to do? Once you fall into the bottomless hells, you will never have an opportunity to leave them. Please go there now by all means," the minister urged heartily.

At that time, the radiance shed by the Buddha in the Sala Forest illuminated the king's figure. King Ajase said, "I heard that at the end of the *kalpa* years, three suns and moons appear and shine. I wonder if these *kalpa* years are ended now and these lights are shining on me."

The minister explained, "King, please listen carefully. A parable tells how parents tenderly care for their many children, including the sick and lame. Can your grave sin of killing your father be compared to the serious illness of a child? The Buddha shows his pity even to one child. The Buddha has released this radiance to help you, the king."

"In that case, I think I will go to see him. But you come with me. Since I have already committed one of the Five Grave Sins,[223] the ground may split open on my way and I may fall into the hell. If that happens, I will grasp you," said the king, finally deciding to visit the Buddha with the minister.

The king began his trip accompanied by many ministers in fifty-two thousand canopied carriages decorated with silk banners on dragonheaded staffs and five hundred great elephants, each transporting the seven kinds of jewels.

The king and his people arrived at the forest and advanced toward the Buddha. As soon as the Buddha saw the king, he asked, "Are you King Ajase?" The king had already become a candidate for Buddhahood, and the Buddha had recorded the fact. The Buddha said

....

223. The Grave Sins include killing one's father, killing one's mother, killing an *arhat*, harming a Buddha's body, and causing disorder in the priests' community.

to the king, "It is impossible to refuse to let you enter the Way. Your arrival proves sufficiently that you have already entered the Way."

Judging by this, merits earned by seeing the Buddha are limitless. Even King Ajase, who killed his father, left the delusions of this world and attained the first stage of enlightenment just by seeing the Buddha.

Thus it was told and handed down.

3:28 HOW THE BUDDHA TOLD HIS PEOPLE THAT HE WOULD ENTER NIRVANA

Long ago, Shaka Buddha converted all kinds of sentient beings in the terrestrial and celestial realms for more than forty years by preaching the Law. When eighty years of age, the Buddha was in the country of Bishari.[224] He said to Anan, "Every part of my body aches. I shall enter nirvana in three months."

"Master, you have always avoided all kinds of sickness. Why do you ache now?" asked Anan.

The Buddha got up and sat in the position of meditation, shedding a great radiance, which illuminated the world. All those who were illuminated by his radiance escaped their sufferings and felt pleasure.

Later the Buddha left the country of Bishari and went to the city of Kushina. He lay under a tree of the Sala Forest in the lion position on his right side, with one leg over the other. The Buddha said to Anan, "I am telling you now. I am going to enter nirvana, just as all those who prosper certainly will decline and those who were born certainly will die."

The Buddha also said to Monju, "I will explain about my backache to the mass of the people. My backache is not due to sickness, but indicates the two karmic relations: one shows my pity for all the sentient beings, and the other offers remedies to the sick. Countless *kalpa* years ago, when I practiced the Way of the bodhisattva, I always benefited people by releasing them from suffering and by offering them medicine. So how could I now be sick! Yet once I hit the back of a deer and now at my entry into nirvana, I am revealing the consequences."

At that time, Bodhisattva Kashō invited Minister Giba and asked

....

224. 毗舍離. Vaiśālī was one of the sixteen great countries in the Buddha's time. See note 175.

about the Buddha's sickness. "The Buddha is almost entering nirvana. Medicine will be of no use," said the minister.

Hearing this, the mass of the people, including Kashō as well as the minister himself, felt immensely sad and grieved. All those in the realms of heaven and of human beings lamented at seeing the Buddha enter nirvana.

Thus it was told and handed down.

3:29   HOW JUNDA'S OFFERINGS WERE ACCEPTED BY THE BUDDHA IN HIS LAST MOMENTS

Long ago, when the Buddha was to enter nirvana, a layman called Junda, a son of a craftsmen of Kushina, was among the crowds surrounding the Buddha.

With his fifteen people, Junda advanced before the Buddha, clasped his hands in prayer, bowed in tears, and said to the Buddha and the people, "Please, our Lord Buddha, pity us and accept our last offerings. After you enter nirvana, who will show mercy and save us? Being poor, we will suffer unbearable hunger some day. For this reason, we wish to follow your teachings and make offerings now so that we will be blessed with food in our future lives. Show pity and accept our offerings before you leave us."

The Buddha said to Junda, "How wonderful. I will free you from poverty, make the rain of the utmost Law fall, generate the power of the Law, and aid you to attain enlightenment by your donations."

Hearing this, all the disciples of the Buddha rejoiced and said, "How wonderful! How wonderful, Junda! The Buddha will accept your final offerings. You have now become a true disciple of the Buddha."

The Buddha said to Junda, "This is your last opportunity to make offerings to me and my priests. I am about to enter nirvana." The Buddha repeated this three times.

As Junda heard the Buddha's recommendation, he raised his voice and said to the people, "Please, everybody, throw yourselves on the ground and ask the Buddha not to enter nirvana!"

"You should not cry. Otherwise you will be more disturbed and confused. I am going into nirvana today because I pity you and all other sentient beings. Laws and teachings do not endure forever, but all will perish someday."

As the Buddha spoke, he radiated blue, yellow, red, white, crimson, and purple rays from his forehead.

Illuminated by these lights, Junda brought various dishes from the feast to the Buddha and said tearfully, "Please, Buddha, stay another *kalpa* year and extend us mercy."

"Rather than trying to retain me in this world, quickly make a final *danharamitsu* offering[225] to me," said the Buddha.

On that occasion, all the bodhisattvas, celestial beings, and other non-human beings said in unison, "Junda has earned great merit. Since we have no blessing, all the offerings that we have prepared are vain."

To realize the wishes and vows of the non-human beings, the Buddha produced countless new Buddhas from his pores. Each new Buddha was accompanied by innumerable priests, who all accepted the offerings of the non-human beings. The Buddha himself stretched forth his hand and accepted the offerings which Junda had prepared. Due to the Mysterious Powers of the Buddha, the offerings increased in quantity to eight *koku*[226] and were sufficient for all the people in the Maka city.

Thus it was told and handed down.

3:30   HOW THE BUDDHA SAW RAGORA[227] WHEN ABOUT TO ENTER NIRVANA

Long ago, when the Buddha was about to enter nirvana, Ragora thought, "Since it will be unbearable to see the Buddha enter nirvana, I will go to another world to avoid such an intolerable sadness."

Ragora traveled through innumerable countries and worlds and finally reached a country of Buddhas. A Buddha of the country saw Ragora and asked, "Your father, Shaka Buddha, is about to enter nirvana. Why are you here instead of watching him at his last moment?"

Ragora replied, "Since I was unable to bear the sadness of seeing my father entering nirvana, I have come to this country to avoid that experience."

"You are really a fool. Your father is waiting for you at this very

....

225. 檀波羅蜜. It refers to *dāna-pāramitā*, which is making a donation, especially a charitable gift to a priestly community.

226. *Koku* is a Japanese measure that equals 4.9629 bushels.

227. 羅睺羅. Rāhula, the son of the Buddha, was one of the Buddha's ten great disciples.

moment. You should immediately return and watch his final moment." Ragora followed the Buddha's suggestion and returned to his country, weeping.

Ragora arrived as the Buddlia asked a disciple if Ragora had come. A disciple said to Ragora, "The Buddha is about to enter nirvana. He has been waiting for you. Go quickly to see him."

In tears Ragora came close to the Buddha, who looked at Ragora and said, "I am entering nirvana and leaving this world forever. This is the last moment when you will see me. Come closer," said the Buddha, and took the hand of Ragora who was overwhelmed by his tears.

"Ragora is my child. Numerous Buddhas of the Ten Directions, please show him mercy." The Buddha entered nirvana as he made this plea.

Judging by this, even the Buddha, who had led the pure life of Buddhahood, held a different relationship with his child than with his disciples. How natural it was, then, for the laymen of this delusioned world to be distressed by anxiety over their children! The Buddha, too, showed us this feeling.

Thus it was told and handed down.

3:31 HOW THE BUDDHA WAS PLACED IN A CASKET AFTER ENTERING NIRVANA

Long ago, when the Buddha was to enter nirvana, he said to Anan, "After I enter nirvana, preserve my body for seven days in an iron casket which is filled with fragrant oil just as they did for King Turning Wheel. Decorate the four sides of the casket with the seven kinds of jewels. Offer the veneration service for me for seven clays with jeweled banners, flowers, and incense.

"Seven days later, take me from the casket and bathe me in various scented waters. Wrap me first with the best *toromen*[228] cloth, then cover me with the fine white *katabira*[229] cloth, place me in the iron casket filled with the refined fragrant oil, close the casket, decorate it with various kinds of jewels, and use the incense of sandalwood and aloe wood. Place the casket in the carriage ornamented with the seven kinds of jewels." After the Buddha spoke, he entered nirvana.

....

228. 兜羅綿. It refers to cotton.

229. *Katabira* cloth in ancient times referred to wooly material for clothing.

Anan and all the other disciples, including the arhats, mourned greatly, raising their voices tearfully. Not a single soul among the bodhisattvas, the celestial beings, the Eight Guardians of the Law, and the numerous sentient beings, including non-human beings, did not grieve over losing the Buddha. The Diamond Deva kings[230] mourned by throwing their bodies on the ground and the Sixteen Good Deities[231] cried, raising their voices. At that time, the earth, the mountains, the great seas, and the rivers all roared and shook.

The color of the sala tree changed, and even the heartless grasses and plants wore sad hues. Even though the heaven and earth mourned together, it was in vain. Afterward, just as the Buddha had requested, his body was preserved in the iron casket for seven days.

Thus it was told and handed down.

3:32   HOW KASHŌ ARRIVED AFTER THE BUDDHA ENTERED NIRVANA

Long ago Kashō heard that the Buddha had entered nirvana and descended Mount Rōshaku.[232] On his way, Kashō met a Niganda[233] ascetic holding a *mondara* flower. Kashō asked, "Have you heard about my master?"

The ascetic said, "Seven days have passed since your master entered nirvana." Hearing this, Kashō and his five hundred disciples cried mournfully with sad tears.

Kashō headed toward the capital of Kushina, crossed the Nirenzen River, and arrived at the Tenkan Temple,[234] where Anan was. Kashō spoke to Anan, "Since the Buddha is not yet cremated, I would like to see him again."

....

230. 執金剛. The diamond holders hold the *vajra* or diamond as a symbol of wisdom. See note 218.

231. "The Sixteen Good Deities" refers to the sixteen *yakṣas* who vow to protect the upholders of the *Mahāprajñā-pāramitā sūtra*.

232. 狼跡山. It refers to Kukkuṭapāda, Cock Foot Mountain, in Magadha, on which Kāśyapa entered into nirvana. He is still supposed to be living there.

233. 尼乾子. It refers to Vardhamāna, the founder of the Jaina religion, born in the fifth century B.C. His religion denied the authority of the Vedas, prohibited rituals, and forbade killing. Since one branch of the sect practiced nudity, it is referred to in Buddhist texts as the Nudist Heresy.

234. 天冠寺. The temple is located to the east of Kuśinagara.

Anan replied, "Though the Buddha is not cremated, he already has been wrapped in five hundred layers of *katabira* cloth and placed in the iron casket as he requested."

Kashō asked Anan three more times, but Anan did not allow him to see the Buddha.

When Kashō approached the casket, he saw the Buddha's gold-colored feet projecting from the casket. Feeling strange, Kashō inquired, "The Buddha's body has a golden hue. Why has his body changed its color?"

Anan replied, "Seeing the Buddha enter nirvana, an old woman shed her tears of grief on his feet, which made his body a different color."

Kashō together with the celestial beings and priests and laymen faced the casket and paid their respects by weeping and crying. Suddenly the Buddha's feet disappeared into the casket. Even though Kashō was a true disciple, he could not see the Buddha at his final moment.

Thus it was told and handed down.

3:33   HOW LADY MAYA DESCENDED TO THIS WORLD AFTER THE BUDDHA'S NIRVANA

Long ago, after the Buddha entered nirvana, Anan was observed mourning and keeping the Buddha's corpse in a casket. Anan ascended to the Tōri Heaven and told Lady Maya that the Buddha had entered nirvana.

Lady Maya collapsed because of her sadness. After a while, she descended to the foot of a sala tree, leading many of her people. When she looked at the Buddha's casket, Lady Maya again passed out and fell to the ground in grief. Her people sprinkled some water on her face, and she soon revived.

Lady Maya went to the casket, paid her respects, and said, weeping, "I have been your mother for a long time, and we never have been separated. Since you have entered nirvana, I will never see you. How sad it is!" Many celestial beings scattered delicate flowers over the casket.

"I wish, my child, the Buddha, would benefit the celestial beings instead of attending to various transient secular matters," said the Lady Maya as she took the Buddha's great robe[235] and stick in her right hand and threw them on the ground. The sound echoed like a great mountain collapsing.

At that time, the Buddha used his Mysterious Powers to open the lid of the coffin. He got out of the casket and faced Lady Maya, clasping his hands in prayer. Thousand of lights shone from the pores of his body, and a thousand Buddhas sat in their radiance. The Buddha said, "Everything ends in this way. Please do not cry and lament over my death."

Seeing the Buddha rise from the coffin, Anan asked the Buddha, "If the people of later generations ask us to explain how the Buddha entered nirvana, what should we answer?"

The Buddha said, "You should explain that after the Buddha had entered nirvana and Lady Maya descended from the Tōri Heaven, the Buddha rose from the golden coffin, faced his mother as he clasped his hands in prayer, and explained the verses for her sake and that of other sentient beings of later generations."

This is called the *Sutra of the Mother Seeing the Child at the Buddha's Last Moment*.[236]

After the Buddha explained this, he and his mother said farewell and the casket lid was closed as before.

Thus it was told and handed down.

3:34   ABOUT THE CREMATION OF THE BUDDHA'S BODY

Long ago, after the Buddha entered nirvana, the people intended to cremate his body as he had requested, just as they did for King Turning Wheel.

There were four strong men in the capital of Kushina. Each of these men wore neck ornaments that contained fires as bright as the seven kinds of jewels and were as large as wheels and shone so as to illuminate everything. Trying to burn the Buddha's corpse, they threw fire into the tower where the casket was kept. The fire became extinguished of its own accord.

Seeing this, Kashō said to the strong men, "The fire of all the

....

235. 僧伽利衣. It refers to *samghāṭī*, the largest of the three priestly robes.

236. 佛臨母子相見経. See *Taishō*, XII (no. 383).

Three Worlds[237] cannot burn the Buddha's casket. How can you expect to burn it with your power?"

Eight yet stronger men in the city threw fire as bright as the seven kinds of jewels on the casket, but it died out; Then sixteen yet stronger men threw fire into the tower, their fire also died out. Finally, each of thirty-six yet stronger men threw the fire on the casket, but in vain.

Seeing this, Kashō said to the yet stronger men and to the massed people, "You should know that even though all the celestial beings tried, they wouldn't be able to burn the jeweled casket of the Buddha. So don't think of burning it."

The great masters of the people, including the men and women in the city and the celestial beings, still missed the Buddha. They brought their belongings as offerings, tearfully paid their respects to the casket, and circled the coffin seven times, raising their voices in mourning. Their voices roared over the entire world. At that moment, the Buddha, because of his strong mercy, produced fire from his heart, which flamed out from the casket. Those who watched thought this most unusual. Finally the casket burned and the tower burned completely in seven days. During these seven days, the grief and mourning of the people continued, and each of them venerated the Buddha.

During that time, the Four Deva Kings thought, "We will extinguish this fire by pouring fragrant water, and take the Buddha's relics for veneration." They immediately filled a jar encrusted with the seven kinds of jewels with fragrant water. They also brought four trees from Mount Shumi which were one hundred *yujun*[238] high and as large as one thousand men's extended arms. With these trees and the jar, the Four Deva Kings descended together to the place of cremation. The trees produced sweet milk. The Four Deva Kings added the sweet milk to the fragrant water in the jar and poured it on the fire. But the fire burned more fiercely and never died out.

Shakara,[239] a dragon king, and the rain god of the great sea, and other gods of rivers and creeks saw the unextinguished fire and

....

237. They refer to the Three Lower Realms of hell, animals, and hungry ghosts.

238. *Yujun* is equated with 120 kilometers.

239. 沙竭羅龍王. It refers to Sāgara, one of the Eight Great Dragon Kings, who causes rain.

thought, "We will bring fragrant water, pour it to extinguish the fire, and take the relics to venerate them." So each god filled a seven-jeweled jar with fragrant water. They went to the place of cremation, and poured the water at the same time.

The fire was not extinguished, but burned just as before. Then Ruzu,[240] the storm god, asked the Four Deva Kings and other gods, "You thought to extinguish the fire by pouring the fragrant water. Wasn't it because you wish to take the Buddha's relics for veneration?" The Four Deva Kings and other gods agreed.

Ruzu said to the Four Deva Kings, "You are greedy. Being in the heaven, if you take the relics to the heaven with you, what will the people on the earth venerate?"

Ruzu also said to the gods of the sea and rivers, "You are living in the seas and rivers. If you take the relics to your places, where do the people on the earth go to venerate them?"

Hearing this, the Four Deva Kings were respectively penitent and returned to the heaven while the gods of the sea and rivers repented of their selfishness and went back to their places.

Later, when Taishaku arrived at the place of cremation with a seven-jeweled jar and other instruments of veneration, the fire died of its own accord. Taishaku opened the jeweled coffin, asked for and took a tooth as a relic to the heaven. Taishaku built a pagoda for it and venerated it.

Thus it was told and handed down.

3:35   HOW THE KINGS OF THE EIGHT COUNTRIES SHARED
THE RELICS OF THE BUDDHA

Long ago when the Maraminju,[241] the people of the country of Ha-ha,[242] heard that the Buddha had entered nirvana, they consulted and decided, "We will go to the capital of Kushina, ask for the Buddha's

....

240. 楼逗. It refers to Rudra, god of tempests.
241. 末羅民衆. It refers to Mallas, who ruled the country of Malla, which was located east of Kapilavastu. Malla included main cities such as Pāvā, Anupriyā, and Kuśinagara as the capital. The country was one of the sixteen great countries in the Buddha's time.
242. 波々国. It refers to Pāvā, a place near Rājagrha.

relics, build a pagoda for them, and venerate them." So they went to the capital of Kushina leading four kinds of soldiers, those on elephants, on horses, in chariots, and on foot.

When they reached the capital, they sent a messenger to say, "The Buddha passed away in this country. However, the Buddha was our master and we respect him greatly. We wish to take his relics to our country and build a pagoda to venerate them."

When the king of Kushina heard the messenger's request, he said, "This sounds reasonable. However, the Buddha passed away in this country, and everybody here wishes to venerate the relics. The people from a neighboring country cannot take the relics."

At that time, various peoples, including the Batsuriminju of the country of Sharaba,[243] the Kuriminju of Rama,[244] the Baramon of Birudai,[245] and King Ajase of Makada, heard that the Buddha had passed away in the Sala Forest. They said, "We will go and get the relics," and all these peoples led their four kinds of soldiers across the Gōga River.[246]

When they arrived near the capital of Kushina, they met a Brahman called Kōshō[247] to whom they said, "Remember our names, go to the capital of Kushina, and tell the Maraminju people that we are on good terms with our neighboring countries and have no intention of fighting. We hear that the Buddha passed away in this country. Since we respect the Buddha, we wish to take his relics to our countries, build pagodas, and venerate them. Let us have some relics. We will preserve them as previous treasures of our countries." Receiving these instructions carefully, Kōshō entered the city and reported to the Maraminju people.

They said, "Truly, what is said is reasonable. Yet, since the Buddha passed away in this country, the people of this country should exclusively venerate him. The relics should not be given to the people of the distant countries."

---

243. 跋利民衆. 遮羅婆国. Batsuri or Sharaba refers to a small kingdom located near Magadha.
244. 拘利民衆. Kuri, the Koliya clan. Rama (羅摩) was located north of Kapilavastu.
245. 舩留提. It may refer to a country called Virasana.
246. 恒伽河. It refers to the Ganges River.
247. 香姓婆羅門. It refers to Droṇa-brāhmaṇa, who distributed the relics of Buddha equally among the eight kings and stopped their quarreling over the relics.

When the kings of the various countries heard this, they consulted with their ministers and decided, "We have come far to ask for the relics. If these people refuse us, our soldiers will take the relics by force. We will not spare our lives."

Hearing this, the ministers of Kushina discussed the matter, "Since these ministers from distant countries have not received the relics, they intend to obtain them by force using their troops. This is truly frightening."

At that time, Kōshō spoke to everyone, "As the Buddha instructed, many holy men preach the Law and vow to give peace to all sentient beings. Now, fighting over the relics, they are going to violate the remnants of the Buddha's body. We should immediately share the relics with these kings of the various countries." The people all agreed, "That is fine."

The decision was reported to these kings from the various countries, who soon came to the place of the relics. They discussed who was qualified to apportion the relics. Everyone recommended, "Since Kōshō is honest and wise, he is the right man to divide them."

The kings said to Kōshō, "You apportion the relics fairly among the eight of us." Immediately, Kōshō went to the relics and paid his respects. He first separated the teeth, placed them to one side, and offered them to King Ajase. Next, he separated the remaining relics, one by one, finishing when the morning star appeared. Kōshō brought a jar which contained stones and measured the relics using this jar. He divided them equally into eight portions. As he finished, he said to the people, "Each can look in his jar, take it to his place, build a pagoda, and venerate his relics."

The people of Hipparaju[248] said, "We wish to have the ashes, to build a pagoda for them, and to venerate them." Everybody agreed to give them the ashes.

The people of Kushina, after getting their share of the relics, built a pagoda and venerated them. King Ajase of Makada and the people of other countries, including Bishari, Kabirae, Birudai, Rama, Sharaba, and Haha, took their shares and built pagodas in which to venerate them.

Kōshō built a pagoda in which to venerate the jar while the people of Hippara built a pagoda for the veneration of ashes. Eight pa-

248. It refers to the *pippala* tree.

godas were built for the relics. The ninth pagoda was for the jar, the tenth for the ashes, and the eleventh for the Buddha's hair, which had been cut while he lived.

The Buddha was born, entered Buddhahood, attained the Way when stars appeared in the sky, and entered nirvana on the eighth day of the second month.

Thus it was told and handed down.

CHAPTER 4

4:1   HOW ANAN ENTERED THE HALL OF COMPILED
       TEACHINGS OF THE LAW

Long ago, after the Buddha entered nirvana, Kashō gathered a thousand arhats to compile the teachings of the Greater and Lesser Vehicles. Among them was Anan, who had many faults.

Kashō questioned Anan to correct his views. "You introduced Kyōdonmi[249] to the Buddha and allowed her to accept the precepts and enter Buddhahood. Because of this, you have shortened the Period of the Correct View[250] by five hundred years. How are you going to justify this error?"

"Four kinds of Buddhists, priests, nuns, laymen, and laywomen, remained after the Buddha entered nirvana," replied Anan.

Kashō continued, "Justify your fault in offering no water to the Buddha at his last moment." "Since five hundred carriages were crossing the river at that time, I could not get water for the Buddha," explained Anan.

Kashō continued, "When the Buddha asked three times whether one should live for one *kalpa* or for many *kalpa*-year periods, you gave no answer each time. How do you explain this fault?" "I did not answer because I was afraid that the Tenma demons and the heretics might interfere with the teachings according to my answers."

Kashō inquired, "When the Buddha entered nirvana, Lady Maya stretched out her hands from the distant Tori Heaven and shed tears

---

249. 憍曇弥. Refer to 1:19.
250. It refers to the Period of the Righteous Law (*shōbō*), when Buddhist doctrines, practices, and enlightenment exist. See note 189.

as she touched the Buddha's feet. Although a disciple of the Buddha, you did not stop her, but allowed a woman to touch his body. How do you explain this error?"

"It was to let the people of later generations know the deep affection between parents and children, children's obligations toward parents, and the rewards for virtue," explained Anan. Since Anan's answers had no fault, Kashō asked no more questions.

When one thousand arhats went to Mount Ryōju to enter the Hall of Compiled Teachings of the Law, Kashō said, "Nine hundred and ninety-nine of the one thousand arhats are holy men who have attained the Way through non-learning. Anan, a man of learning, is an exception. Besides, Anan occasionally attracts women and is not accomplished enough. Quickly go outside the hall!" Kashō took Anan outside the hall and closed the door.

Outside the hall, Anan insisted, "My learning is to benefit the Buddha's Four Kinds of Preaching.[251] I have no attachment to women. So please let me come in and have a seat!"

"Your achievement is still insufficient. As soon as you attain the Way of non-learning, we will let you in and give you a seat," replied Kashō.

"I have already attained the Way of non-learning. Let me in immediately," requested Anan.

"If you have attained the status of non-learning, you should be able to enter the hall by your Mysterious Powers without opening the doors," said Kashō.

Anan entered into the hall through a keyhole and joined the others. Those who were near Anan felt this most extraordinary. On account of this, the other arhats decided to place Anan in charge of the compilers of the teachings.

Anan stepped on the platform to be venerated and said, "I heard this from the Buddha." At that time many priests wondered, "Has our great master Shaka Buddha returned to preach for us?" The priests greatly admired Anan and recited the following verse in unison:

....

251. The four kinds of preaching are preaching according to the audiences' desires, preaching according to the audiences' capacities, preaching by observing the hearer's voice, and preaching by expounding the ultimate truth as the audience progresses.

The Law of the Buddha like the great sea water
Flows into the mind of Anan
Whose face is like the full moon and
Whose eyes are like blue lotus blossoms.

Later, the sutras of both the Greater and the Lesser Vehicles were compiled in Anan's words. People knew that Anan was superior among the Buddha's disciples.

Thus it was told and handed down.

4:2   HOW KING HASHINOKU INVITED RAGORA

Long ago, after the Buddha entered nirvana, King Hashinoku invited and venerated Ragora with a feast of one hundred courses. Both the king and the queen themselves offered the dishes to Ragora. Ragora accepted the food, took a mouthful with his chopsticks, and burst into tears like a child.

Seeing this, hundreds of officials, including the king and the queen, felt strange and said, "We are sincerely venerating you. Why do you cry? Quickly tell us the reason."

"It has not been long since the Buddha entered nirvana. Yet the taste of cooked rice has greatly changed and is bad. Wondering what the people of later generations will eat makes me feel sad and cry," said Ragora and continued to sob.

As the king watched, Ragora reached into the ground with his arm and took a grain of rice from inside the earth. He said, "This is rice from the time when the Buddha was still alive in this world, the food of the holy man who abandoned delusions and attained the Way. Quickly compare this rice with yours."

The king took the rice of Ragora, licked it, and found it tasted marvelous. Compared to the king's rice, the former tasted like a sweet dew, while the latter tasted like a poison.

"After the holy men all have disappeared from this world, for whom is this tasty rice? This good produced from the earth has been buried one hundred *yujun* deep for the earth deity," said Ragora.

The king asked, "When will the earth produce such food?"

"Whenever the lecture on the *Ninōkyō*[252] sutra is given during the later generations," was the reply.

So giving the lectures on the *Ninōkyō* sutra was most important and the best cause for later generations to receive good results.

Thus it was told and handed down.

4:3   HOW KING AIKU KILLED HIS QUEENS AND BUILT EIGHTY-FOUR THOUSAND PAGODAS

Long ago, one hundred years after the Buddha's nirvana, a king of the Iron Wheel,[253] called King Aiku, appeared in this world. He possessed eighty-four thousand queens but had no prince. He lamented greatly and prayed for a child. Soon the second queen, one of his most favored, became pregnant. The joyful king summoned a diviner and asked if the baby would be a boy or girl. The diviner predicted the birth of a boy who would radiate golden beams. The gleeful king attended the queen with utmost care.

The first queen heard the news and thought, "If such a boy is born, my status will surely be inferior to that of the second queen. How can I dispose of the baby?" The first queen reflected and finally devised a plot. "Here is a wild boar. I will exchange the new piglet of this boar for the golden boy who will be killed and buried. And I will say to the second queen, 'You have delivered a wild boar piglet.'" The first queen talked to the wet nurse who was closely attending the second queen.

After anxious waiting, the months of pregnancy were ended, and the second queen had her labor pains. She relied on a midwife to deliver her baby. As instructed by the first queen, the wet nurse told the

---

252. 仁王経. The *ninōkyō*, *Prajñapāramitā-sūtra*, relating about a king who protects his country, has two Chinese translations: one by Kumarajiva and one by Amoghavajra. The sutra is not found in the Tibetan canons, and it is doubtful whether the sutra was compiled in India.

253. 鐵輪聖王. It refers to one of the *cakravartin* wheel-turning kings who rule the world by turning the wheel given by heaven at their enthronement. The four kinds of wheels are gold, silver, copper, and iron. The Gold-Wheel-Turning King rules the four continents; the Silver-Wheel-Turning King rules the eastern, western, and southern continents; the Copper-Wheel-Turning King rules the eastern and southern continents; and the Iron-Wheel-Turning King rules the southern continent.

second queen, "You should not see anything while delivering the baby. If you cover yourself with a robe, you will have an easy delivery."

Following her suggestion, the second queen covered herself, including her head, with a robe and saw nothing during the delivery.

A baby boy was delivered with ease and the second queen took a glance as he truly radiated golden beams. As had been arranged, the wet nurse disposed of the newborn baby with other things and substituted the piglet of a wild boar.

The king was informed, "The second queen has delivered a little wild boar." "This is most extraordinary and regrettable," said the king, and he exiled the second queen to another country. The first queen was immensely pleased at the success of her plot.

Months passed. While visiting another country, the king was wandering and amusing himself on the hunting ground. He saw a woman who appeared to be in the forest for certain reasons. The king summoned her and learned that she was the very second queen whom he had expelled. The pitying king asked her about the delivery of the wild boar piglet.

The queen said, "I am not guilty of anything. I have been thinking of how to tell you this. I am very glad that you have asked me directly without an intermediary." The second queen explained everything to the king so he knew the true story.

The king said, "Oh, I punished an innocent queen, and the death of the golden boy was plotted by the other queens." After the king took the second queen to the palace, he killed the remainder of the eighty-four thousand queens, whether guilty or innocent.

Later, the king reflected from time to time and lamented, "My sin in killing so many queens is very serious. How can I evade falling into hells as the consequence?" The king consulted with Kongi,[254] a priest of arhat status.

The priest said, "Your sin is very serious, and evading its consequences may be difficult. Please build eighty-four thousand pagodas, one for each queen. This may enable you to avoid the sufferings of hell. Merely erecting a pagoda with layers of stone and carved wood earns great merit. There is no doubt that your sins will be forgiven if you make so many pagodas in accordance with the Law."

....

254. The person may refer to Upagupta, otherwise unknown. See note 260.

The king issued orders throughout the country to immediately erect eighty-four thousand pagodas. However, the king regretted that no relics of the Buddha were placed in these pagodas.

A minister suggested, "After his nirvana, when the Buddha's relics were divided, Dragon King Nanda placed the relics which should have been given to the great king, your father, in his dragon palace. You should search for them immediately, bring them here, and place them in these pagodas!"

The king thought, "If I summon various demons and Yakusa[255] deities and have them catch many dragons at the bottom of the sea with iron nets, I surely will be able to obtain the relics."

The king summoned the demon and Yakusa deities and arranged for them to make iron nets. When they were about to pull up the nets, the frightened dragon king came to the sleeping king to accompany him to the dragon palace. Now the king and the dragon king followed by many demon deities went on a ship to the dragon palace. At the palace, the dragon king welcomed the king and said, "At the time of the division of the Buddha's relics, eight kings and four kinds of Buddhists, including priests, nuns, laymen, and laywomen, consulted and received the relics for the expiation of sins. If the king does not venerate these relics as I have done, you certainly will have sinned. I will erect a crystal pagoda and specially venerate it."

The king brought the relics to his country and placed them in the eighty-four thousand pagodas. When the king paid homage to them, the relics shed radiance.

Thus it was told and handed down.

4:4   HOW PRINCE KUNARA[256] REGAINED HIS SIGHT BY THE POWER OF THE LAW AFTER HIS EYEBALLS HAD BEEN GOUGED OUT

The great King Asoka[257] in India had a handsome prince called Kunara who excelled in uprightness and intelligence. The great king dearly

....

255. It refers to *yakṣha*, a female demon.
256. 拘拏羅. It refers to Kuṇāla or Dharmavivardhana, whose son Sampadi became the successor of Aśoka.
257. 阿育王. King Aiku or Asoka was the third king of Mauryan dynasty, reigning from ca. 269 to ca. 232 B.C. See note 139.

loved this prince who had been born to his former queen. The later queen, Taishirasha,[258] the stepmother of the prince, was deeply infatuated with his beauty and could only think of him.

One day, unable to control her desire for the prince, the queen went to his room and embraced him. The confused and shocked prince refused her. "Mother, what are you doing?" he asked, and left the room. The rejected and greatly ashamed queen began to hate the prince and decided to be avenged.

One day she secretly said to the great king, "The prince is in love with me. It is incestuous for one to desire his stepmother. Please pay attention to this matter and scold the prince." The clever king perceived her evil intention and assumed that her story was slanderous.

The great king stealthily called the prince and said, "If you stay in this palace, some evil will befall you. I will give you a distant country which you can govern and where you can spend your life. You had better listen to me. Don't rely on any edicts unless they contain my teeth marks." The king sent the prince to a distant country called Tokushashira.[259] The prince peacefully spent his days there for a long time.

The queen of the palace was not content with this arrangement and plotted against the prince. One night, she gave the king a great deal of liquor and took his teeth marks while the king was intoxicated and sleeping. She sent a messenger bearing an edict to the prince. The edict was marked with the imprint of the king's teeth and said, "Pluck out the prince's eyeballs and expel him from the country."

The prince received the edict. He read it. First he could not believe what he read but was convinced by the teeth marks of his father, the great king. For a while, he could not speak for sadness. "No, no. I shall obey the king's order," and the prince immediately called some men of the *sendara* class, the most debased people of India in those times, and had them pluck out both his eyeballs. Everyone in his country shed tears on hearing this.

The blind prince left his palace with only his wife and traveled toward the boundary of the country. It was a lonely journey for him and his wife. They wandered aimlessly, not knowing the way. The great king had never dreamed that this could happen to his loving son.

....

258. 帝尺羅叉. Taishirasha, Tiṣya-rakṣitā.
259. 德叉尸羅国. The country was famous for academic activities. See note 141.

While traveling, the prince and his wife happened to arrive at the compound of the great king's palace. Unaware that it was his father's palace, his wife led the prince to a hut where elephants were kept. The guard of the hut could not recognize the prince and his wife, who were shabbily dressed in ragged clothes after their long journey. He allowed the exhausted couple to spend the night.

The prince took a lute from one of his few packages of personal belongings and began to play. The soft melancholy tune reached the ears of the great king, who was resting in a palace tower. The playing of the lute resembled that of his beloved prince. The great king immediately called his attendants and ordered, "Search for the one playing the lute." The attendants traced the sounds to elephant hut, where a poor blind man played a lute in the company of a woman.

The attendant asked, "Who are you?" The prince said, "I am Prince Kunara, the son of King Asoka. When I was in Tokushashira, I received the king's edict ordering that my eyeballs be plucked out. Since I was expelled from the country, I have been wandering like this." "What?" exclaimed the startled attendants and could not continue. They immediately reported to the king, who was so shocked that he almost fainted. He called the blind prince and had him explain the whole story.

Having heard his explanation, the enraged king said, "This must have been your evil stepmother's scheme. What shall I do?" and he was going to punish her. The merciful prince, instead of urging vengeance, asked the king to forgive his stepmother.

The great king's heart was terribly pained to have his loving prince blinded. He invited a great arhat from temple of Bodhi Tree, who was famous for his virtue and his mastery of the Six Mysterious Powers.

The king tearfully asked the arhat, "Holy man, please be merciful and use your great influence to restore my son's eyesight." The arhat said, "Fine. I will preach the most effective teachings of the Buddha. Call everyone in the country to listen to my preaching. Each person should bring a bowl in which they will store their tears while listening to the noble teachings of the Buddha."

The king issued an edict and invited all the people in the country to the palace. Even from distant places, the people gathered in the palace like clouds. The arhat began to preach the most noble teachings of the Twelve Causations. Not a single member of the audience failed to shed tears in his bowl. All the tears in the bowls were gathered and placed on a golden plate. The arhat made a vow: "The Law that I am preaching is the ultimate truth of all the Buddhas. If my preaching is false, my prayers will not be realized. If it is true, may the prince regain his eyesight with these tears of my audience and be able to see everything clearly in this world again." As the arhat concluded his vow, he cleansed the prince's eyes with the tears collected on the golden plate. Lo and behold! The prince's eyes opened wide and he could see as clearly as before! The rejoicing king revered the arhat, bowing to him several times.

A stupa about sixty feet high was erected at the place where the prince's eyeballs had been plucked out. It is said that the blind of the country made vows before the stupa and gained their eyesight.

Thus it was told and handed down.

4:5   HOW SINNERS FELL INTO A HELL MADE BY KING AIKU

Long ago, King Aiku in India made a hell in his country and threw in the country's sinners. People who came near the hell were forced to fall in and never returned.

A very noble holy man once came to see the hell. A guard caught him and was about to throw him into the hell. The holy man said, "I have committed no sins. Why should I be thrown into the hell?"

The guard said, "Since the king issued an order, 'Those who come near the hell, regardless of their high or low status, and whether priests or laymen, shall be thrown into the hell,' I am going to throw you into the hell." The guard grabbed the holy man and threw him into the cauldron of the hell. The hell suddenly changed into a pure pond of lotus blossoms.

Seeing this, the astounded guard immediately reported to the king, who also was awestruck with a noble feeling, came near the hell, and paid homage to the holy man.

The guard said, "King, you issued the order, and you told me to throw all those who came near into the hell regardless of their status." The king replied, "When I issued the order, I neither excluded the king nor the guard. So I shall first throw you into the hell." The king threw the guard into the hell and returned to the palace. Later the hell was destroyed since it was regarded as useless.

Thus it was told and handed down.

4:6   HOW UBAKUTTA[260] OF INDIA TESTED HIS DISCIPLE

Long ago, about one hundred years after the Buddha's nirvana, an enlightened arhat, Ubakutta, lived in India. He had a disciple, a priest. Wishing to test his disciple, Ubakutta always warned, "Never approach any women. That will hold you in the cycle of life and death as if between turning wheels." Ubakutta repeated his warning to the disciple at every opportunity.

The disciple asked Ubakutta respectfully, "Indeed, you are my master, but why do you always watch me in this manner? I have already attained arhatship and have long avoided women." Ubakutta's other disciples also wondered, "It is strange of our master to insist on talking like this to such a noble disciple." Ubakutta continued to constantly scold the disciple.

The disciple traveled to a different place for a short time. While crossing a river on his way, the disciple saw a young woman also crossing. When the woman reached the deep part of the river, she almost fell and was swept away. "Priest over there, please help me," asked the woman.

The disciple tried to ignore her but felt such pity at seeing her carried away by the current that he took her hand and dragged her to the bank. Overwhelmed by the soft smooth feeling of the woman's hand, the disciple did not let go even after she reached the bank.

"Please release me. I am going now," said the woman. The priest held her hand more firmly, and the woman became suspicious.

"It is natural of you to feel this way. But I am quite attracted to you. Could you satisfy my wish?" asked the disciple.

"You saved my life when I almost drowned. On account of your virtue, I managed to prolong my life. How can I refuse what you ask?" replied the woman.

"That is what I want," said the disciple as he took her hand and led her into the pampas grass. The disciple placed the woman where no one could see them in the profuse grass. He opened the front of her clothing and of his clothing and entered between her thighs.

Concerned about being watched, the disciple looked back but

....

260. 優婆崛多. It refers to Upagupta, a Sudra by birth, who was renowned as almost a Buddha, who preached the Law for King Aśoka, and was the fifth patriarch, two hundred years after the Buddhaha's nirvana.

saw no one. Relieved, he turned his head to the front only to find his master, Ubakutta, lying on his back and holding the disciple between his thighs. As the disciple looked at his master's face, the master smiled, "How dare you lust in your mind and treat an old master of eighty-some years like this? Do you still insist that you do not intend to approach women?"

Without thinking, the disciple tried to run away. The master would not release him, but held him tightly between his thighs and legs.

The master, Ubakutta, insisted, "Since you have been overcome by your lust, quickly finish with me. Otherwise I will never let you go. How dare you trick me!" Raising his voice, Ubakutta abused his disciple harshly.

The passersby were surprised at Ubakutta's loud voice and gathered. They saw a priest held between the thighs of an old master. Ubakutta said to the people, "This is one of my disciples. Wishing to have intercourse with me, an eighty-some-years-old man, he dragged me into the pampas grass like this." Thinking it extraordinary, the onlookers harshly abused the disciple.

After exposing him to many passersby, Ubakutta got up and took the disciple to a large temple. He struck the bell, gathered many people, and explained in detail about the disciple. All those who heard laughed at the disciple, despised him, and ridiculed him with harsh words.

The disciple was so ashamed and embarrassed that he felt as if his body were broken into pieces. Yet, because of his great lamentations and deep regret for his sinful deed, the disciple finally attained the *arakanka* stage of enlightenment.

Ubakutta's method of leading his disciple into the Way was no different than that of the Buddha.

Thus it was told and handed down.

4.7   HOW UBAKUTTA MET THE YOUNGER SISTER OF KING HASHINOKU

Long ago an enlightened arhat called Ubakutta lived in India. Ubakutta was born after the Buddha's nirvana, and he was extremely anxious to know about the Buddha's life. He traveled, asking people, "Is any one alive who met the Buddha?"

Someone told him, "A nun, the younger sister of King Hashi-noku, now older than one hundred and ten years, met the Buddha in her childhood. She is the only person who knows about the Buddha when alive." Hearing this, the joyful Ubakutta visited the nun.

When Ubakutta arrived at the nun's place, he had someone de-liver his message. When the nun invited him in, she placed a cup of oil by the side of the door. Ubakutta was pleased and excited by the prospect of meeting the nun. He hurried into the room. The skirt of his robe brushed the cup and spilled a little of the oil from the cup on the floor.

When the nun saw Ubakutta, she asked, "Why have you come to see me?"

He answered, "Since I would very much like to know about the Buddha when alive, I have come to hear about him from you."

The nun said, "How sad it is to see such a decline in the Buddhist Law only one hundred years after the Buddha's nirvana! When the Buddha was alive, there was a disciple called Priest Rokugun,[261] who had bad manners and was extremely excitable. The Buddha always admonished and scolded him. On the contrary, you are indescribably noble, maintaining the precepts and having a stately appearance. Yet you spilled a little of the oil when your skirt touched the cup placed by the door. Even the Buddha's excitable disciple whom I mentioned never did such a thing! Judging by this, the teachings of the present day have become considerably degraded compared to the time when the Buddha was alive!"

Ubakutta was so embarrassed to hear this that he felt as if his body were broken into pieces.

The nun continued, "When I was young and small, the Buddha once visited my parents briefly and left. Suddenly my golden hair or-nament was missing. I searched without success. Seven days had passed since the Buddha left, and I found the ornament on the bed. Thinking this strange, I investigated and learned that the golden beams released from the Buddha had lingered at our place for seven days. The glow surpassed the radiance of my hair ornament and made it invisible. On the eighth day, the Buddha's glow disappeared, and the hair ornament

....

261. Rokugun (a group of six) may refer to the six disciples of the Buddha who always practiced evil deeds in a group. So they were called the group of six priests. How-ever, in the *Konjaku* tale, the term is used to identify one person.

finally became visible So the Buddha's beams were radiant for seven days after his visit. Since I was so small, I vaguely recall something like this, but nothing else."

Hearing this, Ubakutta was deeply moved and returned home in tears.

Thus it was told and handed down.

4:8   HOW UBAKUTTA HAD A TENMA[262] DEITY DESCEND

Long ago in India, an enlightened arhat called Ubakutta benefited the people as the Buddha had done. He preached the Law and cultivated those who came to hear his preaching so that their sins were expiated. A great number of people gathered to see him and listen.

Once when Ubakutta was preaching in a garden, a woman of matchless beauty appeared. Those listening to the Law were distracted by their lust. Seeing this woman, Ubakutta thought, "This must be a Tenma deity who has changed himself into a beautiful woman to interfere with people who are receiving benefits from the Law."

Ubakutta called the woman to come closer. When she approached, Ubakutta hung a wreath of flowers around her neck. "Oh, a wreath of flowers!" thought the woman, and she left.

When the woman looked at her wreath again, she found that only the soiled bones of animals, including human beings, horses, and cows, hung there. The disgusting odor was intolerable.

At that moment, the woman's original state, that of a Tenma, was restored. Tenma vainly tried to rid himself of the bones hanging around his neck. Tenma ran from the east to the west and from the north to the south, trying to rid himself of these hanging bones.

The people listening to the Law saw this and thought it most extraordinary. Out of despair, Tenma ascended to seek the help of the Great Jizaiten, the head of the Brahman deities. Tenma pitifully appealed to Jizaiten, "Please rid me of these bones!"

Jizaiten saw Tenma and said, "Since this was done by the Buddha's disciple, I cannot rid you of them. Just ask the person who put them around your neck to remove them."

Rubbing his hands, Tenma returned to Ubakutta and pleaded, "I

---

262. 天魔. Tenma or *māra* demons interfere and distract those who are trying to attain the Way.

regret that I foolishly assumed a woman's form and tried to interfere with the people who were listening to the Law. I will never do this again. Please, holy man, rid me of these bones!"

"Hereafter, never try to interfere with the Law," said Ubakutta, and he removed the bones from around Tenma's neck.

The pleased Tenma asked, "How can I repay you?"

"Have you seen the Buddha?" inquired Ubakutta.

"Yes, I have," answered Tenma. "I very much would like to know about the Buddha while he was alive. Imitate the Buddha's appearance for me," Ubakutta requested.

"Imitating the Buddha is easy, but being worshipped is unbearable for me," said Tenma.

Ubakutta insisted, "I will not worship you; imitate him and show me!"

"Don't ever worship me!" repeated Tenma as he disappeared into the forest. Soon he reappeared. His height was sixteen feet, his head was indigo blue, and his golden-hued body shone like the rising sun.

Although the overwhelmed Ubakutta tried not to worship him, he unconsciously shed tears, lay facedown, raised his voice, and cried.

Then Tenma revealed his original form with the remaining dirty bones hanging from his neck and said in distress, "This is why I warned you!"

Thus it was told and handed down.

4:9 HOW PRIEST DARUMA[263] OF INDIA TRAVELED AND OBSERVED THE BEHAVIOR OF PRIESTS

Long ago, a holy man called Priest Daruma traveled extensively throughout the five countries of India, observed the behavior of many priests, and reported to the people.

Once Daruma visited a temple where many priests lived. He was much impressed by the many noble deeds of the priests who were offering flowers and incense to Buddhas in one living area and reciting sutras in another living area.

Daruma saw one of these living quarters. It was dusty and had thick weeds, and no one seemed to reside there. Daruma went near

---

263. 阤棲摩. Daruma or Bodhidharma, the third son of the king of Kōshi in southern India, was the founder of Chan (Zen) Buddhism.

this area and discovered two old priests about eighty years of age, sitting and playing *go*. Daruma saw no Buddhist statues and no writings about the Law. He left their quarters thinking that playing *go* was the only activity of these two old priests.

On his way, Daruma saw other priests and he said, "I have been to a certain quarter where two aged priests were playing *go*."

The priests replied, "Since their youth, they have done nothing but play *go*. They don't know the Buddha's Way, so the other priests of this temple have not associated with them. They receive food offerings and futilely spend their months and years playing *go*. They are like heretics. Don't go near them."

However, Daruma returned, thinking, "These two priests may have certain reasons," and he entered the living quarters where the two old priests were playing *go*.

Daruma sat to one side between the priests and watched them play. When the *go* game ended, one of the priests rose while the other remained sitting. After a while, the sitting priest suddenly disappeared. Mystified, Daruma saw the two priests reappear together. Then they disappeared again. Soon they reappeared. Seeing the strange doings of these two aged priests, Daruma thought, "The temple priests despise these old priests and treat them as dirt because they play *go*. Their attitude is wrong. These old priests truly must be holy men. I think I will learn more about their activities."

Daruma asked the old priests, "What is this? I heard that you have been spending months and years doing nothing but play *go*. But I watched your splendid performance. Surely you must have attained the Way. I would like to know why you constantly play *go*."

The two old priests answered, "All these years, we have done nothing but play *go*. When the black stones won a game, our delusions increased; when the white stones won, our Bodhi or supreme wisdom increased. As we defeated the black stones, we thought we would increase the white stones of Bodhi wisdom. While doing this, we gradually realized the transiency of our life. Our virtue in recognizing this was immediately rewarded so that we have attained enlightenment."

Daruma greatly regretted his ignorance in not having appreciated these old priests and tears streaked his face like falling rain.

"Despite being regarded as useless wretches, you two priests concealed your merits these many years and have not let anyone of the temple know your virtues. How noble this is!" said Daruma. He reverenced the priests repeatedly and left their living quarters.

When Daruma informed the other priests, they pitifully regretted their past ignorance in despising these noble and enlightened priests.

After Daruma left the temple, he took shelter for the night in a village at the foot of a mountain. That night, he heard someone shout, "Many thieves have broken in and are going to kill me. They have robbed me of all the treasures that I have accumulated in the past. Villagers, come and help me!"

Hearing this, the villagers came out carrying torches in their hands and asked each other, "From where did the voice come?" One said, "The voice came from the direction of the holy man who lives in the forest to the east. Let's investigate that direction!" So the villagers went on noisily, carrying lighted torches and holding bows and arrows in their hands.

"Why on earth would anyone kill an ascetic?" asked anxious Daruma, as he joined the villagers.

In the forest, they saw a hut as small as a large umbrella. They opened the brushwood doors and saw an eighty-year-old priest sitting inside. A patched robe was his only clothing, and his only furniture was an elbow rest before him. They saw nothing that a thief could steal, and there was no thief in the hut.

The villagers questioned him, "We see nothing in your room that a thief would take. Why did you shout?"

"Why do you ask me this? The thief called 'Sleep,' who never set foot in this hut during past years, slipped in at dawn. Since he snatched the seven kinds of treasures in my storehouse, I tried to take them back. As we grappled, I shouted," said the holy man and cried bitterly.

Daruma thought, "While others have been relaxed and asleep, this priest has remained awake a long time and practiced the Way. When he was falling asleep, he shouted to overcome his drowsiness."

Daruma established a close relationship with the old priest and then returned. The villagers also left and returned.

Daruma visited another village. In the forest nearby, Daruma saw a priest who was constantly in motion; he was sitting at one moment, standing the next moment, dashing out, circling around, lying down, and getting up. He turned to the east, next to the south, then to the west, and then faced the north.

After smiling one moment and raging the next moment, the priest was now sobbing. Thinking that he was insane, Daruma approached the priest and asked, "What is happening to you?" The priest replied, "Right after a person is born in the Heavens, he is born in the Human Realm. Right after he is born in the Human Realm, he falls into the hells. Right after the hells, he is degraded and born in the Realm of the Hungry Ghosts. Then he is reborn in the Realm of Ashura, and eventually he is reborn into the Realm of Animals. In general, the unsettledness of things in these worlds and realms is like my state of mind and behavior. Hoping that my unsightly doings will make the people realize the transiency of things, I have been behaving in this way like an insane person for years." Daruma thought that the priest was certainly not an ordinary priest. He paid his respects and left.

Thus Daruma traveled around and observed the behavior of noble priests.

Thus it was told and handed down.

4:10   HOW PRIEST SŌTAKU OF INDIA UNDERSTOOD THE ABSOLUTE TRUTH AND WAS REBORN IN THE PURE LAND

Long ago, a priest named Sōtaku lived in central India. He was an ignorant fool by nature and continued to undergo the sufferings of life and death. Although he appeared to be a priest, he had neither practiced the proper ways of priesthood nor learned the sutras and vows by Buddhas and bodhisattvas. He aimlessly stayed at a temple for years, accepting the people's offerings but sinning by violating the precepts. He was shameless and never thought of his afterlife. The priests residing in the same temple dispised him and did not wish to be near him. They sometimes even tried to drive him from the temple.

However, Sōtaku had a bit of wisdom and relied on the truth of the Buddha's Body[264] of the Buddha and constantly thought of it by

....

264. Among various views about the Buddha's Body (*Buddha-kāya* or *Busshin*), the *san-shin* or the Three Bodies Theory is most commonly accepted in China and Japan. It includes the *hosshin*, or the true body of the Buddha; the *ōjin*, or the physical body of the Buddha adopted out of compassion to save sentient beings; and the *hōjin*, or the rewarded body resulting from his long practice and vows as a bodhisattva.

day and by night. While thus constantly thinking of the virtue of the truth, he finally perceived the Absolute Truth, which naturally affected him. Sōtaku thought of nothing else. He spent months and years solely concentrating on the truth. In his old age, he became bedridden. The priests in the temple scorned him more and treated him as if he were impure and soiled.

In his last moments, many Buddhas and bodhisattvas came to Sōtaku, preached the Law for him, and cultivated him. As his mind improved, his appearance became vivid and alive. Sōtaku got up, earnestly thought of the Buddhas, felt the Absolute Truth, and breathed his last.

Immediately, he was reborn in the Tosotsu Heaven. During that time, a light and delicate fragrance filled the temple. The priests of the temple found that Sōtaku had passed away. He had a vivid appearance and was sitting erect with his palms pressed together.

Seeing this, the impressed priests felt ennobled and pitifully regretted their contempt and disdain. Afterward, the priests sought out the deeds of Sōtaku, which they practiced.

So even if one sees a priest who practices nothing priestly and feels no shame, one should realize that the priest might have a reason, and one should never dispise him.

Thus it was told and handed down.

4:11   HOW AN ARHAT PRIEST IN INDIA WATCHED A MOUNTAINEER STRIKING HIS CHILD

Long ago in India, a traveling arhat priest saw a mountaineer beating a child with a tree branch. The arhat asked the mountaineer, "Why are you hitting this child and making him cry? And who is this child?"

The mountaineer answered, "That is my child. I was teaching him a song. Since he did not learn, I am beating him to teach him."

The arhat laughed at that. "Why do you laugh?" asked the mountaineer. The arhat explained, "You are hitting your child without knowing about your former life. The song that you are now teaching your child was composed by your child long ago when he was born as a mountaineer. Composing and circulating such a song seem clever at this moment, but will not benefit later generations at all. He was born ignorant, does not know about his previous life, and cannot learn the song which he composed.

"On the contrary, although the Buddhist Law appears insignificant at this moment, it enables future generations to recall the past and predicts the future. So one should definitely learn the Law.

"Now I will tell you what happened in the past. Listen to me carefully. Long ago, many travelers on the shores of the southern sea saw a large withered tree standing by the beach. They decided to shelter themselves under the tree for protection from the cold wind. They gathered, made a bonfire, and spent the night.

"Five hundred bats were living in a hollow of the tree. The travelers thought the smoke of the fire would cause these bats to leave the tree. Toward dawn, one of the travelers read the *Abidaruma* treatise.[265]

"Although choked by the smoke, these bats remained in the hollow to listen to the noble recitation of the treatise. When the flames rose, all of the bats were painfully burned to death. Not one remained alive. After they died, they were all reborn as human beings, thanks to their merit in listening to the treatise. They entered Buddhahood, became priests, understood the treatise, and attained arhatship. I am one of these arhats.

"So, you see, one should follow the Law. You should have your child enter the priesthood and learn about the Law." The mountaineer agreed, "We should follow the Law." He did so and had his child enter Buddhahood.

Shortly afterward, the arhat suddenly disappeared. The astounded mountaineer's faith became firmer and has become totally devoted to the Law. This happened some hundred years after the Buddha's nirvana.

Thus it was told and handed down.

4:12   HOW AN ARHAT PRIEST INFORMED A KING OF HIS
        PRINCE'S DEATH

Long ago, the people of a small country in India believed only in their gods and not in the Buddhist Law. The king of the country had a prince, his only child, and greatly loved him as if cherishing a jewel.

....

265. The *Abhidharma-piṭaka* is one of the three divisions of the Buddhist canons. It contains systematic treatises on Buddhist philosophy which are attributed to the Buddha's disciples and the distinguished Buddhist scholars who appeared several centuries after the Buddha.

When the prince was more than ten years old, he became seriously ill. Medicine did not cure the prince, nor did prayer, including that
of the Yin-Yang[266] way, reveal any efficacy.

The distressed king lamented day and night, but the months and
years passed vainly. The prince became more sick and did not improve.

The distressed king finally visited a god worshipped by the people of his country since ancient times.

The king offered the god various treasures heaped like mountains on carriages and as many horses, cows, and sheep as would fill a
valley. The king prayed to the god, saying, "Please cure my prince's
illness." The head priest, the other priests, and the maidens serving
at the shrine took as many treasures as they wished. They finally acquired such quantities that they became surfeited. There was still no
cure for the prince.

A shrine priest possessed by the god came out and said to the
king, "Your prince shall recover completely as you return to your
country. May you maintain the peace and the welfare of your country.
Everyone in your country will rejoice."

Hearing this, the king was overjoyed. Overwhelmed by his happiness, the king gave the great sword he wore to the priest. More
treasures were offered to other priests of the shrine.

The happy king hurried to his palace. On his way, he saw a Buddhist priest. The king asked his people, "What kind of person is he?
His appearance and his clothing are different."

The people answered, "He is a Buddhist priest with a shaved
head, a disciple of the Buddha." "He surely must be knowledgeable.
Summon him," said the king and stopped his carriage. The Buddhist
priest was brought before the king. The king said, "My prince has
been ill a long time. Neither medicine nor prayer has cured him. We
do not know whether he will live or die. What is your opinion?"

"Your child will surely die. There is no way to save him. He
probably will be unable to await your return to the palace," replied
the priest.

"The two priests spoke differently. Which spoke the truth?"
wondered the king. He became anxious and inquired, "A priest of

....

266. Yin and yang are the opposing principles in Chinese philosophy. Yin is the female
or negative principle related to such elements as shady, secret, and dark. Yang is
the male or positive principle related to such elements as light, and superior.

the shrine said the prince would live over one hundred years, but you speak differently. Which of you shall I believe?"

The Buddhist priest replied clearly, "Just to relieve your mind for a short while, the priest of the shrine said what he did not know. Why do you believe the ignorant?"

The king hurried to the palace and inquired about the prince. "The prince died yesterday," said his people. "Don't let any one know," said the king and sent someone to summon the god-possessed priest from the shrine.

Two days later, the shrine priest arrived at the palace. The king said, "My prince's illness is not yet cured. Since I don't understand why, I have summoned you." The priest, again god-possessed, said, "Why do you doubt me? Our god extends mercy and pity to all sentient beings and never ignores their concerns and appeals. The vow of our god is like that of a parent. I never speak falsely. If I do, may the king worship neither me nor my maidens in the service of the shrine," said the priest irresponsibly.

After the king listened, he seized the priest and said, "You have deceived the people for years. You took my treasures as you wished, being god-possessed, and fooled me and my people. You great thief! Quickly cut off his head!" The king had the priest beheaded. The king also sent his soldiers to destroy the shrine, which was thrown into a large river. The greater and lesser priests of the shrine had their hands severed. All of the shrine treasures gained and accumulated by deceiving the people for years were confiscated.

Later, the Buddhist priest was summoned by the king. When the priest arrived, the king himself came out and invited him into the palace, gave him the high seat, bowed to him, and said, "For years, I have been deceived by the shrine priests. I have never known the Buddhist Law, nor reverenced the Buddhist priests. I will never believe others' false words hereafter."

The priest preached the Law. The king and his people listened and felt immensely ennobled. A temple was built immediately in that location. The Buddhist priest and many other priests lived there and venerated the Law.

The temple contained a mystery. A canopy delicately decorated with jewels was placed over the statue of the Buddha. As one walked around the statue, the canopy also turned. When one stopped walking, the canopy ceased to turn.

The people of today don't know the reason and are baffled, saying, "Is it because of the Buddha's Mysterious Powers, or is it due to the excellent skill of the craftsman?"

Maidens have not served in the shrine ever since the time of the king.

Thus it was told and handed down.

4:13   HOW A PRIEST'S CULTIVATION OF AN EVIL DRAGON ENABLED A MAN OF INDIA TO ESCAPE THIS DANGER

Long ago in India, people used to travel with a priest as their guardian.

Once a man on a business trip boarded a boat. A sudden storm almost sent the boat to the bottom of the sea.

The boatman saw a novice in the water beneath the boat. "Who are you?" asked the boatman.

"I am a dragon king and will send your boat to the bottom of the sea," replied the novice.

"Why are you trying to kill us?" asked the boatman.

The novice explained, "The priest on board stayed at my place as a priest in my previous life when I had been born as a man. For years he received my veneration and offerings but never scolded and rectified me. He allowed me to sin and to become reduced to the status of a snake. I now suffer being cut by a sword three times a day. This is solely his fault. Because of my anguish and regret, I want to kill the priest!"

The boatman said, "These sufferings in the status of a snake and your daily agony from the sword cuts all result from the bad karma in your previous life. Why do you try to aggravate those bad results by foolishly harming and killing someone?"

The novice, the dragon king, insisted, "When I think of my former days, I become very confused and am concerned only because the priest did not cultivate me but allowed me to sin. Since I feel very wretched about my bad karma and sufferings, I am going to kill him!"

The boatman suggested, "Stay here for one day and one night. I will let you listen to the Law and leave your condition as a snake."

As he suggested, the dragon king remained for one day and one night. As soon as he listened to the priest's recitation of the sutra, his snake status changed and he was reborn into the heaven.

One should cultivate those who are close by telling them, "Only practice good deeds."

Thus it was told and handed down.

4:14   HOW A KING OF INDIA SAW A NAKED WOMAN AND CLOTHED HER WITH A ROBE

Long ago, a king of India took a large hunting party into the mountains. After a long march, the king and his people were quite exhausted. They saw a large tree in a mountain. Under the tree was a naked woman on a golden seat. The mystified king approached and asked, "Who are you, and why do you sit here like this?"

"I can produce sweet dews from my hands," said the woman. "Quickly produce some," said the king. The woman stretched out her hands and produced sweet dew, which she offered to the king. Being quite fatigued by their long trip, the king imbibed the sweet dew, which satisfied his hunger. He felt very content and happy.

Since the woman was unclothed, the king removed and gave her one of his robes. A fire spontaneously ignited inside the robe, which burned. The king thought the robe had caught on fire accidentally. He removed and gave her another robe. The same phenomenon occurred and the robe was burned. The king gave the woman three robes, all of which burned in the same manner. The woman could not wear any of them.

The astounded king wandered and asked, "Why did those robes burn, and why couldn't you wear them?" The woman explained, "I was once a queen in my previous life. The king venerated priests by preparing delicious food and robes. As a queen, I also venerated many priests by offering food. But I told the king not to offer the robes, and he obeyed. As a result, I now produce sweet dew from my hands but remain unclothed."

The pitying king asked, "How can I change your unclothed condition?"

The woman replied, "Please consider me only by venerating priests and offering them robes."

The king returned to his palace, prepared five robes, and intended to invite and venerate priests. However, that country had no priests to venerate. The distressed king invited a novice who had kept the five precepts, explained the situation, and requested, "Offer a prayer for the occasion and accept this offering!" The king offered the novice a fine robe.

Complying with the king's request, the novice held the robe in his hand and gave a prayer for the occasion. The king sent the robe to the woman. Since the robe had been sanctified, the woman had no difficulty in wearing it.

When a man and wife intend to venerate priests, they should be of the same mind, and not have different intentions as when one of them is opposed.

Thus it was told and handed down.

4:15   ABOUT HOKKI, A WEALTHY MAN OF THE COUNTRY OF SHAE IN INDIA

Long ago, an old man of eighty years lived in the country of Shae of India. Since he was so poor, he barely survived by begging for food. He had a wife whose hair was unequaled for length. People looked at her hair and said regretfully, "How fine it would be if a beautiful woman had this wife's hair." The wife used to say, "This hair embarrasses me."

Time passed. The couple was conversing in bed, "Due to what sort of karma resulting from our previous lives were we born to be so poor? It is because we did not practice good deeds in our former lives. If we do not perform good deeds now, our future lives will be the same. It will be fine if we could do even a little good!" Speaking thus, they lamented their improverished condition. However, they had nothing stored, nor any means to practice good.

The wife said, "I don't benefit by my long hair. I will cut and sell my hair, use that money for good deeds, and accumulate merit for our future lives."

The husband disagreed, "Your hair is your only treasure. Why do you say that you will cut it?"

"Don't you know that this life is transient? Even though one lives to a hundred, what good will hair be after one dies? Eventually my life will end. I am frightened when I think of my future life," said the wife, and cut her hair.

So the old man and his wife sold her hair for one *tō*[267] of rice,

---

267. *Tō*, a Japanese measure of capacity which equals 3.9703 gallons.

which doubled when cooked. They took the rice to the Gionshōja with carefully selected greens.

They first went to the living quarters of a high-ranking priest and said, "We have brought you two *tō* of cooked rice as our offering to the priests."

The surprised and mystified priests asked, "What sort of rice is this?" The wife answered, "We brought some greens and two *tō* of rice obtained by selling my hair. We would like to offer this rice to your disciples."

"Our custom is never to keep offerings for the temple priests in only one quarter. I'll strike the bell, and call more priests. You can fill each priest's bowl with your rice. I would not know what else to do." The priest struck the bell and collected three thousand bowls from the priests.

Seeing the numerous bowls, the confused old couple said to each other, "Because of our scanty offering, we may be caught and tortured by a mob of these priests. What shall we do?" The priests merely answered, "I don't know."

The old man spoke to his wife, "I have an idea. Let's pour all our rice into one bowl and run away." So the old couple poured all the rice from their pail into a bowl. However their pail still contained as much rice as before. Wondering if the bowl were unfilled, the old man looked at the bowl, which was full of rice and was taken away immediately. His pail also was full of rice. The old man filled another bowl with rice and the pail still contained as much rice as before.

The old couple filled all the bowls and completed their offering to the priests. The joyful old couple, still mystified, was about to return home.

At that time, merchants from a foreign country were driven near Gionshōja by winds. Their food was gone and they were exhausted by hunger.

The merchants begged for food, "We heard that a great offering for priests has been made today in the Gionshōja. We are helpless and fatigued from hunger. Please save us."

The old couple had the rice remaining in their pail. They offered it to the merchants. The merchants accepted the offering and finished eating the rice.

"This couple offered us the rice. They appear to be of lowly status. We have extended our lives thanks to their offering. We will be sinning if we do not reward them for their good deeds," said the merchants. Each divided his gold pieces into three portions and gave one portion to the old couple. Some gave the couple fifty *ryō*[268] of gold, others one hundred, and others one thousand. Just imagine how great a total the old couple received!

The old man went home with his wife and the gold pieces and became a man of unequaled wealth. He was called the Wealthy Man, Hokki, Rising Hair.

Thus it was told and handed down.

4:16   HOW IN THE COUNTRY OF KANDARA[269] IN INDIA A
PAINTING OF THE BUDDHA WAS SPLIT IN TWO FOR
THE SAKE OF TWO WOMEN

Long ago, a great king, Hashirika,[270] lived in the country of Kandara in India. The king built a pagoda embellished with seven kinds of jewels. One *ri* east of the pagoda was a half-length painting of the Buddha. A story tells why the painting of the Buddha was only half-length.

Long ago, a very poor woman lived in that country. She developed a pious mind and wished to have a painting of the Buddha. She went to an artist, talked about her wish, and told him to make such a painting of the Buddha.

A woman who lived near the first woman also wished to have a painting of the Buddha done. The second woman, too, went to the artist and told him to make her a painting of the Buddha. Being poor, both women did not offer enough to the artist of their paintings. So the artist made only one sixteen-foot-tall painting of the Buddha.

Days passed and the first woman, wishing to pay homage to her painted image of the Buddha, went to the artist and said, "I would like to worship my painting of the Buddha." The artist brought out the painting. As he showed it to the first woman, the second woman also wished to see and worship her painting of the Buddha. She came and asked the artist, "Have you finished my painting of the Buddha?"

....

268. *Ryō* is a unit of old Japanese coinage.
269. 乾陀羅国. It refers to Kashmir.
270. 波斯利迦. It may refer to King Kaniṣka, ruler of Gandhāra in the northern Punjab, who conquered northern India as far as Bactria. One of his various dates includes the close of the first century A.D.

"This is your painting," said the artist and he showed the second
woman the same painting he had shown the first woman. Seeing this,
the first woman said, "Is this then originally someone else's painting
although you said it was mine?"

The second woman also said, "In that case, this painting of the
Buddha is not mine." The confused women argued about the painting.
The artist explained the situation to the women, "Red paint and gold
dust are very scarce. It is said that both the customer and the artist will
fall into the hells if the painting lacks even one of the Buddha's many
features. Since your offerings were insufficient, I made one painting
for you both to benefit the two of you equally." However, the two
women did not stop arguing.

Finally the artist went to a statue of the Buddha, struck the *kei*[271]
stone, and said, "Since the offerings of these two women were insufficient, I made only one painting. I did not misuse any of their offerings.
But these women argue with each other. Even though I have explained
the situation to them, they do not stop arguing. Please, Buddha, understand our trouble and show us the solution. I am not at all guilty!"

Before the day passed, the painting of the Buddha split of its own
accord into halves above and below the waist.

So the artist with his pure mind had not misused the offerings,
and had appealed to the Buddha for a proper judgment. The Buddha's
image divided into halves of its own accord. The piety and veneration
of the two women who actually witnessed the marvelous power of the
Buddha was increased.

Thus it was told and handed down.

4:17   HOW A BUDDHIST STATUE OF INDIA BENT ITS HEAD
        SO THAT A THIEF COULD REMOVE THE JEWEL FROM ITS
        FOREHEAD

Long ago, a small temple in the country of Sōkara[272] in India had a
man-sized Buddhist statue. It was commissioned by the vow of the
previous king. The statue had a matchless jewel set in the center of its
forehead.

....

271. 啓. The *kei* stone refers to a kind of percussion instrument made of hard stone or
    copper and suspended from a stand before the altar.
272. 僧迦羅. Sōkara, Siṁhala, is present Ceylon.

A poor man thought, "The jewel of this Buddhist statue is priceless. If I take and sell it, my descendants for seven generations will be rich, comfortable, and free from poverty." The poor man thought of breaking into the temple at night, but found it impossible because the guards were constantly checking the names and destinations of those who entered and left the temple.

One night, however, the poor man carefully broke into the lower part of the gate and stealthily stepped through the hole into the compound. The man went to the front of the statue and tried to take the jewel, but the statue was too tall. Stepping on a higher stand, the man made a new attempt, but the statue was a little taller.

"Originally, this statue of the Buddha was man-sized. I wonder if the statue became taller because the Buddha grudges me the jewel," the man wondered as he withdrew, put his palms together in prayer, and bowed respectfully to the statue.

"The Buddha appeared in this world to practice the Way of the bodhisattvas to save us from suffering and to benefit us. I have heard that he would even sacrifice and never begrudged his life to save people. The Buddha practiced various virtuous acts such as saving a pigeon in danger from a hawk, offering his body to seven tiger cubs, plucking out his eyes to offer them to a Brahman, and bleeding himself to offer his blood for a Brahman to drink. Now how can he have begrudged me a jewel like this? His intention is to save the poor and the low.

"One does not remove a jewel from the Buddha's forehead under normal circumstances. I have been reflecting on this and am going to commit a serious sin against my wish. Why has he become taller? Does he begrudge me the jewel? This is contrary to my expectation!" Crying thus, the man appealed to the Buddha.

Then the statue of the Buddha, which looked taller, bent and lowered his head so the man could reach his forehead. "So the Buddha, responding to my wish, is telling me to take this jewel," thought man as he quickly removed the jewel from the forehead and left.

When dawn broke, the temple priests saw the statue and asked each other, "How has the statue lost his jewel from his forehead? Probably a thief took it." They searched for the thief, but did not know who had stolen the jewel.

Later, the man sold the jewel in a marketplace. A person who knew about the jewel saw it and said, "This is the jewel which recently

was stolen from the forehead of the Buddha's statue in that temple."
The person caught and took the man to the king.

At the king's investigation, the man explained everything. The
king did not believe him and sent a messenger to the temple. The
messenger went to the temple, looked at the statue standing with his
head bent, and returned to the palace.

At the messenger's report, the king was deeply moved. He felt
mercy in his heart, called the man who had stolen the jewel, bought
the jewel at the price the man wished, sent the jewel to the temple for
the statue and pardoned the man for his theft.

If one thinks sincerely of the Buddha, the Buddha will extend his
mercy even to a thief. Even today, the Buddha's statue will stand with
its head bent.

Thus it was told and handed down.

4:18   HOW A KING OF INDIA HAD A DRUNKEN ELEPHANT EXECUTE CRIMINALS

Long ago, a king of India released a great drunken elephant to punish
the rascals who violated the king's laws. The elephant, with its red
eyes and wide gaping mouth, threw the criminals down and trampled
them. No criminal remained alive in the country. The elephant was
regarded as the most valuable treasure of the country, and at the news
of this elephant, even enemies in neighboring countries did not dare
attack the country.

Once a fire broke out in the elephant hut. While the hut was being repaired, the elephant was moved to a priests' living quarters. The
head priest in the living quarters always recited the *Lotus Sutra*. As the
priest recited the sutra through the night, the elephant listened. On
the following day, the elephant appeared very restrained.

Meanwhile, many criminals were brought before the elephant.
The elephant was made drunk and released. But it only crawled on all
fours, licked the criminals' heels, and harmed none of them.

The surprised and confused king said to the elephant, "I have
been depending on you during these years. My country has fewer
criminals and no enemy attacks from neighboring countries. If you are
like this, how can I rely on you?"

A wise minister asked the king, "At what sort of place did this
elephant spend the night? I wonder if it was a priest's place?"

"That is correct," said someone. The minister continued.

"This elephant heard the priest reciting the sutra, developed a merciful mind, and will not harm the criminals. Take him near the slaughtering place immediately, have him spend a night there, and try him again."

Following the minister's suggestion, the elephant was sent near a slaughtering place and spent a night there. On the following day, when the elephant saw the criminals, he ground his teeth, opened his mouth wide, strode out, and trampled all the criminals to death. The king was immensely pleased.

We may assume by this that even an animal which listens to the Law will control his evil and develop a good mind. How could a conscientious man, listening to the Law, fail to discard his evil mind?

Thus it was told and handed down.

4:19   HOW A RAT IN THE CEILING OF A PRIEST'S PLACE IN INDIA LISTENED TO THE SUTRA AND OBTAINED BENEFITS

Long ago in India, after the Buddha entered nirvana, a priest always recited the *Lotus Sutra* in his living quarters.

Five hundred old rats were living in the ceiling of the priest's place. They listened to the priest's recitations for many years.

At one time sixty badgers came and ate all five hundred rats. The rats were all reborn in the Tōri Heaven. When their lives in the heaven ended, they all were reborn in the Realm of Human Beings. They met Sharihotsu and finally attained arhatship. Without falling into the Three Lower Realms, they will be reborn again when Miroku Buddha[273] appears in this world. They will be recorded as future Buddhas and will benefit others.

Even rats become like this just by listening to the sutra. If a person sincerely listens, and believes single-mindedly in the sutra, he certainly will achieve the Way and leave the Three Lower Realms.

As is said in a Chinese writing, "A white rat is three hundred years old. A rat will become white after he is one hundred years old, and will know both good and evil things within the span of one year and the

---

273. Miroku or Maitreya-bodhisattva living in Tusita Heaven will come down to this world to succeed Śākyamuni Buddha.

distance of one thousand miles. Such a rat is called Jinso, or the Divine Rat." So even rats could attain the Way by listening to the sutra.

Thus it was told and handed down.

4:20   HOW A KING OF INDIA SUMMONED A MAN'S WIFE AND THE MAN ESCAPED THE DANGER OF SNAKES BY RECITING THE THREE TREASURES

Long ago in a remote place in India, a man had a beautiful wife. He and his wife were deeply in love and lived together for years, cultivating a close relationship.

At one time, the king was searching through the country for a beautiful woman to be his queen without regard to birth or class.

Someone reported to the king, "A incomparably beautiful woman lives in a certain village of a certain district." The king was pleased to hear this and sent a messenger to summon the woman. The man said to the king again, "The woman has been married for a long time. The couple had vowed fidelity for a hundred years. I wonder how we can separate them. If you summon the woman, they will escape into a mountain and hide. You should first summon the husband, prove him guilty of a crime, and then call the wife." "That sounds reasonable," said the king, and he sent his messenger to summon the husband.

As the messenger arrived at the couple's place, he read the king's order. "I have done nothing against the king. Why am I summoned?" asked the husband. The messenger gave him no answer, but escorted him to the palace.

The king saw the husband who had done nothing special of which to be accused. The king thought of sending him on an errand and said, "Four kinds of lotus blossoms are blooming in a large pond to the northeast at a distance of forty miles. Go there and return with the blossoms within seven days. If you bring them, you will be rewarded." Receiving the king's order, the worried husband returned home.

His wife prepared his meal, but the husband did not eat, and was lamenting.

"Why are you sad and why don't you eat your food?" asked the wife. The husband told her about the king's order. "Quickly eat your food," said the wife and the husband ate. Afterward, the wife said, crying, "I have heard that there are demon deities on the way to the pond and that poisonous snakes coil around the stems of the blossoms in the pond. How sad that you and I will be separated while alive. Even if we have pledged ourselves for a thousand years, soon your life will be taken by the demon deities. What use is it for me to remain here alone? I will die with you." The husband coaxed her, explaining, "I wish to take you, but now the king has caused me this trouble, and I may do something contrary to his intention. It is useless for both of us to die. So you remain here."

The husband did his best to stop his wife from accompanying him. Finally the wife understood her husband and advised him, "Many demon deities are on your way. If they ask who you are, say that you are a disciple of the Shaka Buddha of this world. When they ask you what sort of teachings you have learned, tell them that you have learned the teachings of faith in the Buddha, the Law, and the Priests."

The wife packed food for seven days and sent her husband away. She saw him off, he looked back at her several times, and the couple immensely resented their separation.

On the fourth day, the husband arrived at a gate guarded by a demon deity. Seeing the husband, the demon deity was pleased at the thought of devouring him and asked, "From where have you come?" "I am a disciple of the Shaka Buddha of this world. I have come here at the king's order to take the four kinds of lotus blossoms," answered the husband.

"I never heard the name of the Shaka Buddha until now. But, on hearing it, I am changed and am leaving the state of a demon. I will excuse you on account of this. There are more demon deities to the south, and you should tell them the same thing," said the demon and released the husband.

The husband continued on his way and saw another demon, who was also pleased to see him. When the demon asked the question, the husband answered as before. When the husband was asked, "What kind of teachings have you learned?" he recited the teachings of the Three Treasures.

The demon was exalted to hear this and said, "Even though I have lived for innumerable *kalpa* years, I have never heard until now of the teachings of the Three Treasures. Now I have met you and have listened to the teachings with joy in my mind. On account of this, I am leaving the state of a demon and will be reborn in the heaven. If you go farther south, you will encounter many poisonous snakes, which are ignorant and unable to distinguish good from evil. They surely will try to swallow you. Remain here for a while. I will get the blossoms and bring them for you." And the demon deity left.

Soon the demon returned with the four kinds of lotus blossoms, offered them to the husband, and said, "The king told you to bring them within seven days. Five days have already elapsed since you left home. There aren't many days left and you may have difficulties in returning on time. Ride on my back. I will carry you there quickly."

The demon deity took the husband on his back and arrived at the palace in a short while.

As soon as the husband had dismounted, the demon deity disappeared. The husband took the blossoms to the astonished king, who questioned him suspiciously.

As the king listened to the detailed story of the husband, he was overjoyed and said, "I am inferior, even to the demon deities, since I attempted to take your wife by harming you. These demons are superior because they spared your life. I will excuse your wife forever. Quickly go home and uphold the teachings of the Three Treasures," and the king released the husband.

The husband returned home and told his wife everything. The overjoyed wife, together with her husband, continued to uphold the teachings of the Three Treasures.

Thus it was told and handed down.

4:21   HOW A MAN ACCUSED BY A KING ESCAPED HIS PREDICAMENT BY VENERATING THE THREE TREASURES

Long ago, a man in India committed a crime against the king and was accused. The king caught the man. When the man was about to have his head cut off, he appealed to the king, "Please allow me seven more days." The king granted his appeal and allowed the man seven days.

The man returned home and sincerely venerated the Three Treasures for seven days. He went to the king on the morning of the eighth day. The king was pleased to see the man return and was about to have him beheaded.

Just at that moment, the man suddenly assumed the appearance of a Buddha. Observing this, the king stopped the beheading, made a large elephant drunk, and tried to have the elephant trample the man to death. The man released golden rays and five lions from his fingertips, which made the drunken elephant run away.

The king was frightened and awestruck at these mysterious revelations and asked, "What sort of virtue enables you to act like this?"

The man replied, "After I went home, I venerated the Three Treasures for seven days. On the eighth day, I returned to you." The king pardoned the man's faults and became greatly devoted to the Three Treasures.

Venerating and believing in the Three Treasures brings one countless merits.

Thus it was told and handed down.

4:22 HOW A MAN OF THE COUNTRY OF HARANA[274] PLUCKED OUT HIS WIFE'S EYES

Long ago, a man of the country of Harana of India had incorrect views and did not believe in the Buddha's Law. Although his wife was a devoted Buddhist, she had never practiced the Way because of her husband.

At one time, the wife accidentally had met a priest and had secretly learned more than ten lines of the *Lotus Sutra*. Naturally, the husband discovered this and said to his wife, "It's quite noble that you learned the sutra," and left home.

The frightened wife anxiously awaited her husband. He returned home and said, "On my way, I saw a very beautiful woman lying dead in the street. Since she had very good eyes, I plucked them from her face and brought them. Your eyes are ugly and I don't like them. Exchange yours for these!"

The wife grieved intensely, saying, "If my eyes are plucked out, my life will not last. I will die immediately." Her grieving wet nurse said, "You disobeyed your husband and read the sutra against his will. Now you are destroying yourself so futilely."

"My life is transient and I finally will die, no matter how much I resent it. I would rather die for the sake of the Law than to age meaninglessly and become withered," said the wife and cried tearfully with her wet nurse.

The husband in the parlor called the wife in a loud and harsh voice. The wife had no means of escape. When she stepped out of her room, thinking, "Now I am going to die," her husband caught her,

274. 波羅奈国. It was an ancient country in central India. See note 36.

pulled her on his lap, plucked out her eyes, dragged her into the street and abandoned her. The passersby pitied her and gave her something to sit on, which was placed at the intersection of the streets. The wife lay on it and, although without eyes, survived and spent thirty days there.

One day, a priest came and asked her, "Who are you and why are you lying here without eyes like this?" The woman explained her situation to him. The priest heard her story and pitied her. He brought her to a mountain temple and took care of her for ninety days.

One night toward the end of the summer, the blind wife dreamed that the two characters *myō*, marvelous, and *hō*,[275] the Law, of the sutra which she had read became the sun and the moon, descended, and entered her eye sockets. The blind wife awoke. To her surprise, she saw many delightful comforts and pleasures in the higher realms, including the Six Heavens, as clearly as if looking at her own palm. She also saw the various hells, including the Bottomless, and the Black Ropes,[276] and the dying and surviving sentient beings at a distance of twenty thousand *yujun* below this world, as if reflected in a hanging mirror. The rejoicing wife told her dream to her priestly master, who felt it most noble and was immensely overwhelmed with mixed feelings of pity and joy.

The blind wife obtained her mysterious sight by the power in merely ten lines of the *Lotus Sutra*. Just imagine how if one recites an entire copy of the sutra with a sincere mind, his merits will be countless.

Thus it was told and handed down.

4:23   ABOUT DAITEN, A MAN OF INDIA

Long ago, four hundred years after the Buddha's nirvana, a man called Daiten lived in the country of Matora.[277] His father once went abroad to another country on business.

....

275. 妙法. *Myōhō* refers to the first two Chinese characters denoting "marvelous" and "the Law" included in the title of the *Myōhōrengekyō*, the *Lotus Sutra*.

276. The Black Ropes refers to Kālasūytra, or the black-rope hell, the second of the eight great hells where those who committed robberies and murders are tortured by being bound with the chain of hot iron and struck by the hot iron hatchet.

277. 末度羅国. Mathurā, an ancient country in central India, was located southwest of the present-day Jumnā River. It was one of the sixteen great countries at the time

During his father's absence, Daiten thought of looking for a most beautiful woman to be his wife, and searched but could not find such a woman.

Daiten returned home from his search and, seeing his beautiful mother, thought, "No woman is more beautiful than she." He made his mother his wife, and led the life of a man and wife with her for months.

One day Daiten heard that his father was returning by sea and would land soon. He thought, "Since I took his wife as my wife, he will certainly think ill of me when he comes home and sees us." Daiten hurried and killed his father before he came home.

Daiten lived afterward without anxiety. He once took a short trip to another place. Returning home, he discovered that his wife had been with a neighbor for a while. Daiten thought, "My wife may be intimate with the neighboring man." The idea made him furious. Daiten caught his wife, his mother, and beat her to death. Thus he killed both his parents. Out of fear and shame, Daiten left his home and lived in a distant place.

One day, an arhat priest from the Daiten's former place came to where Daiten was living. When Daiten saw the arhat, he was afraid, thinking, "I left my old place since I was ashamed and frightened at having killed my parents. Here nobody knows my past. Now this arhat has come. He may tell everything to the people here. I have no other choice than to kill him." Daiten killed the arhat. Now Daiten had committed three grave sins. Later Daiten [lacuna]

4:24   HOW RYŌJU[278] MADE A MEDICINE OF INVISIBILITY WHEN HE WAS A LAYMAN

Long ago a holy man called Bodhisattva Ryōju lived in India. When still a layman, he learned the teachings of the heretics. Some laymen, including Ryōju, congregated and made a medicine of invisibility. Producing such a medicine required cutting parasitic vines into five-inch lengths and drying them in the shade for one hundred days. The

---

of the Buddha. It was a center of Buddhist activities and contains early remains, such as the three pillars dating from the time of Aśoka.

278. 龍樹. Ryōju or Nāgārjuna, born about the second or third century in South India, was the founder of the Mādyamika school of Mahāyāna Buddhism.

medicine was made from these dried branches. After someone learned certain occult methods and wore the medicine at the base of his hair knot, he would become as invisible as if wearing a magic riding cloak.

The three laymen, including Ryōju, cooperating mentally, wore the medicine on their heads, entered the king's palace, and violated the various queens. The queens were frightened by someone invisible touching them and confided to the king, "Recently, invisible persons have come near and touched us."

The wise king thought, "This is because someone made and is using the medicine of invisibility. The solution is to sprinkle powder or flour over the palace floor. Even though their bodies are invisible, their footprints will tell us where they are." Planning thus, the king ordered a quantity of white dirt like ashes to be sprinkled over the entire floor.

The king had the ashes sprinkled while the invisible men were in the palace and sent many armed men into the palace. Those men swung their swords and slashed at the places where they found the footprints. Two of the invisible men were cut down. The last one, Ryōju, pressed by the slashing swords, had no refuge but to crouch on the floor with a queen's skirt over his head as he made many vows. Perhaps because of this and the capture of the two invisible men, the king stopped the hunt, saying, "So these two are the invisible men."

Later, taking advantage of the relaxation of security, Ryōju stealthily left the palace and ran away.

"The heretical teachings are useless," said Ryōju. He went to [lacuna], entered the priesthood, and learned and transmitted the Buddhist Law. People called him Bodhisattva Ryōju and greatly venerated him.

Thus it was told and handed down.

4:25   HOW THE TWO BODHISATTVAS RYŌJU AND DAIBA[279]
        TRANSMITTED THE LAW

Long ago, Bodhisattva Ryōju lived in the western part of India and was blessed with unlimited wisdom and benevolence. At about the same time, another holy man called Bodhisattva Daiba lived in central

----

279. 提婆. Bodhisattva Daiba refers to Āryadeva, who lived in southern India in the
     third century. He became a disciple of Nāgārjuna and was regarded as the founder
     of the Mādhyamika school in India.

India. He also possessed deep knowledge and had strong convictions about spreading the Law.

Daiba heard about Ryōju and his unlimited wisdom. Thinking of learning the Law from Ryōju and transmitting it, Daiba started to travel to western India.

It was a long journey. Daiba traveled a great distance. He crossed deep rivers, walked over hanging bridges, crawled and climbed through deep mountains, and traversed wide plains. Sometimes he lacked water and at other times lacked food. He only tolerated such hardship because of his strong wish to learn and transmit the unfamiliar Buddhist Law.

After a painful journey of months, Daiba finally reached Ryōju's place. Daiba stood at the gates and waited for someone to lead him. A returning disciple of Ryōju saw Daiba. The disciple asked, "Why have you come?" "I have something to tell your master," answered Daiba.

The disciple reported about Daiba to his master, Ryōju. Ryōju sent another disciple to question Daiba, "Where did you come from and what sort of person are you?"

Daiba replied, "I am from central India. I heard that the great master, Ryōju, possesses unlimited wisdom. This is a distant and difficult place to reach from where I live. I am old and tired. Traveling on foot all this distance was unbearable. Yet I have strong convictions about learning and transmitting the Buddhist Law. I thought I might arrive here if I will have any karmic association with the spread of the Law. So without concern for my health and body, I have come here like this."

The disciple reported what he had heard from Daiba to his master. Ryōju asked the disciple again, "Is he a young or an old priest? How does he look?"

The disciple said, "He must have come a long way. He appears to be thin and quite exhausted, but looks very noble. He is sitting by the gateway."

Ryōju took out a small box containing water and said to his disciple, "Offer this box to the priest." The disciple gave the box to Daiba. Daiba took the box, saw the water, and pulled a needle from the collar of his robe. He put it into the box and returned the box to the disciple. The disciple took the box to Ryōju, who was surprised and greatly confused to find the needle at the bottom of the box and said, "A really wise man truly exists. It was very impolite of me not to receive him promptly, but to have my disciple make many inquiries."

Ryōju immediately had his people sweep a room, prepared a clean seat, and was going to send the disciple to welcome Daiba.

This puzzled disciple addressed Ryōju, "Daiba, a priest from another country, silently remained outside the gates. Master Ryōju asked why the priest had come here. Daiba gave master Ryōju his reason. Master Ryōju offered him a box containing water. I handed the box to Daiba, thinking that he would quench his thirst after the long journey. Instead of drinking the water, Daiba pulled a needle from his collar, put it inside the box, and returned the box to Master Ryōju. I thought that Daiba had offered Master Ryōju the needle, but Master Ryōju left the needle in the box. Now I don't understand why you, Master Ryōju, are inviting Daiba with such courtesy."

Ryōju laughed scornfully and said to his disciple, "Your wisdom is so limited. Daiba told me that he had come a long distance from central India to transmit the Law. Instead of commenting on his reasons, I offered him a box filled with water. I meant that although the box was small, the shadow of the wisdom of Daiba who crossed ten thousand miles would be reflected on the boxed water, and also that my wisdom and knowledge were as limited as the amount of the water in the box. With these intentions, I offered him the box filled with water. Daiba naturally understood my meaning, and placed his needle at the bottom of the water, which meant that Daiba wished to search and know the depth of the great sea of my wisdom by his small knowledge comparable to the needle.

"Even though you have lived and been together with me all these years, your wisdom is so limited that you failed to perceive all these meanings. Despite the fact that Daiba has come from a distant place, he reads my mind very well. The presence or absence of wisdom creates the great difference between these who are superior and inferior." Hearing this, the disciple felt as if his heart and body were shattered.

Obeying Ryōju's orders, the disciple transmitted his master's words welcoming Daiba. So finally Daiba met Ryōju, learned the Law as if water in one jar were completely poured into another jar, returned to his country, and transmitted the Law.

Thus being or not being wise causes a great distinction among individuals.

Thus it was told and handed down.

4:26 HOW THE TWO BODHISATTVAS MUJAKU[280] AND SESHIN[281] TRANSMITTED THE LAW

Long ago in India, nine hundred years after the Buddha's nirvana, a holy man called Bodhisattva Mujaku lived in the country of Ayuja[282] in central India. He had deep knowledge and had made strong vows to save others. At night, he ascended to the Tosotsu Heaven to learn the teachings of the Larger Vehicle from Miroku, and in the daytime descended to this world to spread the Law among the people.

Mujaku's brother, Bodhisattva Seshin, lived in the country of Jōbu of Northern India. He also possessed an extensive knowledge and a benevolent heart. At one time, Binzuru,[283] a disciple of the Buddha, taught Seshin the teachings of the Lesser Vehicle, which Seshin favored. Yet Seshin was ignorant of the teachings of the Larger Vehicle.

In the distance, Mujaku heard of this and wished to encourage his brother to learn the teachings of the Larger Vehicle. He described his wish to one of his disciples and sent him to bring Seshin immediately.

The disciple went to the country of Jōbu[284] and delivered Mujaku's message. Accepting his elder brother's invitation, Seshin prepared for his journey. That night, Mujaku's disciple recited a Larger Vehicle sutra called the *Jūjikyō*,[285] which told about the ten stages of attaining bodhisattvahood.

....

280. 無着. Mujaku or Asaṅga (310–390) was born in Puruṣapura of Gandhāra in North India. After studying the *Mahāyāna sutra*, he expounded the teaching of Yogācāra. His many able disciples included his younger brother Vasubandhu.

281. 世親. Seshin or Vasubandhu, a son of Kaniṣka and a brother of Asaṅga, was first a Hīnayāna devotee, but was converted to Mahāyāna by Asaṅga. He is said to have written one thousand books, five hundred each for Hīnayāna and Mahāyāna. The Yogācāra school founded by Asaṅga and Vasubandhu was opposed to the Mādhyamika school of Nāgārjuna and Āryadeva.

282. 阿輸遮国. Ayuja or Ayodhyā in central India is famous as the site of the epic *Rāmāyaṇa* and the residence of Asaṅga and Vasubandhu.

283. Binzuru may refer to a person of the same name who appears in note 211.

284. 丈夫国. The country refers to Puruṣapura, present-day Peshāwār, an ancient country in North India which was located north of Punjab and northeast of Kashmir. Its king, Kaniṣka, built many temples and stupas there, and it eventually became a center for Mahāyāna studies. It is said to be the birthplace of Asaṅga and Vasubandhu.

285. 十地経. *Jūjikyō*, the *Daśabhūmika-sūtra* or *Shi-di-jing*, is a chapter of the *Avataṃsakasūtra* dealing with the ten stages of a bodhisattva. The Sanskrit text was edited by J. Rahder in 1926.

Seshin heard the recitation, but the meaning of the sutra was too profound for him. Seshin thought, "All these years, I have foolishly preferred the Lesser Vehicle and never heard such a profound teaching of the Larger Vehicle. My sins in slandering the Larger Vehicle must be very grave. Such slander was caused only by my tongue. I will cut off my tongue immediately." Seshin took out a sharp knife and was about to cut off his tongue.

At that moment, Mujaku saw this in the distance by his Mysterious Powers. He stretched out his hands, caught Seshin's hands, and stopped him from severing his tongue. Although the distance was three *yujun*, Mujaku instantly appeared, stood by the side of Seshin, and said, "You are quite foolish in trying to sever your tongue. The teachings of the Larger Vehicle tell the truth and are praised by many Buddhas and holy men. I want to teach you this Law. Don't cut off your tongue, but quickly learn the Law. Cutting off your tongue is not repentance. Once you slandered the Larger Vehicle with your tongue. Now you can praise it with the same tongue!" After saying this, Mujaku vanished as if he were wiped out.

Seshin rejoiced at Mujaku's words and gave up the idea of cutting off his tongue. Seshin later went to Mujaku and, with deep feelings, learned the teachings of the Larger Vehicle for the first time. He learned as well as the water of one jar which is entirely poured into another jar.

Elder brother Mujaku's cultivation was marvelous. Later Seshin composed more than one hundred treatises on the teachings of the Larger Vehicle and transmitted them extensively throughout the world. He was called Bodhisattva Seshin and was highly revered by the people.

Thus it was told and handed down.

4:27   HOW BODHISATTVAS GOHŌ[286] AND SHŌBEN[287] ARGUED ABOUT NON-EXISTENCE AND EXISTENCE

Long ago, Bodhisattva Gohō, a disciple of Seshin, lived in the country of Makada of India. Since he was superior in his knowledge and in

286. 護法. Gohō or Dharmapāla, born in the middle of the sixth century, was one of the great scholars of the Vijñaptimātratā (Yuishiki) school.
287. 清弁. Shōben or Bhāvaviveka, a learned monk who retired from the world to await the coming of Maitreya.

transmitting the Law, he had many disciples. About the same time, Shōben, a disciple of Daiba, also had profound knowledge and many disciples.

Shōben insisted on the view of non-existence, while Gohō took the view of existence. They argued, each defending the truth of his viewpoint. Gohō suggested, "Someone should judge the truth and error of our views. We should quickly ascend to the Tosotsu Heaven and ask Miroku, the Future Buddha."

"Yet, since Miroku is still in the ranks of the bodhisattva and in [lacuna], we should not ask him but should wait until he attains Buddhahood," replied Shōben as he continued to argue with Gohō.

Later, Shōben bathed in water, refrained from eating cereals, went before a Kannon statue, made a vow chanting the *darani*[288] charms of Shūkongō, and prayed, "I shall remain as I am until Miroku appears in this world and I meet him." Shōben prayed thus for three years. Finally Kannon appeared in reality and asked Shōben, "What do you want?" Shōben replied, "I would like to remain in this world until the appearance of Miroku." Kannon said, "One's life does not last forever. Practice good deeds and wish to be reborn in the Tosotsu Heaven." Yet Shōben still insisted, "I only wish to remain here and wait for Miroku."

"In that case, go to the deity Shūkongō, who resides in a mountain cave of the country of Danakachaka.[289] If you pray single-mindedly, chanting the *Shūkongō darani* charms, he will realize your wish," suggested Kannon. Complying with the Kannon's words, Shōben went to the cave, recited the charms, and prayed three years more.

Finally, the deity Shūkongō appeared and asked Shōben, "What do you ask, and why do you do this?" Shōben replied, "I wish to remain in this life and await the appearance of Miroku. Kannon suggested this request."

The deity said, "A palace called Asora[290] is inside the cave. If you pray in the manner prescribed in the Law, the cave wall will open of

288. 陀羅尼. The *dhāraṇī*, mystical invocations which realize the wishes of the reciter of the *dhāraṇi*, are included at the end of the *Prajñāpāramita-hṛdaya-sūtra* (*Taishō*, VIII, nos. 250–255, 257). For an English translation, see *The Manual of Zen Buddhism* by D. T. Suzuki.

289. It refers to Dhanakataka, which was an ancient kingdom northeast of modern Madras.

290. 阿索洛. Asora may refer to the palace of *asura*. See note 103.

its own accord. You can enter the palace through the opening and will see Miroku as you arrive."

"But the interior of the cave is too dark for anything to be seen. Now can I see Miroku appear?" asked Shōben. "When Miroku appears, I will come and tell you," said the deity. Complying with the deity's words, Shōben single-mindedly concentrated in prayer for three additional years. Finally, when he chanted the Charms of the Poppy[291] and struck the cave wall, the wall moved and opened.

At that time, thousands of people came up to the cave, but nobody wished to enter. Shōben, standing by the cave entrance with his legs apart, said to the people, "After my long prayers, I am finally going into this cave to await Miroku. If any of you wish to see Miroku, enter the cave with a sincere mind." Those hearing him became frightened and did not approach the mouth of the cave, but said, "Many poisonous snakes live in this cave. People entering will surely lose their lives!"

"I am going," Shōben insisted, and entered the cave. Only six men followed. After they entered, the cave wall closed.

Some regretted not entering the cave and others were frightened. Thus it was told and handed down.

4:28 HOW THE WHITE SANDALWOOD STATUE OF KANNON OF INDIA APPEARED IN THIS LIFE

Long ago, after the Buddha's nirvana, the country of [lacuna] in India had a temple called [lacuna]. The temple had a white sandalwood statue of Kannon, which revealed marvelous effects and collected many visitors. If one sincerely prayed to the Kannon, observing abstinences and refraining from eating cereals and gruel for seven or twenty-two days, the delicately adorned Kannon would appear from the wooden statue, release lights, and become visible to its devotees. The Kannon would pity them and realize their wishes. Since the Kannon had appeared like this several times, many people had faith in it.

A rectangular fence had been built around the statue at a distance of about seven paces to avoid possible damage by visitors and spectators. The visitors now worshipped the statue from outside the fence and did not come closer.

....

291. The passage reminds us of the well-known command "Open, sesame!" in the tale of the *Arabian Nights*.

When the devotees threw flowers at the statue as offerings, if the flowers hung on its hands or arms, they knew this good omen meant their wishes would be realized.

A priest came from another country to study the Law. He once visited the Kannon, bringing various kinds of flowers as offerings, and prayed for the realization of his wishes. The priest made garlands of the flowers, went to the statue, bowed deeply, knelt, and wished three times. "First, when I return to my country after studying the Law, if my journey will be easy and safe, may the first garland hang from your hands; second, by the good deeds I practice, if I will be reborn in the Tosotsu Heaven and see Bodhisattva Miroku, may the second garland hang from both of your arms; third, certain Buddhist writings say that some do not have the Buddha nature at all. If I have the Buddha nature and will attain the Way after my practices, may the third garland hang from your neck!"

After the priest finished his prayer, he tossed his three garlands at the distant statue. All the garlands hung from the statue as the priest had hoped. He knew all his wishes would be realized, and was ecstatic with joy.

The caretaker of the temple was watching near the priest. He thought this extraordinary and said, "I am sure, holy man, that you will attain Buddhahood. At that time, I hope you will not forgot our present association, and that you will deliver me." The priest promised and left. Those who watched repeated the story.

Thus it was told and handed down.

4:29   HOW A MOUNTAINEER OF INDIA SAW AN ARHAT IN MEDITATION

Long ago there was a mountain with steep peaks in India. After the Buddha's nirvana, thunder caused the mountain to collapse.

A mountaineer crossing the mountain once saw a very thin and withered priest sitting with closed eyes. His long hair and beard hung over his face and down his shoulders.

The mystified mountaineer reported this to the king. The king led his ministers and hundreds of officials to the mountain, paid his respects, and venerated the priest.

"This priest appeared to be very noble. Who is this?" asked the king. A priest among the king's retinue replied, "He is a Buddhist arhat who has entered meditation to extinguish desire. Since he has done this for years, his hair and beard have grown long."

"How can we awaken him and ask him questions?" the king asked the priest.

"His body, which was nourished by ordinary food, will collapse when he ends his meditation. So I suggest that you make a sound and awaken him," said the priest.

The king had someone pour milk over the arhat and sound hammers. The arhat's eyes opened and he said, "Who are you? Even though I appear humble, I am wearing a priestly robe."

The priest replied, "I am a priest."

"Where is my master, Kashō?" asked the arhat.

"He entered nirvana long ago," answered the priest. Hearing this, the arhat grieved and lamented.

After a while, the arhat asked, "Has the Shaka the Buddha attained the Way?" The priest answered, "Yes, he has. He benefited many people and also entered nirvana." When the arhat heard this, he lowered his eyebrows.

Soon afterward, the arhat held his topknot in his hands, ascended into the air, and revealed great Mysterious Changes, burning his own body, emitting fire from his body, and dropping his bones on the ground.

The king picked up the bones together with many people, built a stupa for them, venerated the stupa, and returned to the palace.

Thus it was told and handed down.

4:30   HOW A BRAHMAN OF INDIA TOOK SKULLS TO SELL

Long ago, a Brahman in India took many skulls to the city to sell and shouted, "I have gathered and brought many skulls. Does anyone wish to buy my skulls?" Nobody bought his skulls. Seeing the Brahman unable to sell his skulls and lamenting, many people gathered. They abused and ridiculed him.

A wise man came and bought a skull from the Brahman. The Brahman carried his skulls on a string looped through their ear holes. Seeing the wise man carrying the skull without a string, the Brahman asked, "Why don't you pass a string through the ear holes of the skull?"

"I do not thrust something through the ear holes of the skull of a person who once heard the *Lotus Sutra*," said the wise man as he left with the skull.

The wise man built a stupa, placed many more skulls in it, and offered a service of veneration for them. At that time a celestial person descended, worshipped the stupa, and left.

So the wise man, just to fulfill the wish of the Brahman, bought a skull without any purpose, built a stupa, placed more skulls within, and offered them a service of veneration. The rejoicing celestial beings descended and paid their respects to the stupa.

Thus it was told and handed down.

4:31   HOW A KING OF INDIA DRANK MILK, BECAME ANGRY, AND TRIED TO KILL GIBA[292]

Long ago, a king in India had a mean characteristic. The king always appeared drowsy, was absent-minded, and was constantly napping. The ministers and noblemen noticed that the king was peculiar and said to each other, "Our king does not look normal He must be sick since he always appears drowsy." They summoned eminent medical men and inquired about the king's condition.

"The king is ill. We shall give him milk immediately," said the medicine men. They offered the king milk. The king drank the milk, felt sicker, and became very angry. "This is not a medicine at all but a very evil poison," said the king and had the medicine men beheaded. The king was not cured but became more sleepy as time passed.

Another distinguished medicine man was summoned. The medicine man asked the king's mother, "How were you when the king was born?" The king's mother replied, "I dreamed a large snake violated me and I gave birth to the king." The medicine man was convinced and thought, "The king is the snake's son. This is why he is always so drowsy and sleepy." The medicine man thought of all possible treatments for the king's condition and concluded that the only remedy was milk. The medicine man thought this futile when he remembered the other medicine men who were killed for offering the king milk.

After much thought, the medicine man finally mixed milk with other medicines to mask its appearance and offered the mixture to the king, saying, "This is another kind of medicine."

....

292. See note 221.

The king drank it, but thought it tasted like milk. He became angry and ordered his men, "Catch the medicine man who gave me the prescription and bring him here!" The messengers were sent to catch the medicine man. Anticipating that this might happen, the medicine man who had offered the king the medicine had arranged for a fast horse and fled.

The messengers reported this to the king, who again ordered, "Go and catch him!" The messengers pursued the medicine man, who was now fleeing in a distant place. They finally caught up with him in three days.

As he was being escorted, the medicine man thought, "Having taken my medicine, the king may be cured and feeling better. Yet there is a chance that he is not cured. Returning with these messengers to lose my head is quite useless."

On the way, the medicine man selected herbs which were a deadly poison. He said to the messengers, "These are most delicious," and ate the herbs. Seeing the medicine man eating the herbs, the messengers ate them, too, and died instantly.

The medicine man immediately took an antidote and was saved. Since the messengers had not taken the antidote, they were all dead now.

Thinking that everything had gone as he planned, the medicine man secretly returned to the city and hid for a time. Thanks to the efficacy of the milk mixed with other medicine, the king was finally cured, and his condition became normal. When the joyful king ordered a search, the medicine man timidly appeared. The king summoned him, gave him gifts, and praised him. The people of the country heard about the medicine man and immensely appreciated him. Afterward, milk was offered to the king, who was the child of a dragon.

Thus it was told and handed down.

4:32   HOW AKADA,[293] A MEDICINE, WAS SENT TO A KING OF CHINA

Long ago in the [lacuna] dynasty of China, a king had a prince. The prince was handsome and [lacuna]. So [lacuna], his royal father, greatly cherished him.

---

293. 阿竭陀. "*Akada*" may refer to *agada*, a medicine or elixir of life that rids one of disease.

The prince had been seriously ill for months. The lamenting king offered prayers to the heaven. No medicine was effective in curing the prince, whose sufferings increased.

The king had a minister who was also a distinguished medicine man. The king did not ask the minister's help since they were on bad terms. The king was very confused in his dilemma. He wished to ask the minister's help but had a grudge against him.

The king finally summoned the minister, since the minister was extremely skilled in medicine. The pleased minister came. The king said, "During all these years, we have been estranged and have held grudges. But my prince is suffering from an illness. I have called other medicine men to no avail. Ignoring my grudge, I have summoned you. Quickly cure my prince!"

"Truly, I have received no orders from the king during the past years, and I have felt as if I were existing in the darkness of night. Now that you wish my services, I feel as though I have been directed toward the dawn. I will examine the prince's condition immediately," said the minister.

The king took the minister to the prince's room.

After examining the prince, the minister said, "We should prescribe a medicine to cure him," and left. The minister soon returned with a medicine saying, "If the prince takes this, he will be cured instantly." The pleased king took and looked at the medicine. He asked, "What do you call this medicine?"

The minister really brought a poison, thinking, "This is not a medicine but a deadly poison that will kill instantly as one takes it. I will call it a medicine and kill the prince, taking advantage of the situation and satisfying my grudge of the past years."

When the king asked the name of the medicine, the minister became confused and answered haphazardly, "This is called Akada." The king said, "I hear that those who take the medicine will not die. If one hears the sound of a hand drum which is coated by this medicine, one will get rid of his illness. So if one imbibes it, how can he not be cured?"

With deep faith, the king had the prince take the medicine, Akada. The prince was cured instantly. The minister returned home quite mystified since the prince did not die but was cured instantly. The king rejoiced that the prince was cured by the minister's help.

After night fell, the king heard someone knocking at the door of his room. The suspicious king asked, "Who is it?" "The medicine, Akada," was the reply. Thinking this most extraordinary, the king opened the door and saw a good-looking young man and woman standing there.

The couple came before the king and said, "We are the medicine Akada. Today the minister brought you a deadly poison which would kill anyone instantly. He called it medicine and offered it to kill your prince. When you asked the minister the medicine's name, the confused minister accidentally called it Akada.

When you, the king, with your deep faith, were about to have your prince take the poison, in Mount Hōrai[294] we faintly heard someone calling our name, 'Akada.' Since we did not want people to know that taking Akada would cause instant death, we hurried here and were taken by your prince, who was immediately cured as a result. We have come here again to let you know." As soon as they said this, they vanished.

Hearing this, the astounded king felt as if his heart were crushed. He first called the queen and questioned her. Unable to conceal anything about the minister, she exposed everything. The minister was beheaded. Thanks to the medicine Akada, the prince lived a long life without illness.

So whatever one does should be done with faith. Thanks to the king's deep faith, the prince's illness was cured.

Thus it was told and handed down.

4:33   HOW A WEALTHY MAN AND A BRAHMAN OF INDIA
        HAD THEIR OXEN COMPETE IN A TEST OF STRENGTH

Long ago in India, a wealthy man and a Brahman had their oxen compete in a test of strength. Each bet a thousand pieces of gold on the match. They set the date and examined their oxen. There would be many spectators.

The wealthy man looked at his ox and said, "My ox looks quite bad. His horns, face, neck, and hindquarters appear weak." Hearing his master's complaints, the ox felt ashamed and decided, "Surely I will lose."

When the day came, the wealthy man's ox lost and the wealthy

---

294. 蓬萊. It refers to a Chinese legendary mountain where the immortals live.

man handed one thousand pieces of gold to the Brahman. After returning home, the wealthy man scolded his ox, saying, "Since you lost
the match, my thousand pieces of gold were forfeited. It's a pity that I
can no longer rely on you."

"Your criticism lowered my morale and weakened me. If you
wish to regain your gold, you should arrange another match and praise
me." After listening to his ox, the wealthy man challenged the Brahman to another match, saying, "This time, I will bet three thousand
pieces of gold!"

Relying on his former luck, the Brahman agreed, saying, "So the
second bet will be three thousand pieces of gold!"

As suggested, the wealthy man praised his ox immensely and
had him compete against the Brahman's ox. The two oxen straggled
against each other with their horns. The Brahman's ox lost this time,
and the Brahman gave the wealthy man three thousand pieces of gold.

So praise and compliments will improve matters and bring one
merit.

Thus it was told and handed down.

4:34   HOW TWO BROTHERS OF INDIA CROSSED A MOUNTAIN

Long ago, two brothers lived in India. The two brothers once were
crossing a mountain, each carrying one thousand pieces of gold.

The elder brother thought, "I will kill my younger brother, take
his money, add it to mine, and have two thousand pieces of gold." The
younger brother also thought, "If I kill my older brother and take his
money, I will have two thousand pieces of gold." Thus the two brothers thought the same thing, but had no chance to act on their ideas.

Meanwhile, they crossed the mountain and reached a river. Suddenly, the older brother threw his gold pieces into the river. Seeing
this, the younger brother asked, "Why did you throw your gold pieces
into the river?"

"While crossing the mountain, I thought of killing you for your
money, However, you are my only brother, and I would not think of
killing you if it were not for these gold pieces. So I have thrown them
away," said the elder brother.

"I, too, thought of killing you, older brother. It's all because of
these pieces of gold," said the younger brother, who also threw his
gold pieces into the river.

One loses his life because of avarice for food, while another harms himself by his greed for property. Those who are poor and propertyless certainly should not lament. Circling through the Six Realms results from greed, avarice, and indulgence.

Thus it was told and handed down.

4:35   HOW A DISCIPLE OF THE BUDDHA SAW AN OLD MAN CULTIVATING A FIELD

Long ago, a priest, a disciple of the Buddha, went out and saw an old man and a young man cultivating a field. "So they are farmers," thought the priest while passing. Suddenly, the young man fell on the ground and died. The old man saw this but said nothing and stood, using his hoe. The puzzled priest thought, "The old man saw the sudden death of the younger man. He did and said nothing, but just stands there. How unfeeling he is!"

The priest asked the old man, "Didn't you see the man die? Who is he?" "This is my son," replied the old man. Thinking it more extraordinary, the priest continued, "Was he your first or second son?" "He was neither the first nor the second, but our only child," said the old man. The priest thought it most unusual and asked the old man again, "Does he have a mother, and where is she?" "She lives at the foot of the mountain emitting smoke over there."

"This old man may be a terrible thief. At least I will tell this to the mother," thought the priest and began running.

The priest finally arrived at the mother's house and entered. He saw an old woman with white hair braiding jute.

The priest said, "Your son and husband were cultivating the field over there. Suddenly your son collapsed and died. But the old man ignored him and continued cultivating the field. What is the matter with him?"

The priest thought that the old woman would mourn at the sad news. On the contrary, the old woman showed no surprise, but just continued braiding as she said, "So it should be done."

The puzzled priest reiterated, "The old man was not affected by seeing his son die in front of his eyes. I thought that most strange, hurried here and told you, the mother of the son, about this. Yet, you are not disturbed at all either. Why are you like this? If there is a reason, I would like to know it."

The old woman explained, "We really should mourn over him. But when the Buddha once preached the Law for a year, my husband and I went to hear him. The Buddha preached, 'All lives are void, and thinking them non-void is wrong. So one should understand and regard everything as being void.' Since we heard that sermon, we have understood that everything is nothing. So we remain unconcerned even by the death of our son."

The priest felt very embarrassed to hear this. Even humble farmers believed in the Buddha's Law and did not mourn over their child's death. On the contrary, the priest, the disciple of the Buddha, did not realize this and had incorrect views about the old couple. The priest was ashamed and left.

Thus it was told and handed down.

4:36   ABOUT THE PARROT OF THE COUNTRY OF ANSOKU[295]

Long ago the ignorant people of the country of Ansoku of India did not understand the Law. At that time in the country, a parrot appeared which was yellow, white, and blue and spoke like a human being.

The king of the country and others, including ministers, were amused by the parrot and had him talk. Although the bird was fat, he appeared weak. The people thought that the bird should have food and asked, "What do you eat?" The bird replied, "I will be nourished and become stronger by hearing someone calling 'Amida Buddha!'[296] There is no other food for me. If you wish to nourish me, you should utter the name of Amida Buddha."

So the people of the country, including men and women, the high and the humble, all recited "Amida Buddha." The parrot regained his strength, ascended into the sky, descended to the ground, and said to the people, "Would you like to share the pleasures of paradise?" "Yes, we would," some replied. "If so, ride on my wings," said the parrot. So some of the people rode on his wings. The parrot said again, "I am still weak. Please call Amida's name again and make me stronger." As

....

295. 安息国. Ansoku or Parthia is modern Persia, from which several priests came to China in the Later Han dynasty.

296. 阿弥陀佛. Amida Buddha is the lord of the Pure Land, whose merits are expounded in the *Kanmuryōjukyō*. See *Taishō*, XII (no. 265).

those on his wings recited the name of Amida, the parrot instantly ascended into the air and flew away toward the west.

All the spectators, including the king and the ministers, thought this most extraordinary and said, "The parrot is the incarnation of Amida Buddha, who came to this distant country to cultivate the ignorant people." The parrot and the people who rode on his wings never returned. "Isn't this really an instance of attaining the Way while alive?" The people built a temple on that spot, called it the Temple of the Parrot, and practiced chanting the name of Amida Buddha on every abstinence day.

After that, the people of the country of Ansoku knew a little about the Buddhist Law, and those reborn in the Pure Land of Amida increased.

Thus Amida Buddha led even those who particularly did not think of him with a pious mind. If one thinks of Amida with one's entire heart, one will certainly reach his paradise of Amida.

Thus it was told and handed down.

4:37 HOW A LARGE FISH ARRIVED AT THE BEACH OF THE
       COUNTRY OF SHUSHISHI[297]

Long ago in India, an unknown and isolated island was several miles from the southwestern extremity of the country of Shushishi. More than five hundred families on the island made their living by fishing and had never heard of the Law.

Several thousand large fish once came near the shore of the island. The pleased islanders came to the beach and found that each fish spoke like a person and shouted, "Amida Buddha."

Not knowing the meaning, the islanders called them the Amida fish after the sound of the fish calling out, "Amida Buddha." When the fishermen shouted, "Amida fish," the fish came near the shore. So the fishermen brought many more fish to the shore by frequently shouting, "Amida fish." The fish did not attempt to leave even if the fishermen tried to catch them.

The islanders ate the fish, which tasted delicious. The fish tasted sweeter when "Amida" was shouted more frequently, and tasted bitter

....

297. 執師子. It was a country in present Ceylon.

when "Amida" was shouted less frequently. Soon all the people on the beach indulged themselves in eating and constantly said, "Amida."

Meanwhile, an islander who had eaten the fish first died as his life span ended. Three months later, the man appeared on the beach riding purple clouds which released lights. He said to the people, "I am the oldest of those people who caught and ate the large fish. After my life was ended, I was reborn in the paradise of Amida. This is because I recited Amida's name as I was overwhelmed by the taste of the fish. The large fish was the incarnation of Amida Buddha, who pitied our ignorance, changed himself into the large fish, encouraged us to recite his name, and let us eat him. On account of my association with Amida, I was reborn in the Pure Land of Amida. Those who don't believe me should look at the fish." As he concluded, he disappeared.

The rejoicing people looked and discovered that all the discarded fish bones had become lotus blossoms. Seeing this, the islanders developed pious minds, stopped taking life, and recited the name of Amida.

Since all the islanders were reborn in the Pure Land, the island eventually had no inhabitants and became deserted for a long time. The great arhat [lacuna] Gen went to the island by his Mysterious Powers and repeated the story.

Thus it was told and handed down.

4:38   HOW A POOR MAN OF INDIA OBTAINED WEALTH

Long ago, a man in India was born to a family of high standing, but was poor and had no way to earn his living. He barely lived by begging from others.

The people shunned him and closed their doors. The poor man lamented greatly. Out of his grief, he visited a temple known for the efficacy of Yakushi,[298] the Medicine Buddha there.

The poor man, with a sincere heart, circled the Yakushi Buddha's statue, repented of his sins in his former existence, fasted five days, and remained in front of the statue with his palms together in prayer.

An extremely dainty and noble person who looked like a small priest appeared in his dream and said to the poor man, "Because of your sincere repentance for the bad deeds in your former existence,

....

298. 薬師佛. Bhaiṣajyaguru, Buddha of Healing, resides in the Land of the Pure Emerald in the east. See *Taishō*, IX, 53a–55a.

your bad karma should immediately end and you will obtain wealth. Quickly return to the old home of your parents."

When he awoke from his dream, the poor man went to his parents' house, which had only decayed poles and eaves surrounded by crumbling walls. It did not look like a place where he should remain, even for a short while. Yet the poor man stayed there, believing the words of the small person.

A few days later, the man dug in the ground of the old house with a stick and unearthed treasures. He remained there with these abundant treasures and became rich within a year.

Even though the man's parents owned a great amount of treasure, the man could not inherit them and became poor because of his bad karma from his previous existence. But thanks to the Buddha's help, he could obtain his parents' stored treasures.

Thus it was told and handed down.

4:39   HOW ARHAT MADENJI[299] MADE A STATUE OF MIROKU BUDDHA

Long ago, a temple in Darirasen[300] of the country of Ujōna[301] in northern India had a ten-*jō*[302]-high gilded wooden statue of Miroku Buddha.

The statue had been made by Great Arhat Madenji after the Buddha's nirvana. The arhat said to the statue, "Shaka Buddha entrusted all his disciples to Miroku after his nirvana. Those who offered a handful of food, uttering once, 'Namo, with respect,' as prescribed in the Shaka's teachings, would be delivered from the cycle of life and death at the time of the Three Meetings[303] upon Miroku's appearance in this life. However, Miroku has ascended to the Tosotsu Heaven. How can we sentient beings see Miroku? The statue that I made may not have

....

299. 末田地. Madenji or Mdyāntika, a native of Dahara in India and a disciple of Ānanda, established Buddhism in Kashmir.
300. 達麗羅川. Darirasa, the old capital of Udyāna, present-day Mangir, produced much gold in ancient times.
301. 島杖那国. Ujōna, an ancient country in North India, was in the Swāt Valley.
302. One *jō* equals ten feet.
303. 三會. The Three Meetings refer to the three great Buddhist services for the delivery of all sentient beings. Both the various Buddhas in the past and the future Buddhas deliver sermons at meetings to save those who have failed to be cultivated by Śākyamuni.

the true appearance of Miroku. So with my mysterious powers, I will ascend to the Tosotsu Heaven, look at Miroku three times, and make another statue of him."

At that time, Miroku said to Madenji, "With my mysterious sight, if I see people in all the realms and worlds who wish to make my statues, because of this merit I will save them from falling into the Three Lower Realms. When I attain Buddhahood, they can come to my place with my statues as their guides." Miroku continued praising the arhat, "How wonderful that you will come to my place and make my statue at the end of the five millenia of the Shaka's Correct Views."

The statue ascended into space, releasing a great radiance and explaining verses. All those who heard the verses rejoiced with tears and attained the enlightenment of the Three Vehicles.[304]

Thus it was told and handed down.

4:40   HOW A POOR WOMAN OF INDIA COPIED THE *LOTUS SUTRA*

Long ago a poor woman in India had neither treasures nor children. The woman thought, "At least I intend to have a child on whom I can rely," and prayed the Buddhas and gods for a child. The woman immediately became pregnant and had an incomparably beautiful baby girl. The girl became ten years old. Her mother intensely cherished the girl, and anyone seeing her praised her. However, being so poor, the woman could not find a husband for her daughter.

One day, the mother thought, "More than half of my life has passed, and the remainder may not be long. I will copy the *Lotus Sutra* and accumulate merit for my future life." However, the mother had no money to copy the sutra.

Seeing her mother mourn, the daughter suggested, "I have accumulated no treasures. Although I may live long, eventually I will die and become ashes. My present asset is my long hair. I will sell it to pay for copying the sutra." The mother tearfully regretted spoiling her daughter's appearance. But the daughter was decisive and left home to sell her hair.

As she went from door to door to sell her hair, everybody invited

----

304. 三乗. The Three Vehicles in Mahāyāna include *shōmon, enkaku,* and *bosatsu* (bodhisattva). See note 96.

her in, praised her matchless beauty, and did not want to cut her hair to buy it.

The daughter thought, "Probably, these people do not need my hair. I will go to the king's palace and sell my hair there."

When the daughter was about to enter the palace, she saw a man of the lowly *sendara* class who had a frightening inhuman look. Seeing the daughter, the *sendara* man said, "At the king's order, I have been looking for someone like you for days. Finally I have found you and shall kill you quickly."

"I have done nothing wrong. I am going to the palace to sell my hair and fulfill my filial duty. Why should I be killed?" asked the girl.

The *sendara* man said, "The king has a thirteen-year-old prince who has never spoken since birth. A physician suggested that the prince should take a medicine, the liver of a longhaired incomparably beautiful girl. I have been searching for such a girl throughout the country and there is no one superior to you. I shall take your liver immediately."

The daughter tearfully begged for her life. The *sendara* man insisted, "If I let you go, I will be blamed. I cannot let you go," and the *sendara* man was about to split her bosom with his sword. The daughter appealed once more, "Although you won't release me, at least tell the king about me." The *sendara* man complied with her wish and reported the matter to the king.

The king summoned the daughter and found that she was a matchless beauty. "She can provide the very medicine for which we have been searching," said the king. The daughter appealed to the king, "I don't begrudge giving my life for the prince. But I have a poor mother at home. Since we have no treasures, I decided to sell my hair to have the *Lotus Sutra* copied as my mother wishes. If my mother hears that I have lost my life in the palace, her grief will be intolerable. Please let me go home to tell her of the king's order and I shall return here. I will never disobey the king's order."

"Your suggestion is very reasonable. Yet I want my prince to speak as soon as possible. I cannot send you home!"

The daughter prayed tearfully, "I left home to fulfill my filial duty and now I will lose my life. Buddhas in all directions, please help me." Seeing the daughter behind a hanging screen, the prince felt great pity and spoke for the first time, "Great king, please do not kill the girl."

At the prince's voice, all people present, including the king, his ministers, and other officials, greatly rejoiced.

The king said, "I foolishly intended to kill such a filial daughter. Buddhas in ten thousand directions, please forgive me."

"My prince spoke, thanks to your merit," said the king and gave the daughter countless treasures.

The daughter returned home and told her mother the story. The joyful mother and daughter had the *Lotus Sutra* copied as prescribed in the Law and venerated it. The *Lotus Sutra* had this much efficacy.

Thus it was told and handed down.

4:41   HOW A MAN YEARNING FOR HIS CHILD WENT TO KING YAMA'S[305] PALACE

Long ago in India, a priest practiced the Way but was unable to attain arhat status even though he became sixty years old. He mourned over the situation but could do nothing. He thought, "I have practiced all these years but could not become an arhat. I think I will return to the laity and remain at home," and he became a layman.

Later the man took a wife who gave birth to a most handsome baby boy. The father intensely cherished the boy. The boy suddenly died at the age of seven. The grieving father could not dispose of his son's body. A neighbor came and said, "It is foolish of you not to dispose of your son. You cannot keep the baby forever. You should dispose of it immediately." The neighbor seized the dead son and disposed of the body.

His grief intolerable, the father so much wished to see his son that he considered going to King Yama's palace and asking the king to let him see his son once more.

Since he did not know King Yama's whereabouts, he asked various people. Someone said, "If you go for such a distance in such a direction from here, you will reach a large river by which stands a palace decorated with seven kinds of jewels. King Yama resides in that place."

The father went farther, as instructed. He actually came to a large river and to the palace decorated with the seven kinds of jewels. The joyful father timidly approached the palace. A noble-looking person appeared from the palace and asked the father who he was.

305. See note 84.

The father replied, "My son died at the age of seven. I miss him unbearably and came to appeal to King Yama to let me see my son again. I hope that King Yama mercifully will allow me to see my son."

The person reported this to the king, who granted the father's wish, "Let him see his son, who is in the garden behind the palace."

The joyful father went to the garden and saw his son playing among other children of the same age. The father called his son and said tearfully, "I have missed you so much that I came here to ask King Yama to let me see you. Don't you miss me as much as I miss you?"

Although the father tearfully questioned his son, the son did not seem to have missed him but continued to play without paying attention to his father. The father shed resentful tears, but his son did not appear to feel anything and said nothing. Finally, the father thought his laments were useless and left.

The reason may be that the son had already left this life, but his father who still remained in this world retained a mundane mind and was affected by his yearning and sadness.

Thus it was told and handed down.

CHAPTER 5

5:1   HOW SŌKARA[306] AND FIVE HUNDRED MERCHANTS WENT TO THE COUNTRY OF THE RASETSU[307]

Long ago in India, Sōkara and five hundred merchants boarded a ship for the south sea to hunt for treasure. A sudden gale carried their ship south as fast as an arrow, and it finally went aground on the beach of a large island.

Although the island was unknown, Sōkara and the merchants felt relieved at having arrived on the beach and all got off the ship in confusion.

Shortly afterward, about ten beautiful women appeared and went on singing. Seeing these good-looking women, Sōkara and the merchants, who had just been mourning their unfortunate fate in drifting to an isolated island, were immediately caught by lustful desires and called these women.

The women approached gracefully. At a little distance, they appeared more beautiful and friendly. Sōkara and the merchants said affectionately to the women, "We sailed to the south sea to hunt treasure, and met a sudden gale, which brought us to this unknown island. While bitterly grieving over our situation, we saw you and our worries vanished. Quickly lead us to your place and care for us. Since our ship was destroyed, we cannot return."

"We surely will take care of you as you wish," and the women led the way for Sōkara and the merchants.

---

306. Sōkara is present-day Ceylon.
307. 羅刹. It refers to a demon.

They soon arrived at a stately gateway flanked by high stone walls. After they entered the gateway the doors were locked. The compound had various small buildings. The residents were all women and not a man was in sight. Each merchant took a woman as he wished. They loved each other so much that they did not separate for a single moment.

Thus their days passed The women took daily naps, and their beautiful sleeping faces looked somewhat strange.

Sōkara sensed something peculiar about these women. One day he stealthily got up and investigated the compound while the woman napped. Finally he came to a part of the compound which he had never seen.

It was surrounded by stone walls with a strongly bolted gate. Sōkara carefully climbed the wall and looked inside. To his surprise, he saw many dead and living men, some groaning and others crying. He also saw many bleached bones and red bones with flesh scattered on the ground.

Sōkara called a living man and asked, "What kind of people are these? And why have they become like this?"

The man replied, "I am from southern India. While at sea on a business trip, I was blown by a sudden gale to this island. Indulging in an amorous life with these women, I forgot to return home. All I saw in this country were women. Even though we were very much in love, when a new ship of merchants came to the island, the old husbands were confined in a place like this, had their Achilles tendons cut, and eventually became the food of these women. If another ship arrives, you, too, will become like us. So be careful and escape from here. These women are Rasetsu demons and take a daily nap of about six hours. They won't know if you escape from here. This place is strongly enclosed by iron and we cannot run since our Achilles tendons have been cut. How sad it is! Quickly run away," the man said tearfully.

"So this is why I thought it strange," reflected Sōkara. He returned to his place and went around to tell this to the merchants while the women still slept.

Sōkara hurried to the beach, and the merchants followed him. Since they had no means of escape, they lined up on the beach facing the world of Fudaraku,[308] the place of Kannon. They recited

....

308. 浦陀落. It refers to Potalaka, the land of Avalokiteśvara (Kannon), which is located to the south in the Indian Ocean.

the name of Kannon in unison. Their voices echoed and resounded greatly.

As they recited single-mindedly, a huge white horse appeared out in the sea. The horse galloped, splashing through the waves, and sat before the merchants. "Surely, this can only be the assistance of Kannon," thought the merchants who mounted and clung to the horse as much as they could. The horse went out across the sea.

The women awoke and saw no merchants in the compound. "They have run away," said the women as they raced each other in chasing after the merchants. After leaving their place, they saw the merchants and Sōkara crossing the sea mounted on the horse. Seeing this, the women resumed their original state as Rasetsu demons one *jō* tall and cried aloud, jumping up and down four to five *jō* high. One of the merchants, thinking of his wife's beautiful face, lost his grip on the horse and fell into the sea. The Rasetsu demons immediately went into the water, dragged him out, and devoured him.

Finally, the horse arrived at the beaches of southern India and sat on the ground. As soon as the rejoicing merchants and Sōkara had dismounted, the horse disappeared. They thought, "Certainly Kannon has aided us." They thanked Kannon and each left for his home. But none spoke about this.

Two years later, one of the Rasetsu women, Sōkara's woman, appeared where Sōkara was sleeping alone. The woman appeared several times more beautiful than when he had seen her the first time. She came near and said, "Thanks to a certain karmic relation from our previous lives, we became a married couple and our relation was very deep. Yet you abandoned me. Why did you run from me? A group of violent Yasha[309] demons lives on that island, appears from time to time, and eats people. So we have built high walls and strongly guard our place. Hearing many of you reciting loudly on the beach, these Yasha demons appeared. Seeing these enraged Yasha, you mistook them for us, and thought that we were demons. You were wrong. After you left, my heart ached for you. Haven't you missed me?" The woman wept greatly with tears. If one had not known her real nature, he would surely have trusted her.

Sōkara became very angry, drew his sword, and was about to slash her. The woman developed a great resentment against him and left. She

----

309. 夜叉. It refers to a female demon.

went to the king's palace and said, "Sōkara was my husband for several years, but has abandoned me and has not lived with me. To whom shall I appeal this matter? King, please give us a fair judgment!"

Hearing her appeal, the people in the palace came out and saw the beautiful woman. All of them lusted for her. The king heard about her, secretly inspected her, and was impressed by her matchless beauty. Compared to many of his favorite queens, the woman was a jewel, while his queens were like lumps of clay. The king thought that Sōkara was a fool not to live with the woman and summoned Sōkara and questioned him.

Sōkara replied, "This is a man-eater, a demon. You should not let her in the palace. Quickly chase her out!" The king heard Sōkara but did not believe his words. Deeply affected by his desire, the king secretly called the woman to the great hall, the king's chamber, by the back door. He drew her close to him and found that she looked more beautiful. After embracing her, his lustful infatuation made him neglect state affairs, and he did not get up for three days.

Sōkara came to the palace at that time and said to the people, "A terrible thing will happen. That woman is a demon incarnate. You should quickly destroy her!" But nobody listened to him.

Three more days passed. In the morning, the woman appeared by the edge of the hall. She looked frightening with her unusual eyes and bloody mouth. She looked around for a while, leaped up on the eaves of the hall, flew away like a bird, and vanished into the clouds.

The people hurried to the king to tell him, but heard no sound in his chamber. The suspicious people came near the hanging screen and saw no king but a pool of blood and hair partly crimsoned by blood. The palace became a confused turmoil with crying ministers and officials.

Soon the prince succeeded to the throne. He summoned Sōkara and questioned him about the incident. Sōkara said, "I gave several warnings to kill the demon. I know the country of Rasetsu. With the new king's authorization, I would like to go to destroy that country." The king issued the order, saying, "Quickly go and attack them. I will give you an army as you require." Sōkara said, "Please mobilize ten thousand soldiers with bows and arrows in addition to ten thousand swordsmen and place them aboard one hundred fast ships. I will lead them to the island!" The new king supplied Sōkara with all that he asked.

Leading the twenty thousand soldiers, Sōkara finally arrived at the Rasetsu country. Just as they formerly did, Sōkara sent about ten men masquerading as merchants to the beach to reconnoiter.

Again, about ten beautiful women appeared. They approached and spoke intimately with the men. Just as before, the women led the men, and the twenty thousand soldiers followed them.

As they reached the place, the soldiers mingled with the women, slashed, and shot them. The women remained beautiful for a while, although they showed resentment against these men. However, Sōkara ran about, warning his soldiers loudly against the women. Finally, these women could not hide their original forms and nature and revealed their Rasetsu form. They attacked the soldiers, their mouths gaping wide. The soldiers cut and slashed at their heads, shoulders, and hips. Not a single demon remained whole. The Yasha demons also attempted to fly away but were struck by arrows, and none escaped the clutch of Sōkara's soldiers.

Sōkara and his soldiers set fire to the buildings and structures in the compound and burned the whole city to ashes. When this victory was reported to the new king, he granted Sōkara this Rasetsu country.

Sōkara, as the king of the country, lived there with his twenty thousand soldiers. The country became much more pleasant than before. The descendants of Sōkara now live in the country whose Rasetsu demons were exterminated. The country became called the country of Sōkara.

Thus it was told and handed down.

5:2   HOW A KING HUNTED IN THE MOUNTAINS AND A LION
        TOOK HIS DAUGHTER

Long ago the king of a country in India enjoyed hunting. Leading his men, the king went to the mountains, valleys, and summits to drive out the deer by blowing shell horns and beating hand drums. The king had a daughter, a princess whom he cherished so much that he never left her side for a single moment. The king always took her with him in a carriage.

One time, toward evening, the king and his men tracked deer into a mountain and entered a cave where a lion was. They disturbed the lion by mistake. The surprised lion stood on the other side of the mountain and groaned loudly with a frightful appearance. The terrified king's men fled in confusion. Some fell and others abandoned the carriage when fleeing. The king also dashed away without knowing his directions and barely made his way to the palace.

Later, the king inquired about his princess and was told that the carriage attendants also had run to the palace, leaving the carriage behind. The king was quite distressed and grieved greatly over the situation. He had no other recourse than to send his men back to the mountain to search for his princess. However, the king found that none of his frightened men dared return to the mountain.

Meanwhile the lion, caught by surprise, became agitated and went around the mountain, clawing the ground. Soon the lion saw a carriage in the mountain. He bit off the curtain and looked inside the carriage to see the princess shining like a jewel. The rejoicing lion carried her on his back and returned to his cave. The lion held her and slept with her. The stupefied princess appeared neither dead nor alive.

The lion and the princess lived in the cave for days, and finally the princess became pregnant. After the proper number of months had passed, the princess delivered an ordinary baby, a handsome boy. When the boy became ten years old, he was superhumanly brave, agile, and swift.

Once when his father, the lion, was hunting for food, the boy asked his constantly mourning mother, "You have been weeping and moping all these years. You must have something on your mind. Since we are parent and child, please don't conceal anything from me."

The mother wept more bitterly. After a while she started to explain tearfully, "I am a daughter of the king of the country," and she told the boy everything from the beginning. After listening to his mother's story, the boy, too, was moved and wept. Finally the boy said, "If you would like to go to the capital, please go before father returns. I know how fast he can run. He runs as fast as I do, but not faster than I. I shall take you to the capital, hide you there, and take care of you. Although a child of a lion, I take after you and have the appearance of a human being. I will take you quickly to the capital. Please climb on my back."

The rejoicing mother climbed on her son's back, and the son ran to the capital as fast as a bird. He rented a house from a certain person, hid his mother there, and attentively cared for her.

The father, the lion, returned to his cave only to find that both his wife and son were gone. "So they ran away to the capital," thought the lion and greatly missed them. Sad and grieving, the lion left the cave, faced the capital, and growled so loudly that the people, including the king, were all confused and terrified.

To settle the situation, the king issued an edict, "Anyone who kills the lion and stops him from harrassing us shall be offered half of this country to govern."

The lion's son heard the edict and presented himself to the king, saying, "I would like to kill the lion and have the reward." The king accepted his proposal, saying, "Go and destroy the lion." With the king's order, the lion's son thought, "Although it is a grave sin to kill one's own father, I shall be the king of half of the country and be able to look after my mother, who is a human being."

Armed with arrows the boy went to his father, the lion. The lion was so happy to see the boy that he laid on the ground. When the lion, lying on his back, stretched out his paws and stroked and licked the boy's hands, the boy stuck a poisonous arrow into the lion's side. The lion did not show any anger, but licked the boy more tenderly, shedding tears.

Shortly after, the lion died. The boy cut off his head, took it to the capital, and presented it to the king. The surprised king thought of giving him half of the country, but first asked him how he had killed the lion. The boy thought, "Benefiting by this opportunity, I shall tell him my origin and let the king know that I am his grandson," and he told the king the whole story from the beginning to the end as his mother had told him.

Now the king knew that the boy was his grandson and decided to give the boy the half of the country as promised in his edict. Yet the king thought, "If I reward someone who has killed his own father, I will be implicated in his sin. But if I don't reward him, I will violate my edict. So I will give him a remote country." The king sent both the mother and the son to a distant country. The boy governed the country and his descendants still live in that country, which is called Shūshishikoku,[310] the Country Governed by the Lion.

Thus it was told and handed down.

....

310. 執師子国. It refers to Sōkara, present-day Ceylon.

5:3   HOW A THIEF STOLE A JEWEL WHICH SHONE AT NIGHT

Long ago, the king of a country in India possessed an unusual spherical jewel which illuminated the night. The jewel was kept in a storeroom. One day the jewel was stolen.

The grieving king suspected a man, but had no way to make him confess. So the king carefully developed a plan. First, the king would decorate a high tower with seven kinds of jewels, beaded banners, and canopies. Brocade carpets would be spread on the floor. Beautiful women, elegantly dressed and gorgeously adorned with flowers and ornaments, would entertain by playing instruments, such as harps and lutes, and by singing refined music.

The king would invite the suspect, offer him large quantities of highly intoxicating liquor, and make him fall into a drunken sleep as if dead. The suspect would be carried up the tower and would be dressed in elegant clothes with flowered hair ornaments and a beaded necklace. Since he would be drunk, he would not know what had happened.

He would awaken in an elegantly decorated place like nothing in this world. The fragrance of sandalwood from the four corners of the chamber would reach his nostrils. He would see banners and brocades covering the ceiling and floor as decorations and observe women, as beautiful as jewels, wearing their hair uplifted, wrapped in gorgeously beaded dresses, playing musical instruments, and amusing themselves.

Seeing this, the suspect would wonder, "To what sort of place have I come?" and ask a woman nearby, "Where is this place?" The woman would answer, "This is a heaven," The suspected man would ask again, "Why have I been reborn in a heaven?" "Because you have never told a lie, you have been reborn in a heaven," the woman would answer. Following this, the woman would continue questioning and ask the man, "Have you committed any thefts?"

Since the man had already heard that these who told no false-hoods will be reborn in the heaven, he would think, "I must not tell a lie," and would answer, "Yes, I have." The woman would ask the suspected man again, "Did you steal the treasure of the king, the precious jewel?" The man would answer, "Yes, I did." "Where did you hide it?" the woman would ask. "I hid it in such and such a place," the man will answer. The king would send his men to search the place and recover the jewel. This was the king's plot.

Now, actually, when the man heard a woman say, "Those who tell no lies are reborn in a heaven," the suspect just nodded. The woman next asked, "Have you stolen anything?" The suspect, instead of answering the question, just gazed at the faces of the women around him and carefully remained silent.

The woman repeated the question several times, but the man never answered. Tired of asking the question, the woman had the suspected man descend the tower, saying, "Those who say nothing cannot stay in a heaven!"

The king regretted the failure of his scheme and thought, "I will make this thief my minister. I will cooperate with him, scheme, and devise a new plan." So the king made the suspect his minister. The king confined and consulted with the minister on all matters whether important or trifling. Eventually, they became so intimate that they hid nothing from each other.

On one occasion, the king said to the minister, "I have something on my mind. Last year, one of my matchless treasures, a precious jewel, was stolen. I tried to regain it, but I had no way of finding it. I am thinking of giving the governing of half my country to anyone who finds the thief and returns the jewel. The edict on this matter should be issued immediately."

The minister thought, "I stole the jewel for my benefit. It will be of no use to conceal the fact when I can govern half of the country. I think I will tell about the jewel now." The minister calmly walked close to the king, and said, "I am the one who stole and hid the jewel. If you give me half of the country, I will return it to you."

The king rejoiced to hear this and did not issue the edict. The minister took out and offered the jewel to the king, who said to the minister, "I am so pleased to obtain this jewel. After all these years, my wish is finally realized. Minister, you may govern half of the country for a long time. By the way, last year when I made a high tower and had you ascend it, why did you keep silent and say nothing?"

The minister explained, "Last year when I went to a priest's living quarters to steal, the priest was reciting a sutra. I thought I would wait for the priest to fall asleep. I stood listening by the wall. I heard him recite, 'The celestial persons do not blink while human beings do.' So I knew that the celestial beings do not blink. I did not say anything. The women in the tower were not celestial beings since they all blinked. If I had not committed a robbery, I would never have gov-

erned half of the country. This is solely due to the virtue of robbery,"
said the minister.

Priests also mention that this is what the sutras explain. So good
and bad are the same and are not different. Only the ignorant distinguish them. If Aukutsumara had not cut off the Buddha's finger, he
would not have immediately attained the Way.

Without killing his father, how could King Ajase leave the cycle of life and death? And how could a thief be promoted to minister
without stealing the jewel? Judging by this, one should know that
both good and bad are one.

Thus it was told and handed down.

5:4   HOW HERMIT IKKAKU[311] CARRIED A WOMAN ON
        HIS BACK AND CAME TO THE CAPITAL FROM THE
        MOUNTAIN

Long ago, there was a hermit with a horn on his forehead who was
called Ikkaku, One Horn. For years, he enjoyed his ascetic ways deep
in the mountains. He flew in the sky, rode on clouds, moved high
mountains, and led animals and birds.

A heavy rain fell and the road became very bad. For some reason
or other, Ikkaku could not foretell the coming rain and was walking
on a steep mountain path. He suddenly lost his footing and fell.

Ikkaku became very angry about this accident because of his old
age and thought, "Since it has rained, the road has become slippery
like this and I have fallen. My priestly robe is wet and very uncomfortable. The dragon kings have caused this rainfall." Ikkaku immediately
caught all the dragon kings and put them in a water jar.

The dragon kings were immensely unhappy. Being large, they
were very uncomfortable since they were confined in a narrow jar and
unable to move. Since this was accomplished by the Mysterious Powers of the noble hermit Ikkaku, they could do nothing.

Meanwhile, no rain fell for twelve years and the people of all India suffered greatly from the drought. The kings of the sixteen countries offered prayers to no avail. They did not know the cause of the
drought.

A soothsayer said, "A hermit in a deep mountain to the northeast

---

311. 一角仙人. It refers to Ekaśṛṅgarṣi, an ascetic born of a deer.

caught many dragon kings and confined them. The prayers of the noble saints and ascetics will not surpass the hermit's power." Hearing this, the people of the various countries tried to seek a solution but could not think of a better idea.

A minister suggested, "No matter how noble one may be, no one is unaffected by music and carnal desire. Even the hermit of old times Utsuzuran,[312] although undoubtedly more virtuous than Ikkaku, indulged his desire and lost his Mysterious Powers. If we send lovely women with beautiful voices, selected from the sixteen countries, to the mountain and have them sing on the summits and in the deep valleys, where ascetics and hermits usually live, even Ikkaku may relax on hearing their sweet voices." Everybody agreed with this idea, saying, "That should be done immediately."

Five hundred beautiful women with good voices were selected. They were bathed in water sprinkled with fragrant sandalwood, dressed in sophisticated clothes, and sent to the mountain in lavishly decorated carriages.

It was indescribably elegant to see these five hundred women descending from, the carriages and strolling about the mountain. Groups of ten to twenty sang melodiously, walking about certain caves, under trees, and in the valleys. The summits and valleys trembled at the beautiful echoes, and even celestial beings and demon deities descended.

Soon one of the women saw an emaciated hermit, Ikkaku, in a priestly robe by a deep cave. Anyone would wonder where he had hidden his soul and spirit in his shriveled body of bones and skin. He had a horn on his forehead, which gave him a terribly fearful look.

Leaning on his stick, Ikkaku crawled out like a shadow with a water jar in his hand and a grin on his face. "Who are singing such tasteful songs? I have lived in this mountain for a thousand years, but never have heard anything like this. I wonder if celestial beings have descended or if demons have approached."

One of the women replied, "We are neither celestial beings nor demons. Five hundred of us, called Kekara Women,[313] are going about

....

312. 鬱頭藍. It refers to Udraka Rāmaputra, a Brahman with miraculous powers who was a mentor of Śākyamuni after he left home.

313. Kekara or Kinnara, the musicians of Kuvera are among the eight classes of heavenly musicians. They have crystal lutes and beautiful voices, and the females sing and dance well.

like this in groups throughout India. We heard that this mountain is matchlessly beautiful with various flowers and delightful streams and that a most noble hermit lives here. We thought, 'Since the hermit has been in the depths of the mountain for a long time, he has probably never heard anything like our singing. We decided to sing for him and associate with him.' We have purposely come to this mountain," and the woman continued to sing.

Ikkaku observed the most enchanting appearance of the woman, the like of whom he had never known, and listened to her intently. His eyes glowed. His heart and spirit were touched and excited.

"Would you do whatever I say?" Ikkaku asked the woman.

The woman, thinking "Now, he is relaxing. I will plot and degrade him," replied, "How can I not listen to whatever you say?"

"If I associate with you a little more, I will tell you," said Ikkaku awkwardly as he embarrassedly passed the woman.

Although the woman felt weird with the frightful horned hermit, she tried not to hurt his feelings. She also remembered that the king purposely had sent her and other women to degrade the hermit. She timidly accepted him and did what he demanded.

At that time, the dragon kings, rejoicing at the degradation of Ikkaku, kicked and burst open the water jar and ascended into the sky, which was immediately covered with clouds. The torrential rain fell to the accompaniment of thunder and lightning.

Since the woman had neither a place of shelter nor any way to return, she stayed with Ikkaku for days. Ikkaku became deeply infatuated with her. On the fifth day, when the rain stopped and the sky cleared, the woman said to the hermit, "Since I cannot very well remain here like this, I am going to return."

"If you wish," replied the Ikkaku. Yet he looked sad and pained, resenting his separation from her.

The woman said, "I am not yet accustomed to this mountain and my feet have become swollen by walking along these rocky paths. Besides, I don't know the way back."

"In that case, I will guide you along the mountain paths," said Ikkaku and went ahead of the woman.

It was quite comical and yet frightening to see Ikkaku, clad in his priestly robe, leading the way with his snow-white hair, his horned face wrinkled like serried waves, and his hips bending forward as he wobbled along leaning on a stick as his staff.

After they crossed a valley, they came to a path on a cliffside which was as steep as a standing screen. Down the precipitious cliff a huge waterfall cascaded into a gorge with white foam bubbling up from the deep bottom and producing the extensive mist and fog in the area. Only those with a pair of wings or riding on a dragon could travel such a place.

At that spot, the woman said to Ikkaku, "This is a most difficult place to pass. Just looking down makes me dizzy. How can I take this path? Holy man, you are accustomed to walking in places like this. Please carry me on your back."

The infatuated Ikkaku could not very well refuse her. He said, "You are right. Climb on my back." His shanks appeared so thin that the woman feared they might snap and that she would fall. But she climbed on his back.

After traversing the path, the woman asked Ikkaku to continue to carry her, saying, "A little farther." Finally she entered the capital on his back. The people on the street saw this and said to each other, "The holy man Ikkaku, who has been living in the mountain, has come to the capital carrying a Kekara Woman on his back!"

Many people from the breadth of India, the high and the humble, men and women, gathered to see Ikkaku, with a horn on his forehead, snow-white hair, and bony shanks like needles, carrying a woman on his back and lifting up her buttocks from time to time, his staff in his hand. All laughed at him scornfully.

Finally they entered the king's palace. Seeing them, the king also thought it comical. But since he had heard that Ikkaku was a distinguished and noble ascetic, he said respectfully, "Please return quickly." Ikkaku tried to fly back as usual but this time he fell to the ground and wobbled along. Once such a comical hermit lived in India.

Thus it was told and handed down.

5:5   HOW THE KING WENT HUNTING IN THE MOUNTAINS, SAW LADY ROKUMO, AND MADE HER QUEEN

Long ago, two hermits lived in the mountains called Shōshuyūko,[314] not far from the capital of the country of Harana in India.

....

314. 聖所遊居. It refers to the Snow Mountains in the Himalayas.

One hermit lived on a southern hill and the other on a northern hill. Between the two hills was a fountain by a flat rock.

One day, the hermit of the southern hill sat on the rock, washed his feet and clothes, and returned to his place. A doe came to the spring, drank the water where the hermit had washed his clothes, and licked his urine. Shortly afterward, the doe became pregnant and delivered a human baby girl.

The hermit of the southern hill heard the deer crying, pitied her, and came out to see the doe licking the baby girl. Seeing the hermit, the doe abandoned the baby girl.

The hermit looked at the baby and thought that he had never seen such a beautiful baby. Feeling pity, the hermit wrapped her in his grass robe, took her to his place, and nourished her with fruits and nuts. Months and years passed, and the daughter of the doe became fourteen years old.

When the girl tended the fire, it never died out. So the hermit's place always had fire.

However, one morning, the fire finally died out. The hermit said to the girl, "For years, the fire here has never died out. I wonder why it became extinguished this morning? Quickly go to the hermit of the northern hill, ask for fire, and bring it here."

The daughter of the doe followed the hermit's instructions and started to the northern hill. When she lifted her feet, lotus blossoms bloomed where she stepped. She finally arrived at the place of the hermit of the northern hill and asked for fire.

Seeing the lotus blossoms blooming in her footprints, the hermit of the northern hill thought it most extraordinary and said to the girl, "If you want fire, circle my hut seven times. I will give you the fire after you do that." The girl walked around the hut seven times, received the fire, and returned.

At that time, the great king of that country was deer hunting in that mountain with his ministers and officials. The king saw the lotus blossoms growing about the place of the hermit of the northern hill and was immensely pleased. The king said, "Today, I am so happy that I have come here and seen a most extraordinary sight. How wonderful these blossoms are!"

The hermit spoke, "They are not produced by my virtue, but by the matchlessly beautiful girl reared by the hermit of the southern hill. This morning the girl came here to get fire. Each time she lifted her foot, lotus blossoms appeared in her footprints."

After hearing this, the king went to the place of the hermit of the southern hill and talked with the hermit. "I hear that you have a girl at your place. Let me have her." The hermit replied, "I am poor and she is the only person I have. Yet I shall not resent giving her to you. However, she is still young and has never seen any people outside these mountains. She has lived only in these deep mountains and knows nothing of the outside world. She wears grasses as her clothing and picks fruit for her food. Besides, she was born from an animal." The hermit gave the king the detailed story of the girl.

After hearing the explanation, the king said, "I don't at all mind having a girl born from an animal." At the king's request, the hermit finally brought the girl. The king looked at her and thought that the girl was truly beautiful and that she did not look like a person of common birth.

The king immediately had her bathed in hot fragrant water, dressed her with neck ornaments of hundreds of jewels, had her ride a large elephant escorted by a hundred and a thousand attendants, and took her to his palace to the accompaniment of beautiful music.

On that occasion, the father, the hermit of the southern hill, climbed a high rock to see his daughter leave. He watched her departure without blinking his eyes until she became invisible in the distance, and returned to his place, where he greatly mourned for her.

The king welcomed the girl respectfully at his palace. He made her as his first queen and called her Lady Rokumo, the Doe Mother. Seeing many kings of lesser countries, various ministers, and officials arrive and celebrate the occasion, the pleased king could think of none of his other queens.

The Lady Rokumo soon became pregnant. The king thought that if the child were a boy, he would issue an edict that the boy would succeed to the throne.

Months passed and as everybody waited, Lady Rokumo delivered not a boy but a lotus blossom. The king was enraged and demoted the lady from her position as queen, saying, "She has delivered a useless thing. This must be because she was born from an animal. Quickly throw away the lotus," and he had the flower thrown into a pond.

The person who threw the flower into the pond noticed that the blossom had five hundred leaves. Between each of them, a tiny matchlessly handsome boy was sitting. The person reported this to the king, who immediately welcomed all the boys, reinstated Lady Rokumo in her position as queen, and regretted his treatment of her.

The great king summoned his ministers, hundred of officials, the kings of lesser countries, and various Brahmans and had them hold his five hundred princes. The king also invited a soothsayer and had him predict the princes' fortunes.

The soothsayer explained the signs and said, "All the five hundred princes have noble futures, assured by their virtues in attaining the Way. They will be respected by the people whose fortune they will assure. If they remain as laymen, the demon deities will protect them. If they enter the priesthood, they will leave the karmic cycle of life and death, and obtain the Six Mysterious Virtues[315] of arhatship and the Four Ways so that they enter nirvana and the Four Stages of enlightenment."[316]

The great king was most delighted to hear the soothsayer's words. The king selected five hundred nurses in the country to take care of his princes.

When the princes had grown, they all wished to enter the priesthood. Their parents permitted this, following the soothsayer's suggestion. All five hundred princes entered the priesthood. They lived and practiced their Way in the rear garden of the palace.

Finally, four hundred and ninety-nine princes attained the Way and became Hyakushi Buddhas. They came before their parents, saying, "We have already attained the Way," revealed various kinds of Mysterious Changes, and entered nirvana. Lady Rokumo built four hundred and ninety-nine pagodas, dedicated the bones of these Buddhas and venerated them.

Ninety days later, the youngest prince, too, became a Hyakushi Buddha, came before his parents, and revealed great Mysterious Changes just as his brothers had. Another pagoda was built for him and was venerated.

Thus it was told and handed down.

....

315. It refers to the six kinds of supernatural powers gained by Buddhas and *arhats* through meditation and wisdom. See note 150.

316. They include *shudaonka, shidagonka, anagonka,* and *arakanka.* See note 72.

5:6   HOW THE FIVE HUNDRED EGGS OF KING HANSHARA[317] KNEW THEIR PARENTS

Long ago, the queen of King Hanshara, a great king of the country of [lacuna] in India delivered five hundred eggs. Seeing them, the king felt most strange and the queen felt ashamed. They put the eggs in a small box and jettisoned the box in the Gōga River.

At that time, a king of a neighboring country was hunting. As the king walked along the river and amused himself, he saw small box drifting on the river. He picked up the box, opened it, and saw five hundred eggs. The king took the eggs to his palace.

Days passed and each egg hatched a baby boy. Since the king had been childless, he was immensely pleased to see so many babies. The king carefully looked after them. All five hundred boys became strong, brave, and very superior as warriors. No one in the kingdom surpassed them.

This country and the country of King Hanshara had been enemies from ancient times. As the five hundred princes grew stronger, their father, the king, thought of attacking the kingdom of Hanshara. The king sent a message saying, "We will decide who wins or loses." The king led his army to Hanshara's country and seized the capital. King Hanshara was very frightened.

The queen said to King Hanshara, "Don't be frightened. The five hundred warriors of the enemy are all my children. They will naturally dispel their evil minds as they see their mother. Just as I said, they were born from the five hundred eggs which I delivered." The queen gave a detailed explanation to the king about the eggs and the consequences.

When the enemy army headed toward the city, the queen climbed a high tower, faced the five hundred princes, and said, "You five hundred warriors of the enemy country are all my children. Years ago, I delivered five hundred eggs. Out of fear, the eggs were abandoned in the Gōga River. The king of the neighboring country salvaged them and looked after them. You were born from these eggs. Why are you trying to commit a grave sin by harming and killing your parents?

....

317. 般沙羅. Pañcāla, an ancient country in the Ganges Valley in central India, was one of the sixteen great countries in the time of the Buddha.

"If you don't believe me, face me and open your mouths. I will press my breasts, and my milk will spurt into each of your mouths."

Thus the queen vowed and as she pressed her breasts, the milk entered at the same time into the mouths of the five hundred princes facing the queen on the tower.

Now the five hundred princes believed the queen, paid her their respects, and left for their country. Afterward, the two countries were on friendly terms and ceased to attack each other.

Thus it was told and handed down.

5:7   HOW MINISTER RAGO[318] OF THE COUNTRY OF HARANA ATTEMPTED TO KILL THE KING

Long ago, a great king lived in the country of Harana in India. Once while he was asleep, the guardian deity of a shrine came and warned him, "Minister Rago is going to kill you to usurp the throne. Quickly flee across the boundary." The frightened king told his queen and prince. The royal family stealthily fled across the border.

The distressed and confused king erred and took an extremely difficult route so it would take forty days for them to reach their destination. On their way, their lives nearly ended because of thirst and hunger. Both the king and queen mourned, raising their voices.

The king thought, "The three of us will die soon. If the queen and I are in the same situation. I might as well kill her, eat her flesh, and prolong my and the prince's life." The king drew his sword and was about to kill his queen. The prince said, "I will not eat my mother's flesh. I would rather offer my flesh to my parents."

His hunger unbearable, the king followed the prince's suggestion, and cut some flesh from the prince's body. The prince offered them more flesh from his arms and legs for the rest of their journey.

His wounds began to stink and the odor traveled for some distance. Flies and mosquitoes swarmed down on his wounds to suck out the juices. The prince's pain and suffering were intolerable. The prince said to his parents, "I wish that I could attain the supreme enlightenment of Buddha in my future and release you from your hunger pangs." The king and queen soon abandoned the prince.

At that time, Taishaku, transformed as a beast, came to the prince

318. He is also known as Minister Rāhu.

and devoured his remaining flesh. The prince vowed, "By abandoning this suffering body, I will attain supreme enlightenment and deliver all sentient beings."

Taishaku resumed his original form and said, "You are foolish. Supreme enlightenment is attained only by long ascetic practices. How can one attain it by this kind of offering?"

The prince said, "If my words are false, my body will not recover. But if they are true, my body will revive." The prince's wounds were cured. His flesh recovered and became normal as before. The prince appeared more handsome. He got up and paid homage to Taishaku, who instantly vanished.

Meanwhile, the king and the queen reached the king of a neighboring country and explained their situation. The king of the neighboring country pitied them. He prepared an army and attacked Minister Rago, who was finally defeated.

The king, the father of the prince, returned to his country and regained his throne. The prince, too, returned to his country, succeeded to the throne, and governed the country just as his father had. His name was Prince Susendai,[319] and he is now the Shaka Buddha. Minister Rago is now Daibadatta.

Thus it was told and handed down.

5:8   HOW KING GREAT BRIGHT LIGHT OFFERED HIS HEAD
       TO A BRAHMAN

Long ago, King Daikōmyō, Great Bright Light, lived in India. He was very generous and always made offerings to others. He had no resentments. He even gave away his treasures, which were carried to the people by five hundred great elephants. If someone came to ask for treasures, he never failed to donate them.

The king of a neighboring country heard about Daikōmyō's desiring to make offerings, wanted to kill him, hired a Brahman, sent him to Daikōmyō, and had him ask for the head of Daikōmyō.

Just before the Brahman asked for Daikōmyō's head, the guardian deity of a shrine, who knew about this, told a gatekeeper, who would not let the Brahman into the palace. However, the gatekeeper

....

319. Unknown.

eventually told King Daikōmyō about the Brahman. The king left the palace and rejoiced to see the Brahman just like a child seeing his mother, and asked why the Brahman had come.

The Brahman replied, "I would like to have your head." "You will have it as you wish," agreed the king. The king returned to the palace and told his queen and his five hundred princes that he was going to offer his head to the Brahman. The queen and princes greatly resented this, and strongly insisted that the king should disregard the Brahman's request. The king would not alter his decision.

Clasping his hands, respectfully bowing in all directions, the king prayed, "Buddhas and bodhisattvas in all directions, please pity me and realize my vow today." The king tied himself to a large tree and said, "Take my head and offer it to the Brahman!"

When the Brahman drew his sword and faced the tree, the guardian deity of the tree struck the Brahman's head with his hands. The Brahman collapsed on the ground. The king said to the deity of the tree, "You did not help me in realizing my vow, but interfered with me for your own benefit." The deity no longer interfered.

As the Brahman was beheading the king, everybody in the palace, including the queen, princes, ministers, and hundreds of officials, cried and mourned with excruciating grief. Finally, the Brahman beheaded the king and took the head to his country.

King Daikōmyō is the present Shaka Buddha, and the king of the neighboring country who hired the Brahman is today's Daibadatta.

Thus it was told and handed down.

5:9 HOW KING TURNING WHEEL BURNED HIS BODY IN SEARCHING FOR THE WAY

Long ago, King Turning Wheel, who lived in India, was searching the Law to benefit sentient beings. He issued an edict, asking, "Does anyone in this world know the Buddha's Law?"

The king received a response, "A Brahman in a small country in a remote place knows the Buddha's Law." The king sent a messenger to summon the Brahman, who immediately came to the king's palace.

The king was greatly pleased, prepared a seat for the Brahman, and intended to venerate him with hundreds of dishes at a feast.

The Brahman neither took the seat nor accepted the proffered veneration, but said, "Great King, if you wish to venerate me and hear the Law, cut off your flesh at a thousand places on your body, place animal fat with taper threads in each of your wounds, and burn the tapers in veneration. I will accept only such veneration and preach the Law. Otherwise, I am leaving." And the Brahman was about to go.

The great king held the Brahman by his arm and said, "Great master, please remain here for a little while. Even though I have gone through numerous lives and deaths since before the heavens and earth were separated, I have never given up my life for the sake of the Law. Now is the time."

The king returned to his palace and spoke to his many queens and five hundred princes: "I will give up my life to hear the Law. Now is the time to tell you farewell."

One of the princes was matchlessly brilliant and was blessed with limitless wisdom. He also had a handsome and noble appearance and an upright mind. The king loved this prince as though cherishing a jewel, and the people of the kingdom appreciated and followed this prince like grasses and plants bent by winds. The king said to the prince, "Separation is inevitable with love and attachment in life and death. Never lament over this."

Hearing this, both the queen and prince grieved intensely with tears. The great king, as suggested by the Brahman, made a thousand cuts on his body, filled the wounds with animal fat, placed tapers made with five kinds of woolen material in them and lighted the tapers.

Meanwhile, the Brahman recited a verse saying, "Death is attained through life and release is attained through death." Hearing these verses, the rejoicing king offered great mercy to various sentient beings. The people, who heard the verses, said, "Our king is like our merciful parents. He is undergoing hardship and suffering for us. We should copy and record this." As they said this, the people copied and wrote the verses on paper, or rocks, or tree trunks, or bricks, on grass blades and in places to which many people came.

Those who heard and saw the verses all developed piety to attain the supreme enlightenment. The light of the tapers which were burned on the king's body illuminated the ten thousand directions of the world. All those who reflected the light developed piety.

At that time, the Brahman finally resumed his original form as

Taishaku, released radiance, and asked the great king, "What do you wish because of such unusual veneration?" The king answered, "I don't seek pleasure in the realms of the heavens and of human beings. I only wish the supreme enlightenment. For that, I would not mind placing a glowing iron ring on my head. In spite of such ascetic practices, my yearning for enlightenment will not weaken."

"Even though you say such a thing, it's hard to believe," said Taishaku. "If my words are untrue and deceive Taishaku, my thousand wounds will never be cured. But if my words are true, my blood will turn to milk and my wounds will be healed." As soon as the king said this, his wounds were healed and he was recovered completely. Taishaku vanished instantly. The Shaka Buddha is the great king of that time.

Thus it was told and handed down.

5:10   HOW A KING WAS STABBED WITH A NEEDLE FOR SEEKING THE LAW

Long ago, an Indian king abdicated to seek the Law. He went to a mountain and engaged in ascetic practices. A hermit appeared and said to the king, "I have known the Law. What do you think of my teaching you the Law?" "I have been practicing in the mountains because I seek the Law. Teach me immediately," said the king.

"If you follow what I say, I will. If not, I won't," replied the hermit. The king said, "I would not grudge even my life for an opportunity to learn the Law. Why should I withhold anything else?" "If you allow your body to be stabbed by a needle five times a day for ninety days, I will teach you the noble Law," proposed the hermit. "I don't mind being stabbed for a hundred or a thousand times a day for the sake of the Law," said the king as he accepted the proposal and entrusted himself to the hermit.

The hermit stabbed the king fifty times with a needle, but the king showed no pain. The hermit stabbed the king five times a day for three consecutive days and asked the king, "Isn't it painful? If so, go away. I am going to stab you like this for ninety more days. How about it?"

The king replied, "When I fall in the hell, am burned by the molten copper and undergo the sufferings of walking on the sword mountains and through flaming trees, can I evade my sufferings just by saying, 'Since it's painful, I will go away?' No, I cannot. The pain of a needle cannot be compared to one hundred quadrillionth of the sufferings in hells. So I feel no pain," said the king.

The king withstood his hardship well for ninety days.

Later, the hermit taught the king the verses of eight syllables saying, "Practice all the good but not the evil."

The king of that time is the Shaka Buddha, and the hermit of that time is Daibadatta of today.

Thus it was told and handed down.

5:11   HOW FIVE HUNDRED MERCHANTS SUFFERED THIRST IN A MOUNTAIN

Long ago in India, five hundred merchants and a priest were passing through a mountain on a business trip to another country. By mistake, they took the wrong route and went deep into the mountains, where they saw neither inhabitants nor water. The merchants had not drunk water for three days and were almost dying of thirst.

The merchants said to the priest, "Buddha has vowed to save all sentient beings. He would even substitute for his devotees in undergoing the suffering of the Lower Realms. With your shaven head and priestly robe, you accompany us as a disciple of the Buddha. Five hundred of us may soon perish because of thirst. Please save us!"

The priest asked, "Can you achieve salvation by developing a sincere mind?" "Our lives solely depend on you," said the merchants.

The priest climbed a high summit, sat by a rock, and said to the merchants, "Although I have shaved my head, I have not engaged in ascetic practices and have no power to save others." However, the merchants insisted, "You are the Buddha's disciple. Please help us," and asked him for water.

The priest, feeling helpless, vowed, "Please, various Buddhas of all directions and generations, change my brain to water and save the life of these merchants," and the priest hit his head against the rock. The blood from his head turned to water and quenched the thirst of the merchants and their cattle.

The priest of that time is the present Shaka Buddha. The five hundred merchants are his disciples of today.

Thus it was told and handed down.

5:12   HOW FIVE HUNDRED PRINCES INSTANTLY ENTERED PRIESTHOOD

Long ago, a king of India had five hundred princes. The king went on an outing with the princes leading the way. They saw a priest playing a lute on the road ahead. The five hundred princes stopped simultaneously before the priest, instantly entered priesthood, and received the precepts. Seeing this, the king was immensely astounded and confused.

A minister said to the king, "A priest was playing a lute on the way ahead of the princes. As soon as they heard the sound of the lute, they immediately entered the priesthood. The music of the lute said, 'Everything is like an illusion. All pleasures and comforts in the world are as vain as clouds.' Listening to the music, all your five hundred princes instantly perceived the transiency of life and death. Leaving the pleasures of this world, they entered the priesthood."

The lute-playing priest is the present Shaka Buddha. The five hundred princes are the five hundred arhats of today.

Thus it was told and handed down.

5:13   HOW THREE ANIMALS PRACTICED BODHISATTVAHOOD AND THE RABBIT BURNED HIMSELF

Three animals, a hare, a fox and a monkey, were practicing the Way of the bodhisattva in India. Each thought, "We three were born as lowly animals into this world because of grievous sins in our previous existences. Because we were greedy, did not pity living beings, and did not share our possessions, we went to hell to suffer for a long time and have been reborn to atone for the rest of our sins. In this existence, we will avoid self-centeredness."

Accordingly, they practiced unselfishness, regarding the old as their parents and elder brothers, and showing pity and mercy to the young as their younger brothers. Thus they detached themselves from the ways of the world and thought first of others.

Observing their deeds and determination, the heavenly deity Taishakuten reflected, "Though animals, they have honorable minds. Some creatures born as human beings kill even their parents, hold grudges against their brothers, and steal. Others hide their evil minds behind a smile. Anger lurks beneath their mercy. How can I trust that these animals have true hearts? I will test them and see."

Taishakuten transformed himself into a feeble old man, suffering from hunger and exhaustion, and appeared before the three animals. He said, "I am unable to feed myself since I am so old and tired. I am poor and have neither food nor children. You three animals, please take care of me. I have heard that all of you are very merciful."

The three animals replied, "This is exactly what we have wanted to do. Let's take care of his needs quickly." No sooner had they said this than the monkey climbed trees, bringing assorted nuts and fruit such as chestnuts, persimmons, pears, and all kinds of tangerines. The monkey went to the village and got melons, eggplant, soya beans, red beans, cowpeas, millet, and corn, and prepared them as the old man liked. The fox went to the graveyard and took the offerings of rice cake, mixed rice, and various fish, including abalone and bonito. The monkey and the fox fed the old man anything he wished, so that he became quite full. Several days later, the old man concluded, "Those two animals, the monkey and fox, are truly pious and sincere. They are true bodhisattvas."

However, the hare found no food, although he searched everywhere. He made every effort with a sincere heart, carrying torches, burning incense, pricking up his ears, opening his eyes widely, arching his back, raising his short front paws, and dilating his anus.

The monkey and the fox, as well as the old man, humiliated the hare with laughter and scorn at one moment and encouraged him the next moment. But the rabbit had no way of finding anything for the old man. Then the rabbit thought, "I should go to the mountains and villages to get food for the old man, but I am so afraid of the beasts and human beings who will surely kill and eat me. That would cost me my life to no purpose. I would rather give my body to the old man to eat and leave this life forever."

So the rabbit went to the old man and said, "I am going to search for something delicious. Gather some wood and build me a fire." The monkey gathered some wood, and the fox lit the fire, which burned as they waited for the rabbit.

Soon the rabbit returned empty-handed. The monkey and fox complained angrily, "You lied to us, had us gather the wood and build the fire with which you are thinking to warm yourself! You hateful rabbit!" The rabbit answered, "I am not able to find food. So please, old man, roast and eat my body!" The rabbit jumped into the fire and was burned to death.

At that moment, the old man transformed himself into Taishakuten and moved the rabbit's body to the moon to be seen by all sentient beings. So the cloudlike forms on the surface of the moon are the smoke of the fire in which the pious rabbit died. And, looking at the moon, one can see the rabbit and remember this story.

Thus it was told and handed down.

5:14   HOW A LION PITIED THE YOUNG MONKEYS AND CUT OFF HIS FLESH TO GIVE IT TO AN EAGLE

Long ago, a lion lived in a mountain cave in India. The lion thought, "I am the king of the beasts. I should be merciful and protect all animals."

A monkey couple, husband and wife, lived on the same mountain and reared their young. As their little ones grew, the monkey parents worried, "When our young ones were very small, we held one and carried the other as we gathered fruit and berries. Now that they have become bigger, we can no longer hold and carry them while looking for food. Without food, how can we raise them and survive? If we leave them in our nest, birds from the sky will fly down to snatch them or the beasts of the earth will seize them." Disturbed and worried, the monkey couple became exhausted and nearly starved to death while seeking a solution.

Finally an idea came to them. They thought, "The lion lives in a cave of this mountain." We will entrust our young ones to him while we search for food. The couple went to the lion and said, "You are the king of beasts and should care about the various animals. We are animals needing your protection. We have two young ones. When they were small, we carried them on our backs while gathering fruit in the fields and mountains. Now they have become too big for us to carry. Since we are afraid that other beasts will harm our young ones, we cannot very well leave them at our place while we are out. Being worried and disturbed, we have not gathered food for days. Our lives will soon end in exhaustion and starvation. We beg of you, lion, that you will take care of our young ones while we gather food."

The lion understood and replied, "You may leave your children with me. I will watch them until you return." So the pleased monkey couple left their children with the lion and went into the mountains.

While the lion was watching the young monkeys, he fell asleep. An eagle had been hiding in a tree in front of the cave as he waited for the slightest chance to snatch the two young ones. As soon as the eagle saw the lion sleeping, he flew down, seized the young monkeys, and flew back to the tree.

At that moment, the lion awoke and was surprised to miss the young monkeys. Confused, the lion left the cave and saw the eagle perched in the tree, holding a young monkey in each claw.

The disturbed lion went under the tree and called to the eagle, "You are the king of the birds and I am the king of the beasts. Each of us should be merciful. A monkey couple came to my cave and told me how they wished to gather food to feed their young ones. The couple entrusted me with their children and went into the mountains. While I was sleeping, you took the young monkeys. Please release them. Since I have agreed to take care of them, if I lose them I would feel heartbroken. Besides, you cannot very well refuse to listen to me. If I become angry and roar, you won't be safe."

The eagle replied, "What you say is reasonable. However, these monkeys are my food for today. If I give them up, I'll have nothing to eat today. Though I am afraid of you, I also have to think of my life."

"What you say is reasonable," agreed the lion. "I will give you some of my flesh in place of these two young ones. Here, take and eat it as your food." As he spoke, the lion used his claws, which were as sharp as swords, to cut out a portion of his thigh. He rounded it into the size of the two young monkeys and offered it to the eagle.

"After what you have done, how can I not return the two young monkeys to you?" asked the eagle as he returned them to the lion.

Covered with blood, the lion went to his cave with the two young monkeys. Just then, the mother monkey returned from gathering fruit and berries. When the lion explained what had happened, the mother monkey shed tears like falling raindrops. The lion continued, "It was not the gravity of your situation, but the question of my honor in keeping my word. Besides, I have deep feelings toward other animals."

It is said that the lion was the contemporary Shaka Buddha, the male monkey was Kashō Buddha, and the female monkey was Nun Zengo. The two small monkeys were Anan and Ragora, and the eagle was the contemporary Daibadatta.

Thus it was told and handed down.

5:15 HOW A PRIEST DID NOT MOURN OVER A BURNING PALACE OF INDIA

Long ago, a palace caught a fire in India. As the fire spread from one side to the other, the confused king, queens, princes, ministers, and other officials gathered and began to carry out the treasures.

The king very much relied on a priest as his guardian. At outbreak of the fire, the priest was pleased, nodded his head, and stopped the king's people who were carrying out the treasures.

The bewildered king asked the priest, "Why aren't you sorry to see the fire breaking out of the palace? Why are you pleased to see our treasures burning? Did you start this fire? If so, your sin is grave!"

The priest replied, "I did not cause the fire. I am afraid, great king, that you may fall into the Three Lower Realms because you are so much attached to your treasures. If all the treasures are burned and you lose them today, you will be detached from what will cause you to descend into the Three Lower Realms. This is most joyous. Attachment to mundane treasures, which are comparable to a mere handful of dust, links one to the cycles into the Three Lower Realms and the Six Realms."

Finally the great king understood the priest and said, "What the priest said is very correct. Hereafter, I will not resent the loss of the treasures."

Thus it was told and handed down.

5:16 HOW A PERSON OFFERED A FRUIT TO A KING WHO LOVED FRUIT

Long ago, a king of India loved and enjoyed delicious fruit. Once a guard of a shrine discovered a fine fruit by a pond. Remembering that the king loved fruit, the guard offered the fruit to the king. The king ate the fruit and found it very sweet, unlike any other fruit.

The king summoned the guard and said, "The fruit you offered me was matchlessly sweet. Where did you find it? You must know the place. Hereafter, bring me the fruit all the time. Otherwise, you will be punished."

The guard explained in detail how he had found the fruit by

chance, but the king refused to listen. The lamenting guard went to the pond and sat weeping tearfully.

A person appeared and asked the guard, "Why are you sitting and moping here?" "Yesterday, I found a fruit by this pond, which I offered to the king. The king ate it and told me to offer the same fruit again, otherwise I shall be punished. Since I have no way to find the same fruit again, I am crying here like this," replied the guard.

The person said, "I am a dragon king and the fruit that you found here yesterday was mine. I will offer the king as much as one load carried by a horse. In return, let me hear the Buddha's Law." The dragon king gave the guard the fruit and said to him again, "Remember, if you don't let me hear the Buddha's Law, I will make this country into a sea within seven days."

The guard offered the fruit to the king again and reported the story of the dragon king. The distressed king, minister, and hundreds of officials said to each other, "From old times to the present, we have never heard nor seen anything called the Buddha's Law in this country. If anyone in our country or in other countries knows about it, let us know." They searched widely and vainly for anyone who knew the Law.

Finally the king summoned a one-hundred-and-two-year-old man and said, "You are already very old. Have you ever heard about the Buddha's Law in your young days?" The old man replied, "I have never known the Buddha's Law, but my grandfather said, 'When I was small, I heard that there was something called the Buddha's Law.' The grandfather also had an unusual shining pole standing at his house. When I asked him about it, he answered that the pole had been erected long ago when the Buddha's Law was known."

Hearing this, the pleased king immediately had his people bring the pole, broke it, and in the pole found two lines of verses about the Eight Precepts and Taking Meals.

When the king and his people had faith in the verses as a teaching of the Buddha, the verses released radiance in every direction and benefited the people. The dragon king also rejoiced at it. Since that time, the Buddha's Law has been popularly known in that country and the people have enjoyed peace, wealth, and comfort.

Thus it was told and handed down.

5:17   HOW A KING OF INDIA WON A BATTLE THANKS TO
THE RATS

Long ago, a country called Kusshana[320] was small in size but rich in material wealth and treasure. Although India was large, food was scarce, the roots of grass and trees were regularly on the menu, rice and soya beans were luxuries, and rice was hardly obtainable.

In contrast, both food and clothes were abundant in Kusshana. Moreover, the handsome king of Kusshana had been born from a cleft in the forehead of the Bishamonten deity. A wet nurse had originally been chosen for the baby, but he had refused her milk and all other food. The people lamented, "The baby drinks no milk and eats no food. How shall we raise him?" And they prayed to an image of Bishamonten for help.

Suddenly the side of the image bulged out and grew into the shape of a human breast. The wondering people asked, "What is the matter?" Then the baby approached the side of the image, extended his hand, and scratched open the tip of the breast. Something like milk spurted forth and dribbled down. The baby immediately drank and eventually grew into a handsome man. After becoming an adult, he ruled as king.

The king's strong mind and keen intelligence resulted in military tactics that defeated the neighboring counties, subjugated many peoples, and expanded his domain. His power and influence became incomparable.

On one occasion, evil men in an adjacent country plotted against Kusshana, gathered approximately a million troops, and suddenly crossed the frontier. The invaders spread into the open fields. The surprised king of Kusshana tried to quickly mobilize his soldiers, who were far inferior in number. Leading forty thousand men, the king headed toward a place where he could fight. Soon darkness fell and they did not fight that day. That night, the king's soldiers camped to one side of a tumulus beyond which the well-equipped enemy troops lurked.

The soldiers of Kusshana were intelligent, but the sudden at-

....

320. 喎遮那国. Kusshana, Kustana, also Uton, is present-day Khotan, where Mahāyāna Buddhism flourished.

tack had not given them time to make preparations. "What shall we do?" lamented their bewildered king. Then a large rat of a golden hue appeared and ran about the king as it ate something. This gave the watching king an eerie feeling, and he asked, "What kind of rat are you?" The rat replied, "I am king of the rats here, and I live in this tumulus called the Rat Mound." The king approached the tumulus, faced it, and said, "Your form does not seem to be that of an ordinary rat. Though you have the shape of an animal, you may be a supernatural being. Please listen carefully. I am king of this country, in which the king of the rats also lives. Please help me win this battle. If you assist me, all the people of this country will faithfully hold an annual festival with services in your honor. If you do not support me, I will destroy and burn this mound and kill all of you."

That night, the king dreamed that the golden-hued rat appeared and said, "King, you need not be bewildered. I will help and let you win the battle. Just do this. Attack the enemy at dawn."

The king awoke very pleased and had his troops spend the remainder of the night preparing for battle, putting saddles on the elephants and horses, checking the chariot wheels, and examining their bowstrings and quivers as they awaited the dawn.

As dawn broke, his forty thousand armored soldiers attacked with firm determination and high spirits, holding spears, waving flags, beating large drums, and riding horses, elephants, and chariots.

The enemy had expected the Kusshana army after sunrise. At the onset of the sudden attack, they tried to place the howdahs on their elephants and discovered that the tails of their animals and the reins and harnesses as well as arms and equipment had been chewed to pieces by rats. Nothing had been left undamaged. The rats had also gnawed the bowstrings, the ties of the quivers, the bindings of the swords, and the lacings of the armor plates. The enemy remained uncovered and naked. Without reins and harness, the horses and elephants all ran away. Even the chariots had suffered from the rats. The shields were like baskets with large holes through which even a man could crawl and offered no protection against arrows. So one million soldiers of the enemy were in great confusion and didn't know what to do. Most of them ran off helter-skelter and hardly any would confront the Kusshana army. Those who appeared all had their heads struck off. Thus the king of Kusshana won the battle and returned victorious to his palace.

Afterward, the tumulus was dedicated at an annual festival and all the population of the country paid homage to the rats. Kusshana became very peaceful, and its people enjoyed tranquility. If they needed something, they went to the tumulus and prayed. It is said that there was nothing that was not granted and no assistance ungiven.

Thus it was told and handed down.

5:18   HOW A NINE-COLORED DEER CAME OUT OF A
        MOUNTAIN AND SAVED A MAN FROM DROWNING

Long ago, a nine-colored deer with a white horn lived on a mountain in India. Nobody in the country knew about the deer. A crow had also lived intimately for years with the deer on that mountain.

A man was crossing a large river by the foot of the mountain. Being carried by swift currents, the man floated and sank repeatedly and almost drowned. He caught a tree branch in the river and cried loudly while being carried downstream, "Mountain, tree, dragon and other deities, why won't you help me!" But no one helped him.

At that time, the deer came out of the mountain by the river, heard the man crying, and said, "Don't be afraid. Climb on my back and grasp my horn. I will carry you to the shore." The deer, carrying the man on his back, swam to the shore, and saved him.

Clasping his hands, the rejoicing and grateful man said to the deer, "Thanks to your virtue, my life is saved. How can I repay you?" The deer replied, "Are you asking how to repay me? Well, there is one way. Don't ever tell any one that I live in this mountain. I have an unusual nine-colored hide and a horn as white as snow. If the people know about me, they will kill me to get my hide and horn. Fearing this, I have been hiding myself deep in this mountain and have let no one know about me. Yet today, when I heard you crying faintly in distance, I felt great pity for you, came out of the mountain, and saved you." The man promised not to tell any one and left, tearfully repeating his promise.

The man returned to his village and stayed for days and months, but did not repeat the story.

At that time, the queen of the country dreamed of a large deer with a nine-colored hide and a white horn. After she had awoke, she so much wished to have the deer that she finally became bedridden.

The king asked, "Why can't you get up?" The queen said, "I

dreamed of such and such a deer. Surely such a deer must exist in the world. I would like to have its hide and horn. Great king, please catch the deer for me."

The king immediately issued an edict, "Anyone who catches such and such a deer will be rewarded with treasures of silver and gold, as he wishes." The man who was saved by the deer heard the edict and was caught by irresistible avarice. He forgot his obligation to the deer and finally reported the deer to the king: "The nine-colored deer lives in such and such a mountain of such and such a country. Since I know the place, my lord, I can capture it with your army and offer it to you."

The king rejoiced. "I myself should go to the mountain with an army," and the king headed toward the mountain, leading his army. The man guided them, walking by the king's carriage. Finally they arrived at the mountain.

The nine-colored deer, utterly unaware of this, was soundly sleeping in a cave of the mountain. A friendly crow saw the king's army, was surprised, and flew to the deer in confusion. The crow cried loudly, but the deer did not awaken. The crow left the tree and pecked at the deer's ears, and finally the deer awakened.

"The king of this country has surrounded this valley with his army to capture you for your colorful hide and your horn. Even if you run now, you won't be able to save yourself," said the crow and flew away.

The surprised deer saw the king truly approaching and leading soldiers. The deer had no way to escape. He walked to the front of the king's carriage. The king's soldiers all took bows and arrows to shoot the deer.

The king said, "Don't shoot the deer for a while. He appears to be a most unusual deer. He has come to the front of my carriage fearlessly. Let him do as he wishes for a while and watch him." The soldiers detached their arrows from their bows and observed the deer.

Kneeling before the king's carriage, the deer said, "Being fearful for my rare colorful hide, I have been hiding in a deep mountain and allowed no one to know about me. Great king, how did you learn about me?"

The king replied, "I haven't known you and your place during these years. But this scar-faced man escorted me and told me about you."

The deer heard this, and looked at the scar-faced man by the carriage. He was the very man whom the deer had saved. The deer said to the man, "When I saved you, you were so grateful for the favor and repeatedly promised me not to tell anyone. But now you have forgotten your promise and told the king about me, and you are going to let the king kill me. Why are you doing this to me? When you almost drowned, I carried you on my back and swam to shore, risking my own life. It is most regrettable that you lack a sense of obligation." Speaking tearfully, the deer lamented intensely.

Hearing the deer's story, the man had nothing to say. The king issued an order, "Hereafter, no deer shall be killed in this country. If someone violates this order and kills a deer, he shall be killed and his house shall be destroyed." The king returned to his palace leading his army. The relieved deer returned to the mountain.

Afterward, the country became abundant in the five kinds of cereals, with sufficient rainfall and no stormy winds. It had neither rich nor poor people.

Some men forget their obligations, while some animals remember and help men. This is true just as in old times. The nine-colored deer is the present Shaka Buddha, while the friendly crow is Anan. The queen is Sondari,[321] and the drowning man is Daibadatta of today.

Thus it was told and handed down.

5:19 HOW A TORTOISE OF INDIA REPAID HIS OBLIGATION TO A MAN

Long ago, a pious person saw a man carrying a tortoise. The person asked the man to sell the tortoise. He bought and released it.

Years later, when the person was in bed, he heard something stealthily moving near his pillow. "What is this?" asked the person, lifting his head from his pillow, and he saw a three-foot-long tortoise near his pillow.

"What kind of tortoise are you?" asked the startled person. The tortoise replied, "I am the tortoise which you released the other day. Once I was caught by a man and was about to be killed. You bought and freed me. All these years I have been thinking of how to reward you. I let months and years pass without a chance to do so. Today I

....

321. 孫陁利. Sondari became Nanda's wife.

have come to inform you of an impending catastrophe in your vicinity. The river before your house will rise and wash away people and cattle. Your house will lie sunken at the bottom of the river. Quickly arrange for a boat. When the river rises upstream, board the boat with the people close to you and save your life!" The tortoise left.

The person considered this extraordinary, but thought, "It could be possible." The person arranged for a boat, moored it before his house, and waited. That evening, a torrential rain began to fall with strong winds and continued through the night. Toward dawn, the water upstream increased and flowed down.

The person and his people quickly boarded the boat. As they rowed away, looking for higher places, they saw a large tortoise drifting down. It said, "I am the tortoise who came to see you the other night. Let me aboard."

"Quickly," the person said with pleasure, and he brought the tortoise aboard the boat.

Soon they saw a large snake drifting and shouting, "Help me, I am going to be drowned." Although the people did not suggest letting the snake aboard, the tortoise insisted that the person save him, "The snake will die. Please let him aboard." The person said, "No, we should not. Even a small snake is frightening. How dare we let such a large one aboard with us? We may be swallowed up. It's absurd."

"No, he will not swallow you. Just let him aboard. It's good to save a life." Since the tortoise insisted that no harm would come, finally the person let the snake aboard. The snake coiled at the bow of the boat. Since the boat was large, the snake did not seem to take much space on board.

While rowing, they saw a fox drifting down. Seeing the boat, the fox asked for help just as the snake had. At the tortoise's suggestion, the fox was also saved.

Shortly after, they saw a drifting man, who looked at the ship and cried for help. The person was going to row near the man to try and help him.

The tortoise said to the person, "You should not let him aboard. Animals understand the meaning of obligation, but a man does not. You won't be guilty of his being drowned."

"We allowed even a fearsome snake on board from mercy. How can we refuse someone belonging to our own kind?" asked the person as he rowed near the drowning man and brought him aboard. The rejoicing man tearfully thanked the person.

As they were resting and waiting at a certain place, the river water finally receded to its normal height, and everybody on board got off and left.

Some time later, when the person was walking, he saw the snake he had saved from the river. The snake said, "Though I have been waiting these days, I have had no chance to extend my gratitude to you for saving my life. Now I see you again. Please follow me," and the snake crawled ahead of the person. The person followed the snake, which finally crawled into a large tomb. The snake said, "Follow me." Although he was frightened, the person entered the tomb. In the tomb, the snake said to the person, "The abundant treasures in this tomb are all mine. I am offering them to you to show my gratitude. You may take as much as you wish," and the snake left. So the person brought his people to the tomb and had them carry all the treasures from the tomb to his place.

While the person was enjoying his treasures, which he could use as he pleased, the man whom he had saved in the river visited him.

"Why did you come here?" asked the person. "I have come to thank you for saving me," said the man. He saw the many treasures piled in the house and asked, "What kind of treasures are these?"

The person explained in detail, "So you have obtained these unexpectedly. Let me share them," said the man. The person gave him a part of his treasures. "This is so little. After all, you did not spend years in accumulating these treasures, but got them so easily by chance. Give me half!" insisted the man.

"It's most unreasonable of you to say that. I have obtained these treasures as a reward for saving the snake. Unlike the snake, you don't think of repaying your obligation to me. Instead, you demand to share what I have. Although it was quite unreasonable for me to give you even a portion of my treasures, you demand half. This is most extraordinary and unreasonable." When the person said this, the man became angry, threw down the treasures he had gotten, and left.

The man immediately reported to the king, "Such and such a person took treasures from a tomb." The king sent his men, caught the person, and imprisoned him.

The person was forced to lie flat on his stomach on the ground with his limbs tightly bound, and had no relief at all. The person was immensely confused and distressed. He cried, raising his voice.

That night, the person heard a stealthy sound near his head. It was the tortoise he had saved. "Why have you come here," asked the person. The tortoise replied, "I came to see you because I heard that you are being punished because of unreasonable consequences. Didn't I tell you that you should not save a man? A man does not have a sense of obligation. But it's of no use to mention that now. Yet you should not undergo these hardships for a long time."

The tortoise, the fox, and the snake had conspired to save the person who had saved him. They made an arrangement, saying to each other, "Foxes will cry in the palace. The king will be surprised to hear the foxes cry and will have a soothsayer determine whether the foxes' cry is a good or a bad omen. We will make the soothsayer say that the king's cherished princess should be confined carefully. Later we will play a trick to make the princess seriously ill."

From the following day, many people gathered in front of the prison and said to each other, "Since a hundred and a thousand foxes are crying in the palace, the confused king consulted a soothsayer, who advised the king to look carefully after the princess. The princess has been critically ill with a swollen stomach. The palace is in a turmoil now!"

Meanwhile, a jailer came and said, "When the king questioned the soothsayer about the cause of the princess' illness, he said that it was due to the imprisonment of an innocent person. So the king wishes to know if the prison contains an innocent person."

All the prisoners were investigated one by one until they came to the case of the person. "This is the very one," said the jailer and reported to the king. The king summoned the person immediately and inquired regarding his case.

The person explained everything from the beginning. "We have punished an innocent person. Let him go quickly," said the king and released the person.

The king also said, "The man who wronged this person should be punished." He summoned the man and punished him severely. So the person finally realized that the tortoise's words, "A man does not understand obligation," were correct.

Thus it was told and handed down.

5:20   HOW A FOX IN INDIA CALLED HIMSELF THE KING OF THE ANIMALS, RODE ON A LION'S BACK, AND KILLED HIMSELF

Long ago in India, a priest lived in an old temple and was constantly reading a sutra. A fox listened to the recitation of the sutra, which said, "In general, a man as well as an animal will become a king if he maintains a haughty air and attitude."

The fox thought, "So by maintaining a haughty air, I may become the king of the animals." As the fox left the temple, he met another fox on his way. Lifting his head high, the first fox threatened the second fox. The second fox was overawed by his haughty attitude. The first fox ordered the second fox to come close to him and rode on his back.

As they went on, they met another fox, who noticed the haughty air of the first fox riding the second fox and felt awed, thinking, "He must be quite a fox." The first fox called the third fox and had him attend the second one. Thus the first fox made all other foxes he met on his way his followers and went on accompanied by a thousand foxes.

On their way, the foxes met a dog, who also thought, "He must be our king," and was respectful. The first fox summoned the dog as he had the foxes. Since many more dogs gathered, the first fox now rode on the first dog and had other dogs attend him as grooms. Next he gathered tigers and bears and rode them alternately. Thus the fox went on leading many animals as his related subjects.

An elephant came, who also thought the procession extraordinary and showed his respect. The first fox summoned the elephant, rode on his back, and had many other elephants follow him. So the first fox became the king of many animals ranging from foxes to elephants.

Finally, they met a lion. He was also impressed by the fox, who was now riding on an elephant and being followed by thousands and tens of thousands of animals. The lion thought, "He must be someone," and remained respectfully kneeling by the roadside.

Being a fox, this seemed as far as he could elevate himself. Yet the fox thought arrogantly, "Since I have made so many animals follow me, I now will become king of the lions." The fox summoned the lion, who came before him obediently.

"I am going to ride you. Let me on quickly," said the fox. "Since you have become king of the animals, I have nothing to say and will do as you wish," replied the lion.

The fox rode the lion thinking, "Being a fox myself, I never expected to become king of the elephants. To be king of the lions is most remarkable!" So the fox continued on his way, riding the lion, holding his head higher, pricking his ears erectly, flaring his nostrils widely, and looking down at the world and the other animals.

"Now I am going to gather many more lions," the fox thought as he crossed a wide field with flanking elephants as his grooms.

The elephants and other animals thought, "The lion's roar alone usually disturbs other animals, destroys their morale, and even frightens some of them to death. But our lord the fox, thanks to his virtue, has become friends with the lion and closely associates with him. This is most unusual!"

Lions customarily roar once a day. When it became noon, the lion suddenly held his head high, breathed hard from his flaring nostrils, and glared about with a disgruntled air. All the animals, including the elephants, became frightened, thinking, "What will happen now?" and felt as if their hearts and bodies had frozen to ice.

At the sight of the lion's erect mane and pointing ears, the fox on the lion's back became afraid of falling. But the fox still maintained his lofty air and crouched on the lion's back, thinking, "After all I am the lion's king!"

Just at that moment, the lion, raised his front paws high and bellowed with a horrible roar, which resounded in the distance like a rolling thunder.

The fox on his back instantly fell headfirst to his death on the ground. The elephants closely attending the lion and many other animals collapsed on the ground as if dead.

The lion thought, "I considered the fox to be the king of the animals and had him ride on my back. At my little roar, he was so confused that he fell to his death. If I became really angry and roared my loudest, what would happen to him? He wouldn't be able to bear it. I have been tricked and fooled by an insignificant creature and gave him a free ride." The lion calmly stalked off.

Some animals revived after having fainted and staggered from the place absentmindedly. Some did not recover but remained dead like their king, the fox.

Riding an elephant went well for the fox, but riding a lion was too much for him. A man also should consider his status and refrain from anything beyond that.

Thus it was told and handed down.

5:21   HOW A FOX OF INDIA ASSUMED THE PRESTIGE OF A TIGER, WAS THREATENED, AND DEVELOPED A PIOUS MIND

Long ago, a fox and a tiger lived in a country of India. The fox assumed the tiger's prestige and power, and threatened many animals.

Hearing this, the tiger went to the fox and pressured him saying, "Why do you threaten other animals by assuming my prestige?" The fox tried to make excuses, swearing by the gods of heaven and earth, but the tiger did not believe the fox. Feeling helpless, the fox ran off.

Suddenly the fox fell into a lion pit, which was so deep that the fox could not climb out. Lying at the bottom of the pit, the fox was aware of the transiency of life, and single-mindedly generated a pious mind, thinking, "Prince Satta of old times developed a pious mind and offered his body to a tiger. I am just like him."

At that time, the earth tremored greatly, and all of the Six Heavens were shaken. On account of this, both Monju and Taishaku transformed themselves into a hermit, came to the pit, and asked the fox, "What sort of mind and vows have you adopted?"

"If you wish to know what is in my mind, first pull me up. Then I will tell you," said the fox. The hermit helped the fox out of the pit. As soon as the fox was out, the hermit urged him, "Tell me quickly," but the fox forgot about his piety and thought of running away without repeating his vows.

The hermit perceived the fox's evil intention, immediately assumed the appearance of a demon deity, and threatened the fox with a sword and a spear. Finally the fox told his complete story.

Listening, the hermit pitied and commended the fox. "After your life ends, because you have developed sincere piety, you will become a bodhisattva with two names in the world of the Shaka Buddha. One name is Great Benzaiten,[322] and the other is Earth Deity

<hr>

322. 大弁才天. Benzaiten or Sarasvatī, originally the deification of a river, is closely associated with music and grants eloquence in speech, wisdom, longevity, victory on the battlefield, and protection from calamities.

Kenrō.[323] You will benefit all sentient beings and have eighty-four thousand demon deities as your servants." And the hermit vanished.

The hermit of that time is the present Monju, and the fox is the bodhisattva or present Earth Deity Kenrō, who appears an as eight-handed figure one thousand *jō* tall. Two of his hands are in the attitude of prayer with the palms together, and six hands respectively grasp farming instruments, including a sickle, plow, spade, and rake. Attended by nine hundred million, four thousand demon deities, he benefits all sentient beings by the five cereals. So the piety developed single-mindedly has had a marvelous effect. A popular saying "The fox assumes the tiger's prestige" was derived from this story.

Thus it was told and handed down.

5:22   HOW PRINCE ZENSHŌNIN[324] OF THE COUNTRY OF TŌIKI[325] ASSOCIATED WITH PRINCESS ASHŪ[326]

Long ago, King Myōkyōengen[327] of the country of Tōiki had an unmarried son, Prince Zenshōnin.

The king of the country of Saiiki had a matchlessly beautiful princess, Ashū. Zenshōnin heard about Ashū and decided to visit to her country. He made a three-foot-high Kannon statue and prayed. "Protect me from the dangers of my voyage."

The country of Shae lay between the two countries of Tōiki and Saiiki[328] and was across two great seas. The voyage from Shae to Tōiki or Saiiki required seven days.

When Zenshōnin was crossing the sea between his country and Shae, a sudden gale rose and his boat was about to be blown to an unknown country. Zenshōnin tearfully prayed to Kannon for help. The adverse gale died down, and a gentle breeze blew him toward his destination. Rejoicing, Zenshōnin voyaged three more days and arrived at Port Mui.[329] From there, he sent his people, including his

....

323. 堅牢地神. It refers to the Earth Deity, who solidifies the earth.
324. Unknown.
325. Unknown.
326. Unknown.
327. Unknown.
328. Saiiki (西域). Central Asia. It *includes India* and usually means Turkestan.
329. Unknown.

attendants, back to his country and began to cross the other sea alone. On the fifteenth day, Zenshōnin finally arrived at the palace of the king of Saiiki.

Zenshōnin stood by the gate. Meanwhile, Ashū, who had heard of Zenshōnin's coming, left the palace and looked outside the gate. She saw a handsome man standing there. Thinking that he must be Zenshōnin, Ashū asked, "From where did you come?" "I am Zenshōnin, prince of the country of Tōiki," replied Zenshōnin.

Rejoicing, Ashū secretly brought him into her chamber and spent days alone with him. On the seventh day, the king, the father of Ashū, sent a messenger to Ashū asking who was in her chamber. Ashū replied that it was Zenshōnin, the prince of the country of Tōiki.

The king summoned Zenshōnin, found him matchlessly handsome, and decided to look after him with care. After a time, Ashū became pregnant.

The king's queen was Ashū's stepmother and did not accept Zenshōnin as her son-in-law. The stepmother gave Zenshōnin pure white rice when the king was present, but mixed the rice with other grains in the king's absence.

One day Zenshōnin said to his wife, Ashū, "I have countless treasures in my country. I will go and bring them to you."

"I am already pregnant with your child. If you don't return, what shall I do?" asked the worried Ashū. Yet, a month later, Zenshōnin returned to his country.

Eight months later, Ashū delivered male twins. The king greatly cherished the two boys. The older boy was called Jūyū, and the younger was Myōyū.

Zenshōnin was supposed to return sooner, but he was unable to, as he wished to be with his own father, whose life came close to its end. A few years passed and the two boys became three years old. One day, Ashū said to her boys, "I will not look for another husband. I think I will go to your father, Zenshōnin. Even if he is dead, I will not marry another man."

She secretly took five *shō*[330] of rice and headed for the country of Tōiki. She carried one boy on her back and had the other walk before her. Seven days passed and the five *shō* of rice were exhausted. She took off one of her unlined robes, sold it for four *shō* of rice, and continued

330. A *shō* equals 1,805 liters.

their trip with the rice. On the day when they arrived at Port Mui, Ashū became seriously ill and lay on the roadside.

The two boys stood weeping by their mother. Ashū instructed the boys, "My life is ending today. After my death, remain here, and beg passersby for food. If someone asks whose children you are, reply that your mother was Ashū, the daughter of the king of the country of Saiiki, and that your father is Zenshōnin, the prince of the country of Tōiki." As soon as she had spoken, Ashū passed away.

Following their mother's instructions, the two boys remained by their mother's corpse in the bush and spent a month begging for food.

At that time, Zenshōnin came from the country of Tōiki, leading several ten thousands of men. The children left the bush and begged him for a cup of rice. When they got the rice, they turned back, crying out, "Oh! Our father! Our father!" Zenshōnin heard this and asked, "Who are your parents?" The children replied, "Our mother is Ashū, the princess of the country of Saiiki, and our father is Zenshōnin, the prince of the country of Tōiki."

Zenshōnin held the children and said, "You are my children and I am your father. Where is your mother?" "She is dead under a tree to the east of here," said the children.

Zenshōnin was led to the place by his children. Parts of Ashū's corpse were scattered among the green grasses. Zenshōnin grieved greatly, held the corpse, and said, "It is only for you that I brought so many treasures. Why did you die?"

Zenshōnin invited ten wise men to the spot and had them copy twenty rolls of the *Birushana* sutra[331] and venerated them.

Later, Zenshōnin and his children passed away at the same place. Presently the Shaka Buddha called the place the Place of Perceiving the Truth of Equality. There the Buddha preached, "Zenshōnin of old times is the present Bodhisattva Zenken;[332] Ashū of old days is the present Bodhisattva Kichijō.[333] The older brother, Jūyū, of old times

....

331. 毗盧遮那経. The sutra refers to the *Mahāvairocana-sūtra*, the fundamental scripture of the Tantric school, translated by Shan Wu-wei in 724 in seven fascicles and thirty-six chapters.

332. 善見菩薩. Bodhisattva Zenken refers to King Ajātaśatru.

333. 吉祥菩薩. It refers to Śrīmahādevī, the wife of Vaiśravaṇa, a daughter of Takṣaka, who brings happiness and virtue to men.

is Tamonten[334] of today, while the younger brother, Myōyū, is Jiko-kuten[335] of today."

Each of the bodhisattvas maintained and guarded the Buddhist Law and benefited all sentient beings.

Thus it was told and handed down.

5:23 HOW A NOSELESS MONKEY OF THE COUNTRY OF SHAE VENERATED TAISHAKU

Long ago one thousand monkeys lived in a large tree on a mountain of the country of Shae of India. All these monkeys venerated Taishaku with the same mind. Nine hundred and ninety-nine monkeys were noseless; only one monkey was an exception.

All the noseless monkeys congregated and greatly abused and ridiculed the one with a nose: "You are a freak. You should not associate with us." They would not let the monkey who had a nose be in the same place. The monkey with a nose lamented greatly.

The nine hundred and ninety-nine monkeys once venerated Taishaku by offering unusual fruits. Taishaku did not accept their veneration, but accepted the offering made by the monkey with a nose. The nine hundred and ninety-nine monkeys asked Taishaku, "Why did you reject our offerings and accept that of the freak?"

Taishaku replied, "Since you slandered the Law in your previous lives, you are imperfect in the Six Roots[336] of your bodies and are noseless. Thanks to his virtues in his former lives, the other monkey was born perfect in his Six Roots, including his nose. He temporarily remains in the Realm of Animals because of his ignorance and for doubting his master in his previous lives. However, he will soon enter Buddhahood. You nine hundred and ninety-nine abnormal monkeys ridiculed and scorned the perfect one. This is why I did not accept your offerings."

Hearing this, the nine hundred and ninety-nine monkeys admitted their deficiencies and stopped abusing the perfect monkey.

....

334. 多聞天. Tamonten, one of the four dava kings, protects the north. See note 12.
335. 持国天. Jikokuten protects the east. See note 12.
336. The Six Roots (六根) include the sense of audition, the sense of smell, the sense of taste, the sense of touch, and the faculty of the intellect.

Using this story as a parable, the Buddha compared the situation to lazy and wayward people slandering diligent people who maintained the precepts. When they talked about the noseless monkey they were referring to this story.

Thus it was told and handed down.

5:24 HOW A TORTOISE DISREGARDED A CRANE'S WORDS AND FELL TO THE GROUND, BREAKING HIS SHELL

Long ago in India, a terrible drought dried up the water and killed greens and grasses. A tortoise lived in a pond whose water had evaporated long ago. The tortoise was going to die.

A crane came to the pond to search for food. The tortoise came out and said to the crane, "The Buddha explains that you and I, the tortoise and the crane, are a pair on account of our association in our former lives. We are frequently compared and mentioned as a pair in the Buddhist teachings and writings.

"This severe drought has continued. The water in this pond has dried up, and my life is coming to its end. I hope you will help me."

The crane replied, "What you said is true, and I understand your pressing trouble. Your life may not last until tomorrow, and I feel sorry for you. I can fly around the world, high or low, as I wish. I have seen beautiful and colorful flowers and grasses under the spring sky, profusely growing plants and vegetables in the summer fields, exquisite views of red autumn leaves in the mountains, and the frozen mirror-like streams and rivers in the winter frost and snow. There is nothing more beautiful than the scenes that reflect changes of the four seasons.

"I have seen the pools of paradise adorned by the seven kinds of jewels. On the contrary, you don't even know anything in this small pond. When I look at you, I feel truly sorry for you. So before you asked me, I was going to bring you to water. However, I have no strength to hold you in my arms, to carry you on my back or in my mouth. The only thing that I can do is to have you hold one end of a stick in your mouth while I hold its other end. Thus the two of us can fly.

"But one thing worries me. You are very talkative by nature. If you ask me a question while flying, I may answer you by mistake. If both of us open our mouths, we will lose our stick. You will fall and lose your life. What do you think of this?"

The tortoise replied, "If you take me, I will be as silent as if my lips were sewn together. Is there anyone who does not consider his life?"

Yet the crane was still worried and said, "A long-time habit is hard to lose. I still cannot trust you." The tortoise assured the crane, "No, I will say nothing. So take me."

The crane and the tortoise got themselves a stick. Each held an end in his mouth and they flew high.

The tortoise, who had only stayed in the small pond, was immensely impressed with the fascinating views of mountains, rivers, and valleys. Unable to suppress his excitement, the tortoise asked the crane, "Where is this?" The crane, also forgetting himself, opened his mouth, saying, "This place is..." The tortoise instantly fell to his death.

Judging by this, one who is talkative will not consider his welfare. This is indicated by the Buddha's teaching "One should restrain and be careful of one's mouth, will, and body."

What people say about an unreliable tortoise breaking his shell has this meaning.

Thus it was told and handed down.

5:25   HOW A MONKEY TRICKED A TORTOISE

Long ago in India, a monkey lived on nuts and berries in a mountain near a beach. A married tortoise couple lived in the sea near the beach.

One day the tortoise wife said to her husband, "I am pregnant with your child. Since I have been sick to my stomach, I surely will have difficulties in delivering my baby. If you give me medicine, I will deliver your child safely."

The husband asked, "What would be the best medicine for you?" The wife replied, "I heard that monkey liver is the best medicine for stomach sickness."

The husband went to the beach, met the monkey, and asked, "Do you have many things at your place?" "I always lack food," replied the monkey.

"My place in the sea always has abundant nuts and berries throughout the four seasons. Oh, how I wish I could take you there and have you eat these foods until you are tired of them!" said the tortoise.

The monkey, unaware that he was being tricked, was pleased to hear this and said, "I want to go there now." "Then come with me," said the tortoise, and he carried the monkey on his back.

On the way, the tortoise said to the monkey, "Don't you know that my wife is pregnant, but has a stomach sickness. Since we heard that monkey liver would make a good medicine, I have tricked you like this to get your liver."

The monkey replied, "Oh, how regrettable that you have kept this a secret until now. Don't you know that we monkeys do not keep our livers in our bodies but hang them on nearby trees. If you had told me there, I could have offered you not only my liver, but those of other monkeys. Even if you kill me, you will find no liver. It would be quite useless and regrettable!"

The tortoise believed the monkey and said, "In that case, let's return. Get your liver and let me have it." "If I can only go back to where I was, it will be easy to do," said the monkey. The tortoise returned to the beach with the monkey on his back.

As soon as the monkey got off the tortoise's back, he dashed to a tree, climbed to the top of a branch, looked down at the tortoise, and said, "Tortoise, what a fool you are. Is there any liver without a body?"

"He tricked me cleverly," thought the tortoise, but he could do nothing except look up at the monkey in the tree and reply, "Monkey, how foolish you are! Tell me which great sea bottom has nuts and berries?" Saying this, the tortoise returned to the sea.

In old times, animals were foolish like this, and foolish people are no different from them.

Thus it was told and handed down.

5:26   HOW AN ELEPHANT IN A FOREST OF INDIA TREATED
       HIS BLIND MOTHER WITH FILIAL PIETY

Long ago, a blind elephant and her young elephant lived in a forest of India. The young elephant had been caring for his blind mother by finding berries and nuts as well as water for her. Thus the two elephants lived in the forest for years.

One day, a man lost his way in the forest and could not leave. Seeing the man in trouble, the young elephant felt pity, came out, showed him the right way, and sent him away. The rejoicing man left the forest and returned home.

The man told the king about the elephant, "I know a forest where an unusual elephant lives that releases fragrance. The king should quickly capture it."

At this suggestion, the king himself led an army and went to the forest to hunt the elephant with the man as his guide. When the man stretched out an arm to indicate to the king where the elephant lived, his arm broke off of its own accord as if severed. The king thought this extraordinary but continued hunting, captured the young elephant, took it to the palace, and secured it.

The young elephant refused to take water and grass. A stableman thought this strange and made a report to the king. The king himself came to the elephant and asked, "Why don't you take water and food?"

The elephant replied, "I have a blind mother who cannot walk. She has relied on me for years. Now I am captured and she has no one to care for her. She soon will die of starvation. How can I eat and drink when I feel so sad to think of her?"

The king was touched to hear this, became merciful, and released the elephant. The rejoicing elephant returned to the wood.

The young elephant is the present Shaka Buddha. The elephant used to live by the pond to the north of a stupa. The stupa was in a large forest beyond the River Nirenzen to the east of the Bodhi Tree.

Thus it was told and handed down.

5:27   HOW AN ELEPHANT SCHEMED TO MAKE A MAN PULL
        THE STAKE OUT OF ANOTHER ELEPHANT'S FOOT

Long ago, a priest was passing through a deep mountain. He saw a large elephant. The frightened priest quickly climbed a tall tree and hid himself in the dense leaves. The elephant came under the tree and unexpectedly found the priest, who thought he was well hidden.

The elephant began to dig at the base of the tree. The frightened priest prayed, "O, Buddha, please help me." Finally the tree fell as if uprooted. The elephant held the priest aloft with his trunk and went deeper into the mountain. Not knowing his destination, the priest felt that his life was near its end.

They finally arrived at an inner part of the mountain, where the priest saw a much larger elephant. The first elephant approached before the larger one and lowered the priest. "So the first one brought me here to feed the large one," thought the priest, anxiously anticipating his last moment.

The larger elephant lay down before the first elephant and rolled over, showing his immense joy. Seeing this, the priest became more intimidated, thinking, "He is very happy because I was brought here." The terrified priest felt as if he were no longer alive.

The priest soon noticed that the larger elephant did not stand but just stretched out a foot, which was pierced by a big stake.

As the larger elephant held out his injured foot ingratiatingly before the priest, the priest understood, "Now he wants me to pull the stake from his foot." He grasped the stake and pulled with all his might. Finally the stake came out.

The larger elephant rejoiced greatly, rolling over and over. "He is happy because I pulled out the stake for him." thought the priest and felt relieved.

The first elephant again lifted the priest with his trunk and carried him to the opening of a large grave at a distant place. Although mystified and frightened, the priest entered into the grave and found abundant treasures. "He is rewarding me with these treasures for helping the other elephant," thought the priest and took out all the treasures.

The elephant again carried the priest with his trunk. He lowered the priest at the tree where he originally had found the priest and left for the mountain.

Now the priest realized, "The larger elephant who stepped on the stake is probably a parent of the first one. The first one brought me there to help his parent, and gave me the treasures from gratitude."

So the priest obtained unexpected treasures and returned home.

Thus it was told and handed down.

5:28   HOW FIVE HUNDRED MERCHANTS OF INDIA
        ENCOUNTERED A WHALE IN A LARGE SEA

Long ago, a man and five hundred merchants of India were voyaging for treasure. On board, an oarsman asked a watchman on the tower, "Do you see it or not?" The watchman replied, "I saw two suns and white mountains, and water flowing as if sucked into a large hole." The oarsman said, "Don't you know that the king of the fish has appeared? The two suns are his eyes; the white mountains are his teeth. The flowing water is being sucked into his mouth. Nothing is more frightening than that fish.

"Maintain the Five Precepts, everybody, and recite the Buddha's name single-mindedly so that we will be preserved from this coming calamity. If the ship goes near the fish, we won't be able to return. You should know how swift the water is by the fish."

All the five hundred merchants, with one mind, recited the names of the Buddha and Kannon, appealing, "Please deliver us from this disaster!" The fish suddenly closed its mouth and submerged. The merchants traveled peacefully and returned to their homeland.

People also said that the fish, after his existence in this life ended, was reborn in the Realm of Human Beings, became a priest, and attained arhatship.

Thus it was told and handed down.

5:29   HOW FIVE MEN CUT AND ATE THE MEAT OF A HUGE FISH

Long ago, a huge fish was stranded on a beach of India. Five mountaineers happened to pass by, saw the fish, and cut and ate the meat.

Others heard about the fish and came to the beach. They cut and ate the meat. Shaka Buddha had become the fish to give meat to the traveling mountaineers. Resuming his original state, Shaka Buddha first cultivated the five hundred mountaineers who ate the fish meat and had them attain the Way. These five mountaineers included Priest Kurin,[337] Meshō[338], Makanan,[339] Kashō,[340] and Prince Kuri.[341]

Thus it was told and handed down.

5:30   ABOUT THE HERMIT WHO HEARD THE VOICE OF LADY SHASHI[342] OF TAISHAKU

Long ago, Shashi was a daughter of King Ashura[343] and the wife of Taishaku. Before the Buddha's appearance in this world, Taishaku always went to a hermit, Daibanaen,[344] and learned the Way.

....

337. 拘隣. Priest Kurin refers to Kaundinya.
338. 馬勝. It refers to Aśvajit, one of the first five disciples of the Buddha, who influenced Śāriputra to become the Buddha's disciple.
339. 摩訶男. It refers to Mahānāman. Refer to 1:21.
340. 迦葉. One of the ten great disciples of the Budhaha. See note 38.
341. It refers to Mahānāman, thus the disciple named Bhadrika is omitted from this story.
342. 舍脂夫人. Refer to 1:30.
343. 阿修羅王. See note 217.
344. 提婆那延. It may refer to Arhat Devasena.

Lady Shashi thought, "Surely Taishaku is not learning the Law, but must be seeing another woman." She secretly followed Taishaku and found that he was truly sitting before the hermit. Noticing his wife stealthily following, Taishaku scolded her, "The hermit's teachings never should be heard by women. Return quickly!"

As he spoke, Taishaku hit the lady with a lotus stalk. Suddenly Lady Shashi intimately showed herself to Taishaku. The hermit heard the flirting and enticing voice of Lady Shashi. His mind was contaminated, he immediately lost his Mysterious Powers as a hermit, and was degraded to a mere common man.

A woman is a great hazard for the Way of hermits.

Thus it was told and handed down.

5:31   HOW A COWHERD OF INDIA ENTERED A CAVE, WAS
        UNABLE TO COME OUT, AND BECAME A ROCK

Long ago, a cowherd lived in India before the time of the Buddha. Among his several hundred animals was one which left the others and disappeared from time to time. The cowherd did not know where this cow could go. When the cowherd looked at this cow before returning home at sunset, she appeared especially beautiful and unlike the others. Her mooing, too, sounded somewhat different. Other members of the herd, noticing this strangeness, did not approach her.

Many days passed, and though the cowherd recognized her strangeness, he did not know how to discover the reason. One day, the cowherd followed her, wishing to know where she went. The cow entered a cave in the side of a mountain. The cowherd followed for a distance of four to five *ri* and came to a bright field. Although out of season in India, he found blooming flowers and fruit. The cow was grazing in the field. The cowherd looked up at the trees, which bore red and yellow fruit which was like gold. He picked one, but did not dare to eat it.

After a time, the cow started to return. The cowherd also headed back, following her. Just before the cowherd went through the mouth of the cave, an evil demon tried to snatch the fruit that he had brought. The cowherd quickly put the fruit into his mouth. When the demon began to feel down his throat, the cowherd swallowed the fruit. His body grew larger as soon as the fruit entered his stomach and became so great that only his head projected from the cave. His body filled the rest of the cave. The cowherd hailed passersby, but no one could help him.

His family heard about this and came there, only to be frightened by his changed form. The cowherd told his family what had happened in the cave. His family gathered many people, and all of them tried to pull the cowherd from the cave, but they could not budge him. The cowherd died several days later. As the months and years passed, he became petrified.

Later, the king understood and told his minister, "The cowherd was changed because he took the medicine of a hermit. Though a rock, he is also a divine spirit. Send someone to cut off and bring here a small piece of the rock." The minister obeyed the order and went to the rock with a craftsman. But after ten days, they had not chiseled off even a pound of the rock. So it is said that the rock still has its original form.

Thus it was told and handed down.

5:32 ABOUT THE COUNTRY WHICH EXILED PEOPLE OLDER THAN SEVENTY YEARS OF AGE

Long ago, a country in India exiled people who became more than seventy years of age.

A minister of the country had cared for his old mother in the mornings and in the evenings for years. Finally his mother became older than seventy. The minister thought, "When I see her in the morning, but do not see her in the evening, I miss her and worry about her very much. How could I bear sending her to a distant country and not seeing her for a long time?"

The minister excavated a corner of his room to make a cell and secretly hid his mother there. He let no one know, not even the people of his household.

Several years passed. A neighboring country sent two very similar female horses and proposed a difficult question, "Which of these two horses is the parent? If you cannot tell us, we will attack your country within seven days."

The king of the country summoned the minister and asked, "What shall we do? If you have any idea, let me know."

"This is not an easy matter. I will tell you after reflecting at home," said his minister. He thought, "Since my mother is old, she may have heard of something like this." The minister hurried home and stealthily went to his mother and inquired.

"When I was young, I heard of something like this. I understand that the way to detect the parent of two similar horses is to place grass between them. The one who eats first is the offspring. The one who eats in a relaxed manner, letting the other take as much as it wishes, is the parent, "said his mother.

When his minister returned to the palace, the king asked, "Do you have an idea?" The minister offered the king his mother's suggestion as his own idea.

"That sounds reasonable," said the king, and he immediately had his men place grass between the two horses. One of the horses quickly got up and energetically ate the grass, while the other leisurely ate what remained. Seeing this, the king put identifying placards on each horse and returned them to the neighboring country.

Later, the neighboring country sent a well-chiseled and lacquered piece of wood and asked which end had been the base and which the top.

The king again summoned and consulted his minister, "What shall we do about this?" The minister returned home and asked his mother's help as before.

The mother said, "It is very easy. Float the piece of wood in water. The end which sinks slightly is the base." The minister returned to the palace and told the king. The king had his people put the piece of wood in water, made the determination, and returned the wood properly identified.

Some time later, an elephant was sent from the neighboring country with a message, "Determine the weight of this elephant." The king again consulted his minister, "This is difficult. What shall we do?"

"Indeed. I will think of some solution at home," said the minister and left. The king became suspicious. "It is quite inconceivable that the minister never discovers a solution while with me, but always at home. I wonder what he does at home?"

When the minister returned, the king asked, "How about it?" wondering whether the minister might have had difficulty. The minister replied, "I have reached a solution quite easily. The elephant should be placed aboard a boat in the water. Mark the side of the boat with ink of soot at the level to which it sinks. Have the elephant removed from the boat, load the boat with stones until it sinks to the depth of the mark. Then unload the stones and weigh them. The total weight of all the stones will equal that of the elephant, and you will know how heavy the elephant is!"

The king did as instructed, wrote down the elephant's correct weight, and returned the animal to the neighboring country.

The people there were immensely impressed by a country which gave them perfect solutions to three most difficult problems. They praised it: "That country has many wise men. They discover answers to problems which are insoluble for men of ordinary talents. If we are antagonistic and attack them, we may be tricked and destroyed by them. We should maintain a friendly relationship."

So the neighboring country abandoned its long-cherished intention of challenging the first country, had an exchange of official correspondence, and maintained good relationships.

The king of the first country summoned his minister. "Thanks to your virtue and merit, we are out of our predicament and have altered our neighbor's antagonistic feelings. I am immensely pleased with you. How did you find the solution to these difficult problems?"

The minister confessed to the king, wiping his tears with his sleeves, "This country has an ancient custom to exile all those who become older than seventy. I have a mother of more than eight and seventy years. I have secretly cared for her in an underground cell. Since older people usually have heard more and know more, I asked my mother about these problems, hoping that she might have some solutions. If it were not for an older person like my mother..."

Hearing this, the king said, "Why is there an ancient custom in this country to abandon old people? Considering the situation, older people should be respected. I shall issue an order to recall all old people, regardless of sex and rank, who have been sent away. And the name of our country, the Country that Abandons the Old, should be changed to the Country that Cares for the Old." The king issued the edict.

Afterward, the country was governed in a tranquil manner, and its people enjoyed peace and bountiful living.

Thus it was told and handed down.

APPENDIX

The list includes all abbreviations used for materials related to the *Konjaku Monogatarishū* of India:

CHI	*Daichidoron*	大智度論
H	*Hōonjurin*	法苑珠林
HO	*Hōbutsushū*	宝物集
I	*Kyōritsuisō*	経律異相
IN	*Kakogenzai ingakyō*	過去現在因果経
KN	*Kengukyō*	賢愚経
NE	*Daihatsu nehangyō*	大般涅槃経
S	*Sangokudenki*	三国伝記
SAN	*Sanbōkannō yōryakuroku*	三宝感応要略録
SEI	*Daitōsaiikiki*	大唐西域記
SEN	*Senjūhyakuengyō*	撰集百縁経
SH	*Shishūhyaku innenshū*	私聚百因縁集
YO	*Shokyōyōshū*	諸經要集
ZA	*Zappōzōkyō*	雑宝蔵経

1:1–IN (1), H (8:4[2]), S (1:1)
1:2–IN (1)
1:3–IN (2), H (10)
1:4–IN (2), H (10), SH (2:4)
1:5–IN (2, 3)
1:6–IN (3), H (11), I (4)
1:7–IN (3)
1:8–IN (3)
1:9–KN (10:48)
1:10–H (9:5[2]), I (20:5), CHI (14)

1:11–CHI (8), H (33), I (41:11)
1:12–H (42:39[2:9]), I (35:8), SEI (9)
1:13–H (55:16 [Inshōbu:2]), S (1:13), SH (2:6)
1:14–NE (14), S (8:9)
1:15–H (58:67 [Hibōbu:3]), NE (30)
1:16–H (7), I (8:8, 17:10), KN (11:52), S (4:16)
1:17–I (7:6, 7:15)
1:18–HO (4), I (7:8), S (8:12), *Shasekishū* (7)
1:19–I 7(7:4)
1:20–[lacuna]
1:21–*Shibunritsu* (4)
1:22–H (22:13 [Inshōbu]), YO (4[Nyūdōbu-inshōbu :4])
1:23–SAN (1:2)
1:24–[lacuna]
1:25–The direct sources are unknown.
1:26–I (35:4), KN (4:22), SH (2:1)
1:27–KN (4:22)
1:28–H (22:4), S (5:13)
1:29–SEN (1:10)
1:30–H (64:74), I (46:1)
1:31–H (56 :64[3], 39:36[2:1]), I (3:2), S (1:10), SH (3:3)
1:32–SEN (6:55), I (30:6, 34:1)
1:33–SEN (1:5)
1:34–H (55:62), I (15:12)
1:35–H (36:34[4])
1:36–H (37:35[5])
1:37–I (37:9)
1:38–I (5:14), NE (16), SEI (6), SH (4)

2:1–I (7:2)
2:2–I (7:3), S (2:4)
2:3–H (95:95[Tanbyōbu :3])
2:4–I (31:3), S (3:10), SH (1:14)
2:5–*Rokudojūkyō* (4:26)
2:6–H (56:64[Hinjobu:5])
2:7–H (56:64[Hinjobu:5]), KN (5:26)
2:8–H (56:63[Inshōbu:2]), KN (5:21)
2:9–I (18:6), KN (2:11)
2:10–I (18:4), KN (2:9)

2:11–H (37:35), SEN (9:83)
2:12–H (35:31[Inshōbu:2])
2:13–I (23:2), KN (5:26), S (1:22), SEN (8:73)
2:14–H (81:86[Zaisebu:9]), KN (3:17), SH (1:13), *Sanbō ekotoba* (3:9)
2:15–I (38:3), KN (13:58)
2:16–I (36:12)
2:17–SEN (7:61)
2:18–SEN (9:88)
2:19–H (35:31 [Inshōbu:2]), S (8:18)
2:20–H (42:39[Sefukubu:93]), I (37:8)
2:21–I (19:2), S (6:4), I (19:2)
2:22–H (36:32[Inshobu:2]), 37:35[Kanpukubu:4])
2:23–H (56:63[Inshōbu:23])
2:24–H (68:78[Inshōbu:5]), ZA (2:21)
2:25–KN (1:6), SEN (10:98)
2:26–I (18:1), KN (5:28)
2:27–H (91:90[Inshōbu:2]), I (36:8)
2:28–I (7:12), *Shibunritsu* (41)
2:29–H (73:4[Inshōbu:2]), I (15:7)
2:30–H (73:84[Sesshōbu:4, Inshōbu:2]), KN (7:32)
2:31–H (58:67[Jusobu:2]), KN (3:16)
2:32–H (64:73[Inshōbu:2])
2:33–I (36:6), KN (5:24)
2:34–H (76:84[Akkōbu:8]), KN (10:44)
2:35–CHI (34:3)
2:36–SEN (5:50)
2:37–H (76:84[Akkōbu:8, Inshōbu:2])
2:38–H (77:84[Kendonbu:11, Inshōbu:2])
2:39–SEN (10:94)
2:40–KN (6:29)
2:41–H (77:84[Kendonbu:11, Inshōbu:2]), 1 (36:14)

3:1–*Bussetsu yuimakekkyō* (1)
3:2–SAN (3:1)
3:3–CHI (10:1[15]), H (25:17[Inshōbu:2])
3:4–CHI (2:1[4]), I (14:7)
3:5–H (25:17[Inshōbu:2])
3:6–The direct sources are unknown.

3:7–CHI (17), SEI (1)
3:8–SEI (2)
3:9–H (35:30[Sainanbu:4])
3:10–The direct sources are unknown.
3:11–SEI (3)
3:12–H (17:7[Chōhōbu:2]), KN (12:51)
3:13–H (10:5[Kyūkonbu:3])
3:14–I (34:2), KN (2:8), SEN (8:70)
3:15–I (32:4), KN (2:14)
3:16–The direct sources are unknown.
3:17–H (57:65[Inshōbu:2]), S (3:16), ZA (2:19)
3:18–The direct sources are unknown.
3:19–H (79:84[Jakenbu:13])
3:20–*Bussetsu ōmukyō, Chūagonkyō* (40:4)
3:21–H (94:94[Benribu:4]), I (17:18), KN (6:30)
3:22–H (77:11), The *Jataka* (No. 535), *Ujishūi monogatari* (1:85)
3:23–H (77:84[Kendonbu: 11]), I (5:10), S (11:25), SH (3:6)
3:24–H (56:63[Inshōbu:2]), YO (6:10[Inshōbu:2]), I (14:13)
3:25–H (21:12[Zokujobu:2]), I (29:7)
3:26–ZA (9)
3:27–H (49:50[Gogyakubu:2]), *Hōbutsushū* (1), SH (2:3)
3:28–H (12:5[Nehanbu:14])
3:29–I (4:5), *Shasekishū* (4:4)
3:30–*Daihikyō* (2)
3:31–*Bussotōki* (4), I (4:4)
3:32–I (4:5)
3:33–*Makamayakyō* (3), *Bussotōki* (4), SEI (6)
3:34–NE (3), I (4:5)
3:35–*Makamayakyō* (3), *Chōagonkyō* (4), H (40:37[Binpōbu:4]), I
     (6:1)

4:1–H (12:15[Sennin-kesshūbu:3])
4:2–SEI (6), SH (3:15)
4:3–H (37:35[Inshōbu:2])
4:4–H (91:91[Inshōbu:2]), I (33:4), SEI (3), SEN (no. 100), S (7:4)
4:5–I (24:12), S (6:1), SEI (8)
4:6–*Aikuōkyō* (10), *Fuhōzōinnenden* (4), *Ujishūi monogatari* (13:14)
4:7–*Fuhōzōinnenden* (3), CHI (10), *Ojōyōshū* (3:3)
4:8–*Fuhōzōinnenden* (3), KN (13:67)

4:9–H (34:28[Inshōbu:2]), Hōbutsushū (6), Ujishūi monogatari (no. 137)
4:10–The direct sources are unknown. Variants in Hōbutsushū (6), SH (1:19)
4:11–S (12:7), SEI (2)
4:12–SEI (12)
4:13–Shūgyōsen zatsuhiyukyō (3:30,31), S (10:22)
4:14–Kyūzatsuhiyukyō (1:3), I (46:4[4])
4:15–I (45:1, 36:5), ZA (4:48)
4:16–SEI (2)
4:17–SEI (11)
4:18–H (17:6[5]), S [Chōhōbu:2]), SH (3:2)
4:19–SAN (3:13), S (12:4)
4:20–I (37:2), S (8:27)
4:21–I (37:3)
4:22–I (44:15)
4:23–Abidatsuma daibibasharon (99), S (3:28)
4:24–H (53:58[Bosatsubu:2]), Uchigikishū (13), S (2:19)
4:25–SEI (10), Ujishūi monogatari (no. 138)
4:26–SEI (5)
4:27–SEI (10), Shingonden (2:1)
4:28–SAN (3:16)
4:29–SEI (12)
4:30–H (17:7[Chōhōbu:2]), Shasekishū (2:8)
4:31–Shibunritsu (40)
4:32–The direct sources are unknown.
4:33–H (76:84[4, Akkōbu:8, Inshōbu:2]), I (47:4)
4:34–H (77:84[5, Kendonbu:11, Inshōbu:2])
4:35–H (52:56[Rishōbu:4]), Shasekishū (8:4)
4:36–SAN (1:17)
4:37–SAN (1:18)
4:38–SAN (1:23), S (11:7)
4:39–SAN (3:11), SEI (3)
4:40–I (45:1)
4:41–H (52:56[Airenbu:2])

5:1–H (31:24[Inshōbu:2]), SEI (11), I (43:3), The Jataka (no. 196), Ujishūi monogatari (6:9)
5:2–SEI (11)

5:3–SEN (8:80), *Uchigikishū* (15), S (4:19)
5:4–H (71[Ayokubu:4]), *Taiheiki* (37), S (2:28), The *Jataka* (no. 526)
5:5–ZA (1:8)
5:6–ZA (1:8, 9), SEI (7)
5:7–H (49:49[Taishibu:3]), KN (1:7), ZA (1:2)
5:8–I (25), KN (6:30)
5:9–I (24:6), KN (1:1 [2])
5:10–KN (1:1[3]), CHI (49), S (1:4)
5:11–The direct sources are unknown.
5:12–H (91), I (2), YO (6)
5:13–I (33:5)
5:14–H (64:74[Chikushōbu:4]), I (11:5)
5:15–The direct sources are unknown.
5:16–SEN (6:59), KN (1:3)
5:17–SEI (12)
5:18–H (50:52[Inshōbu :2]), YO (8:3)
5:19–H (50:51[Inshōbu:2]), I (11:1, 44:4)
5:20–H (54:60[Sachikubu:6])
5:21–The direct sources are unknown.
5:22–The direct sources are unknown.
5:23–The direct sources are unknown.
5:24–*Kyūzatsuhiyukyō* (3:39), The *Jataka* (no. 215)
5:25–I (23:13), The *Jataka* (Nos. 57, 208, 342)
5:26–SEI (9), ZA (2:15), The *Jataka* (no. 455)
5:27–SEI (3)
5:28–*Shūkyōsen zatsuhiyukyō* (3:25), H (34:28[Inshōbu:2]), I (43:15), SEI (8)
5:29–KN (7:33), I (11:15)
5:30–I (39:13)
5:31–*Daijionji sanzōhōshiden* (4:1), H (5:4[Shurabu-kanōen:1]), *Uchi-gikishū* (20), *Ujishūi monogatari* (171)
5:32–ZA (1:4), KN (7:32), *Uchigikishū* (7)

SELECTED BIBLIOGRAPHY

Japanese-language works, including primary sources (unless otherwise stated, all Japanese-language works were published in Tokyo)

(1) TEXTS

Akanuma Chizen 赤沼智善 and Nishio Kyōo 西尾京雄, eds. *Hyakuyukyō* 百喩経, in *Kokuyaku issaikyō* 16 国訳一切経. Daitō Shuppansha, 1930.
———. *Kengukyō* 賢愚経, in *Kokuyaku issaikyō* 16 国訳一切経. Daitō Shuppansha, 1930.
———. *Senjū hyakuengyō* 撰集百縁経, in *Kokuyaku issaikyō* 14 国訳一切経. Daitō Shuppansha, 1929.
Akutagawa Ryūnosuke 芥川龍之介. "Konjaku monogatari kanshō" 今昔物語鑑賞, in *Nihon bungaku kōza* 日本文学講座 6. Shinchōsha, 1927.
Haga Yaichi 芳賀矢一, ed. *Kōshō konjaku monogatarishū* 放證今昔物 語集. Fuzanbō, 1913–21.
Inone Mitsusada 井上光貞. *Nihon jōdokyō seiritsushi no kenkyū* 日本浄土教成立史の研究. Yamakawa Shuppansha, 1975.
Inone Mitsusada 井上光貞 and Ōsone Shōsuke 大曽根章介, eds. *Ojōden Hokkegenki* 往生伝法華験記. Iwanami Shoten, 1974.
Iwamoto Yutaka 岩本裕. *Bukkyō setsuwa kenkyū josetsu* 仏教説話研究序説, *Bukkyō setsuwa kenkyū*, I. Kyoto: Hōzōkan, 1967.
Kanda Hideo 神田秀夫 and Kunisaki Fumimaro 国東文麿, eds. *Nihon no setsuwa 2* 日本の説話. Tokyo Bijutsu, 1973.
Kasuga Kazuo 春日和男. *Konjaku monogatari kō* 今昔物語考, in Nihon bungaku kenkyū shiryōsōsho 日本文学研究資料叢書, ed., *Konjaku monogatarishū* 今昔物語集. Yūseido, 1970.
Katayose Masayoshi 片寄正萎. *Konjaku monogatarishū no kenkyū* 今昔物語集の研究. Geirinsha, 1974.
———. *Konjaku monogatarishū ron* 今昔物語集論. Geirinsha, 1974.
Koizumi Tōru 小泉道. *Nihon ryōiki* 日本霊異記. Sumiya Shobō, 1969.

Kunisaki Fumimaro 国東文麿. *Konjaku monogatarishū* 今昔物語集. Kōdansha, 1978–.

———. *Konjaku monogatarishū seiritsu kō* 今昔物語集成立考. Waseda University Press, 1962.

Kuroita Katsumi 黒板勝美, ed. *Konjaku monogatarishū* 今昔物語集, in *Shinteizōho kokushi taikei*, 新訂増補国東大系. Yoshikawa Kōbunkan, 1930–31.

Mabuchi Kazuo 馬淵和夫. "Konjaku monogatarishū ni okeru ketsubun no kenkyū" 今昔物語集における欠文の研究, in *Kokugo kokubun*, December 1949, pp. 173–85.

Mabuchi Kazuo 馬淵和夫, Kunisaki Fumimaro 国金文麿, and Konno Tōru 今野達, eds. *Konjaku monogatarishū* 今昔物語集, in *Nihon koten bungaku zenshū* 21–24. Shogakukan, 1971–76.

Maruyama Jirō 丸山二郎, ed. *Konjaku monogatarishū* 今昔物語集. Iwanami Bunko, 1952–54.

Masuda Katsumi 益田勝美. *Setsuwa bungaku to emaki* 説話文学と絵巻. Kyoto: Sanitsu Shobō, 1971.

Nagai Yoshinori 永井義憲. *Konjaku monogatari no sakusha to seiritsu* 今昔物語の作者と成立, in *Nihon bungaku kenkyū shiryō sōsho: Konjaku monogatarishū* 日本文学研究資料叢書今昔物語集. Yūseido, 1970.

———. *Nihon bukkyō bungaku* 日本仏教文学. Shima Shobō, 1963.

Nagano Jōichi 長野嘗一, ed. *Konjaku monogatari* 今昔物語, in *Nihon koten zensho*. Asahi Shinbunsha, 1953–57.

Nihon Bungaku Kenkyū Shiryō Kankōkai 日本文学研究資料刊行会, ed. *Konjaku monogatarishū* 今昔物語集. Yūseido, 1970.

Nishio Kōichi 西尾光一. *Chūsei setsuwa bungakuron* 中世説話文学論. Shima Shobō, 1963.

Sakaguchi Tsutomu 坂口勉. *Konjaku monogatari no sekai* 今昔物語の世界. Kyōikusha, 1981.

Sakai Kōhei 坂井衡平. *Konjaku monogatarishū no shinkenkyū* 今昔物語集の新研究. Meicho Kankōkai, 1965.

Sakakura Atsuyoshi 阪倉篤義, Honda Yoshinori 本田義憲, and Kawabata Yoshiaki 川端義明, eds. *Konjaku monogatarishū* 今昔物語集. Shinchōsha, 1978.

Satō Kenzo 佐藤謙三, ed. *Konjaku monogatarishū* 今昔物語集. Kadokawa Bunko, 1954–65.

Seki Keigo 関敬吾. *Mukashibanashi no rekishi* 昔話の歴史. Shibundō, 1966.

———. *Nihon mukashibanashi shūsei* 日本昔話集成. Kadokawa Shoten, 1950.

Takahashi Mitsugu 高橋貢. *Chūko setsuwa bungaku kenkyū josetsu* 中古説話文学研究序説. Ōfusha, 1974.

Takakusu Junjirō 高楠順次郎, ed. *Hōonjurin* 法苑珠林, in *Taishō shinshū daizōkyō* 53. Taishō Issaikyō Kankōkai, 1928.

————. *Myōhōki* 冥報記, in *Taishō shinshū daizōkyō* 51. Taishō Issaikyō Kankōkai, 1928.

————. *Zappōzōkyō* 雑宝蔵経, in *Taishō shinshū daizōkyō* 4. Taishō Issaikyō Kankōkai, 1924.

Takase Shōgen 高瀬承厳. *Nihonkoku genpō zen'aku ryōiki* 日本国現報善悪霊異記, in *Kokuyaku issaikyō* 61. Daitō Shuppansha, 1938.

Uematsu Shigeru 植松茂. *Kodai setsuwa bungaku* 古代説話文学. Shima Shobō, 1964.

Watanabe Tsunaya 渡辺綱也 and Nishio, Kōichi 西尾光一, eds. *Ujishūi monogatari* 宇治拾遺物語, in *Nihon koten bungaku taikei* 27. Iwanami Shoten, 1960.

Yamada Yoshio 山田孝雄 et al., eds. *Konjaku monogatarishū* 今昔物語 集, in *Nihon koten bungaku taikei* 22–26. Iwanami Shoten, 22–26.

Yoshida Kōichi 吉田幸一, ed. *Sanbō ekotoba* 三宝絵詞. Koten bunko, 1965.

(2) WESTERN-LANGUAGE WORKS, INCLUDING A PARTIAL LIST OF TRANSLATIONS OF VARIOUS TALES FROM *KONJAKU MONOGATARISHŪ*

Aarne, Antti, and Stith Thompson, eds. *The Types of the Folktale*, Helsinki, 1961.

Brower, Robert H. "The Konzyaku monogatarisyū." Ph.D. dissertation, University of Michigan, 1952.

Cowell, E. B. *The Jataka*. Cambridge, 1897.

Dykstra, Yoshiko Kurata. "Jizō, the Most Merciful: Tales from *Jizō Bosatsu Reigenki*," *Monumenta Nipponica* 33 (1978): 179–200.

————. "Miraculous Tales of the Lotas Sutra: The *Dainihonkoku Hokkegenki*," *Monumenta Nipponica* 32 (1977): 189–210.

————. *Miraculous Tales of the Lotus Sutra from Ancient Japan*. Osaka: Kansai Gaikokugo Daigaku, 1983.

————. "Tales of the Compassionate Kannon: The *Hasedera Kannon genki*," *Monumenta Nipponica* 31 (1976), 113–43.

Frank, Bernard. *Histoires qui sont maintenant du passé*. Paris: Gallimard, 1968. Translations of fifty-eight stories.

Gjertson, Donald E. "A Study and Translation of the *Ming-pao-chi*: A T'ang Dynasty Collection of Tales." Ph.D. dissertation, Stanford University, 1975.

Hammitsch, Horst, ed. *Erzählungen des aiten Japan aus dem Konjaku monogatari*. Stuttgart: Reclam, 1965. Translations of twenty-three stories from chapters 17–31.

Jones, S. W. *Ages Ago: Thirty-Seven Tales from the Konjaku Monogatari Collection*. Cambridge, Mass.: Harvard University Press, 1959.

Kelsey, W. Michael. "Konjaku Monogatari-shū: Toward an Understanding of

Its Literary Qualities," *Monumenta Nipponica* 30 (1975): 121–50. Translations of four stories from chapter 19.

———. *Konjaku monogatarishū*. Boston: Twayne's World Authors Series, 1982.

Kobayashi, Hiroko. *The Human Comedy of Heian Japan: A Study of the Secular Stories in the Twelfth-Century Collection of Tales, Konjaku Monogatarishū*. East Asian Cultural Series 19. Center for East Asian Cultural Studies, 1971.

Konishi, Jin'ichi, Robert Brower, and Earl Miner. "Association and Progression: Principles of Integration in Anthologies and Sequences of Japanese Court Poetry, A.D. 900–1350," *Harvard Journal of Asiatic Studies* 22 (December 1958), 67–127.

Mills, D. E. *A Collection of Tales from Uji: A Study and Translation of Uji Shui Monogatari*. Cambridge University Press, 1970.

Nakamura, Kyōko Motomachi. *Miraculous Stories from the Japanese Buddhist Tradition: The Nihon Ryōiki of the Monk Kyōkai*. Cambridge, Mass.: Harvard University Press, 1973.

Seki, Keigo. *Folktales of Japan*. Chicago: University of Chicago Press, 1969.

———. "Types of Japanese Folktales," *Asian Folklore Studies* 25 (1966): 1–220.

Smith, Robert. "On Certain Tales of the *Konjaku Monogatari* as Reflections of Japanese Folk Religion," *Asian Folklore Studies* 25 (1966): 221–233.

Speyer, J. S., ed. *Avadānacataka*. St. Petersburg, 1909.

Thomas, Edward J. *The Life of the Buddha as Legend and History*. London: Routledge and Kegan Paul, 1956.

Thompson, Stith, and Jonas Balys. *The Oral Tales of India*: Bloomington: Indiana University Press, 1958.

Thompson, Stith, and Warren E. Roberts. *Types of Indic Oral Tales*. Helsinki, 1960.

Tsukakoshi, Satoshi. *Konjaku: Altjapanische Geschichten aus dem Volk zur Heianzeit*. Zurich: Max Niehans, 1956.

Ury, Marian. *Tales of Times Now Past: Sixty-two Stories from a Medieval Japanese Collection*. Berkeley: University of California Press, 1979.

Wilson, William Ritchie. "The Way of the Bow and Arrow: The Japanese Warrior in *Konjaku Monogatari*," *Monumenta Nipponica* 28 (1973): 177–233. Translations of the stories from chapter 25.

INDEX

317

CPSIA information can be obtained
at www.ICGtesting.com
Printed in the USA
LVHW012243080721
692040LV00007B/67